— OLD-TIME —
COUNTRY
WISDOM & LORE

FOR HEARTH AND HOME

OLD-TIME
COUNTRY WISDOM & LORE

FOR HEARTH AND HOME

1000s
of Traditional Skills
for Simple Living

JERRY MACK JOHNSON

VOYAGEUR
PRESS

First Published in 2021 by Voyageur Press, an imprint of The Quarto Group, 100 Cummings Center, Suite 265-D, Beverly, MA 01915, USA.
T (978) 282-9590 F (978) 283-2742 QuartoKnows.com

Voyageur Press titles are also available at discount for retail, wholesale, promotional, and bulk purchase. For details, contact the Special Sales Manager by email at specialsales@quarto.com or by mail at The Quarto Group, Attn: Special Sales Manager, 100 Cummings Center, Suite 265-D, Beverly, MA 01915, USA.

25 24 23 22 21   1 2 3 4 5

ISBN: 978-0-7603-6932-6

Digital edition published in 2021
eISBN: 978-0-7603-6933-3

Library of Congress Cataloging-in-Publication Data is available.

Design and page layout: Tango Media Publishing Services, LLC
All images are from the Voyageur Press Archive with the exception of the following: Clipart.com: 69 (bottom); Florida Center for Instructional Technology: 38, 53, 57, 60, 63, 69 (top), 70, 72, 73, 74, 76, 99, 169 (left), 170; *Graphic Ornaments* by The Pepin Press: 5–7 (border), 9 (border), 89 (border), 90–99 (border), 169–176 (border); Library of Congress: 86 (bottom)

Printed in China

IMPORTANT, PLEASE READ:
Any recipes or "health cures" are intended as a historical reference only. They are NOT recommended by the editors or publisher of this book. They have been compiled as a historical narrative for historical purposes only. The publisher assumes no responsibility whatsoever for any injury or damage resulting from reader's use of any of the material or information contained in this book.

We recognize, further, that some words, model names, and designations mentioned herein are the property of the trademark holder. We use them for identification purposes only. This is not an official publication.

PREFACE

s I was growing up in the ranch country of West Texas, I accepted as fact that Nature could satisfy almost any need, if we but had the knowledge of her secrets. My elders appeared to exhibit an unending supply of that vital knowledge with their ability to heal with herbs, to predict weather and animal behavior, and to locate underground water with a forked twig.

We didn't have bottled air fresheners in those days; instead, they sprang from the ground. I remember Mother picking mint sprigs from around an old water spigot, drying them, and crumbling their brittle leaves into small china pots, placed strategically throughout the house.

I can't forget the way our house gleamed, despite the lack of today's highly touted cleansers. Homemade soap and plenty of elbow grease kept both clothes and home sparkling.

Many an old recipe handed down from before Grandma's time was responsible for the tantalizing smells that permeated our kitchen.

Much of what we had then we made ourselves. There seems to be in all of us an elemental desire to create with our own labor something useful from the earth's materials. Nothing affords so much satisfaction in its ownership and use as a thing we have made with our own hands. In their making, economy and pleasure are bound up together.

This book contains wisdom and know-how that has been passed from generation to generation by word of mouth from folks in every corner of our country. Although this book by no means contains all the knowledge that has been passed down to us, it is a representative sample.

There is no work of humans that cannot be aided by the proper reading of Mother Nature's signs. Nature says, "be still and look at me. Listen to me, for I have many things to show and tell you." Every day, every hour, every minute, nature is talking to each of us. We only need to look and listen.

"Of this fair volume which we World do name
If we the sheets and leaves could turn with care,
Of Him who it corrects, and did it frame,
We clear might read the art and wisdom rare."
—W. Drummond
"The Lessons of Nature"

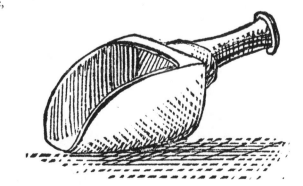

CONTENTS

PART II: THE COUNTRY TABLE — 89

PART I

HEARTH AND HOMESTEAD

1 | SCENTS, SALTS, AND SUCH

Hair Care

Shampoos and After-Shampoo Rinse

Old-Time Shampoo

Prepare a shampoo by dissolving 1 ounce of salts of tartar in 2½ cups of soft water. To this add 4 ounces of bay rum and 1 ounce of Castile soap shavings. The salts of tartar will remove dandruff; the bay rum will cut oil and act as a preservative for the shampoo; and the soap will cleanse scalp and hair.

Rosemary-Lavender Shampoo

  1 cup rosemary leaves
  ½ ounce lavender oil
  ⅛ ounce Castile soap

Sprinkle 1 cup rosemary leaves into a vessel holding 4 cups of water; simmer for fifteen minutes. Strain the contents, returning the liquid to the vessel. Put in the soap; heat until dissolved. Take the pot from the stove and add the lavender oil, beating it in until well blended. Bottle for use.

Natural Shampoo Rinse

Churn the following ingredients in a blender:

  1 ounce olive oil
  1 egg
  1 tablespoon lemon juice
  ½ teaspoon apple cider vinegar

Wash your hair with this natural shampoo. Rinse.

After-Shampoo Rinse

Steep 2 teaspoons of dried nettles in boiling water. When the solution

is lukewarm, strain it for use as the final rinse after shampooing your hair.

Natural Hair Dyes and Styling Products

Blond

To lighten blond hair that has begun to darken, prepare a safe vegetable rinse. Put ½ cup of chopped rhubarb roots into 3 cups of water. Leave the saucepan uncovered and simmer its contents for thirty minutes. Steep overnight; then strain the liquid.

Towel dry the freshly shampooed hair. Pour the plant bleach through it several times, and squeeze out the excess liquid. Drying your hair in the sun will heighten its color.

Light Brown

If gray or white hair doesn't become you, mix the following formula to achieve a light-brown color: In separate saucepans, boil onionskins and black walnut skins in enough water to cover them. Combine the resulting juices, using ¼ onionskin juice to ¾ walnut-skin juice. When a deeper shade of brown is desired, use more walnut juice; for a redder color, add more onion juice.

An old-time treatment for coloring gray hair light shades of brown is tag alder bark. It can be purchased from botanical supply houses. Simmer 2 ounces of the chips in 1 quart of water for sixty minutes. When the liquid cools, strain it.

Use the whole quart to shampoo and rinse your hair. Usually, you will need to apply the coloring once a week for a few weeks before desired results are apparent.

Dark Brown

Gather black walnuts during the summer while the hulls are still soft and green. Pry the hulls from the nuts, and press their juice into a jar. Wear rubber gloves to prevent staining your hands. If a walnut tree doesn't grow close by, the hulls can be purchased at health food stores or herbalist shops.

Stir in a small amount of powdered cloves and a little purified alcohol. Close the jar, and let the mixture steep for a week. Occasionally shake it.

At the end of a week, pour the jar's contents through porous cloth

to filter out any solid particles. Bottle the dye, and add a bit of salt as a preservative. Store it in a cool place.

Wear rubber gloves to avoid staining hands and scalp. Apply this harmless dye to the hair only.

Black

Blend the juice of green walnut hulls with neat's-foot oil. Add one part of oil to four parts of juice. For very oily hair, reduce the amount of oil a bit; for exceptionally dry hair, add a little more oil.

Natural Hair Spray

Chop a whole lemon. Put the pieces in a saucepan and cover them with hot water. Boil the mixture until the liquid is reduced to one half. Let it cool; then squeeze the lemon and liquid through cheesecloth. If the resulting lemon solution is too thick, mix in a little water. Preserve the hair spray by adding lavender water or cologne. You may prefer to prepare a smaller amount at one time, using half a lemon, and to eliminate the need for a preservative by storing the grooming aid in the refrigerator.

To use, lightly spray it on your hair from a pump-valve bottle.

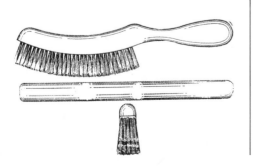

Hair Tonic

Into 1 pint of good alcohol put 4 ounces of oil of sweet almonds, 2 drams of oil of bergamot, and 1 dram of oil of citronella. Then add 8 ounces of rye whiskey, 4 ounces of aqua ammonia, and ½ ounce of gum camphor. Mix well. Shake before using as an excellent hair tonic.

Pomade

Melt 1 ounce of spermaceti in 4 ounces of oil of sweet almonds. When it is cool, perfume it by stirring in oil of neroli (the oil of orange blossoms) or oil of lemongrass. Put the pomade in a large-mouthed bottle for easy access by the fingers. Keep it corked. It is a fine pomade for hair or for chapped hands and lips.

Skin Care

Skin Lotions and Paste

Almond Milk

Shell enough sweet almonds to amount to an ounce. Put them in a strainer, and dip it first in boiling water, then in cold to blanch the nuts. Slip off their skins.

After drying the almonds, reduce them to a powder with mortar and pestle. (A bowl and old china doorknob can substitute for the mortar and pestle.) To achieve speedier results, first grind the nuts in your blender at its highest speed. Then pour the resultant coarse powder into your mortar to further refine the powder, or you can pour it on a piece of clean muslin, producing the desired fine powder with a rolling pin.

Return the powder to a bowl or mortar, and blend in, several drops at a time, 1 cup of distilled water. Grind the almond powder until a milky, smooth liquid forms. Strain it through cheesecloth to eliminate any coarse particles. Bottle for use.

Almond milk has been used for generations to smooth and protect the complexion.

Almond Complexion Paste

Crush 4 ounces of bleached sweet almonds with a rolling pin. Then pulverize them in a marble or earthenware mortar. Almonds may more easily be reduced to paste in a mortar by moistening them with rose water before grinding with a pestle.

Or the almonds may be heated in a saucepan of water until they become a granular mass, similar to cooked oatmeal.

Now add one egg white and equal portions of alcohol and rose water to make a smooth paste.

Sweet almonds contain about 50 percent almond oil. The oil is a gentle emollient that softens and feeds the skin.

Cucumber Milk

Finely mince one cucumber. Cover it with ⅓ cup of boiling water in a saucepan. Put on the lid, and simmer the contents for thirty minutes, using minimal heat.

Strain the mixture into a bowl, and add tincture of benzoin in drops until the liquid takes on a milky appearance. Add ⅓ cup of boiling water. Put the lotion in a small jar. Close it securely, and shake the contents to blend them thoroughly.

Cucumber milk provides a cooling, soothing lotion for various skin conditions.

Honey-Whey Lotion

Beat ½ teaspoon of rose water into 1 teaspoon of whey. Continue beating until the whey dissolves into the rose water. Stir in 1 teaspoon of honey. Thoroughly blend the mixture.

Apply this soothing facial lotion to troubled skin, leaving it on for ½ hour. Then wash it off with tepid water followed by a cold rinse.

Watercress Lotion

Wash a handful of cress. Simmer it for ten minutes in 2 cups of water. Strain the solution into a bottle.

To smooth rough skin, bathe the face with this soothing lotion. Allow it to dry; rinse with warm water followed by cool.

Lettuce Lotion

Remove the deep green outer leaves from a head of any type of lettuce but the iceberg variety. Wash them well. Put the leaves in a saucepan (do not use an aluminum one). Pour in enough boiling water to cover them. Then put on the lid, and let the contents simmer for about forty minutes.

Beat the leaves in the water, and strain the liquid into a jar. Add several drops of tincture of benzoin. After the addition of each drop, beat the liquid to blend it thoroughly. The lotion will now have a milky appearance.

Apply this cooling facial lotion to help your skin retain moisture.

Sesame Milk

Ladies of an earlier era found that sesame seed milk, applied externally, could soften, nourish, and cleanse their skin. Today, used as a substitute for commercial suntan oil, it can also help to protect the skin from burning or too rapid tanning.

Make this skin aid by grinding one handful of sesame seeds in your blender. Add sufficient water to cover them, and blend for about sixty seconds. Strain the resulting milk into an appropriate container.

Use it to revitalize your complexion or for overall body care. When you wish to remove the milk, rinse your skin with warm water, followed by cool. Blot dry.

Since a little of the sesame seed milk goes a long way, it is not an extravagance. Keep it in the refrigerator.

Sunburn Remedy and Suntan Lotion

Sunburn Remedy

Whip one egg white; then beat in 1 teaspoon of castor oil until the mixture is well blended.

Apply it to sunburned areas on face and body.

Suntan Lotion

Beat one egg yolk until it becomes lemon-colored. Gradually beat in 8 ounces of vegetable oil. Whip until thick. Add 1 tablespoon of vinegar and 1 tablespoon of wheat germ. Thoroughly beat the mixture.

Apply the preparation to all skin areas that will be exposed to sunshine. This speeds the tanning process, reducing the time necessary to acquire a tan and thus limiting exposure to ultraviolet rays.

Mouth Care

Preparation for Chapped Lips

Melt 1 ounce of spermaceti and 2 ounces of beeswax in a glass double boiler (a glass bowl set in a saucepan of hot water will also do). Keep the heat very low. Add ¼ cup of honey, and blend it in well. Slowly pour in ½ cup of sweet almond oil.

Take the upper part of the double boiler from the stove, and stir the contents until cool. Before the mixture solidifies, pour it into a small, shallow jar and put on the lid.

Use this preparation as a remedy for chapped lips.

Toothpowders and Paste

Charcoal-Sage Tooth Powder

Scrape the charcoal from burnt toast, and crush it to fine powder. Reduce an equal amount of dried sage leaves to a powder. Blend both ingredients well.

Dip a moistened toothbrush in the mixture to clean teeth.

Soda-Salt Tooth Powder

Make an effective tooth powder by mixing well baking soda and salt, in a proportion of three parts to one. If you prefer flavored tooth powder, add several drops of wintergreen or peppermint oil. Keep the compound in a small-mouthed container.

Toothpaste

To make toothpaste, add 3 teaspoons of glycerin and about 15 drops of some flavoring (cinnamon, peppermint, wintergreen, etc.) to each 4 ounces of homemade tooth powder. Blend the ingredients thoroughly in a bowl, and then add only enough water to turn the mixture into paste form. Spoon the toothpaste into a plastic squeeze bottle for use.

Bath Enhancers

Old-Fashioned Beauty Bath

1 pound barley
1 pound bran
1 pound oatmeal
1 pound brown rice
½ pound bay leaves
½ pound dried lavender flowers

Boil all of these ingredients in 4 quarts of rainwater for sixty minutes. Then strain the mixture.

Use 2 quarts of the liquid for each tub of bath water. An extra rinse after this herbal bath is unnecessary and would deprive you of some of its benefits. Follow it with a vigorous towel drying.

Bubble Bath

Make effervescent salts for your bath by mixing well these materials: 4 tablespoons of cornstarch, 15 tablespoons of cream of tartar, and 18 tablespoons of bicarbonate of soda. You may want to add several drops of water-soluble perfume.

About 2 tablespoons of the mixture will give you a tub full of bubbles. Store it in a tightly closed glass or metal container.

Bath Vinegars

Put 1 cup of some fragrant plant material—lavender flowers, rose petals, violet leaves and blossoms, etc.—or a combination of your choice in a 1-pint jar. Heat 8 ounces of white vinegar until it just begins to boil. Pour it into the jar and put on the lid.

Then let it stand for two weeks, shaking it several times each day.

After two weeks, strain the contents and bottle in attractive containers.

For a spicy bath vinegar, try blending ½ cup of lavender, ½ cup of dried rosemary, a pinch of sage, and 3 teaspoons of bruised, whole cloves.

One cup of perfumed bath vinegar will scent your bath water and leave your body clean, refreshed, and free of soap film.

Afterbath Powder

You will need a shoe box, 2 ounces of orrisroot powder, and a 1-pound box of cornstarch. Mix the orrisroot and cornstarch. Line the box with aluminum foil. Put in the powdered mixture, and directly over it lay a section of cheesecloth somewhat bigger than the bottom of the box.

Collect fragrant, fresh materials: bark, blossoms, flower petals, leaves, roots, seeds, and stems. Shake them lightly to remove any moisture, and place them right on the piece of cheesecloth. Cover the box snugly. Every two or three days, examine the plants for mold. If any are so affected, discard them. Whenever you find new petals or other aromatic materials, put them in the mix. Continue adding to the box in this way, occasionally stirring its contents. The orrisroot will absorb and hold the combined fragrances.

When a pleasing scent is achieved, take out the plant material. Allow the powder to dry if it has soaked up any moisture. Then package it in attractive containers, and close them tightly.

Hand Care

Fingernail Paste

1½ ounces spermaceti
¼ ounce white wax
2 ounces alkanet root (powdered)
12 ounces oil of sweet almond
½ teaspoon rose oil

Melt the spermaceti and the wax in the top portion of a double boiler. Mix in the alkanet root and almond oil. Beat the ingredients until well blended. As the mixture is cooling, stir in the rose oil.

For best results, buff clean, unpolished nails with an old-fashioned chamois buffer before applying the rose paste. Then rub in the paste, and gently buff again to develop a rosy sheen. Daily treatment will increase the health, luster, and beauty of your nails.

Hand Paste

An easily prepared paste to soften hands requires these ingredients:

2 egg yolks
¼ pound honey
¼ pound sweet almond oil
2 ounces blanched almond meal

Beat together the egg yolks and honey until a smooth paste is formed. As you continue to beat the mixture, gradually add the sweet almond oil. Then slowly mix in the almond meal. Store the unused portion in the refrigerator.

Hand Lotion

Warm 4 ounces of honey in a double boiler. Thoroughly blend in 8 ounces of lanolin. Take the pot from the stove, and allow the contents to cool somewhat. Then beat in 4 ounces of sweet almond oil.

Bottle the preparation, and use it for good hand care.

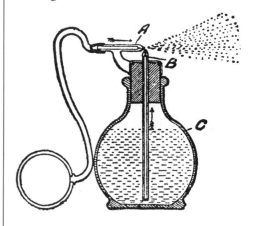

Scents and Salts

Toilet Water

Long ago the famous mineral baths of Budapest found favor with the Queen of Hungary. The Queen herself was renowned for a perfumed toilet water she had concocted for use after bathing. This preparation, known as Hungary Water, has been passed down from mothers to daughters for generations.

To prepare old-fashioned Hungary Water, put 1 dram (¹⁄₁₆ ounce) of essence of ambergris and ½ ounce of oil of rosemary into a pint jar. Add 2 cups of deodorized 95 percent alcohol. Close the jar tightly and shake thoroughly. Open it and allow to stand for twenty-four hours. Again close the jar tightly and let stand for six weeks, shaking it every five days. Transfer the contents to a suitable tightly stoppered bottle for use.

Solid Perfume

Melt 2 ounces of beeswax chips in the top of a double boiler. Using a wire whisk, slowly blend in ¼ cup of sweet almond oil. As you continue stirring, add 2 tablespoons of distilled water. Take the pot from the stove. Add 8 dropperfuls of your favorite cologne, and blend thoroughly with the whisk.

Pour the mixture, while still warm, into 4-ounce pimento jars or other suitable small containers that can be closed tightly. You may divide this recipe in half, perfuming each portion with a different scent.

Pomanders

Scent your linen and clothes closets with pomanders. To make them you will need large, well-shaped oranges, a few boxes of whole cloves, ground cinnamon, a roll of ¼-inch-wide cellophane tape, colored ribbon, a nutpick, and some silver foil.

Let the fruit dry for several weeks. Then fasten a strip of cellophane tape around the center of each orange. With the nutpick, pierce holes in the skin about ¼ inch apart, avoiding the tape. (Since the oranges will shrink more as they continue to dry, a small space should remain between each hole.) Push a clove into each hole. Now dust the oranges lightly

with powdered cinnamon. You may use ground allspice or orrisroot for dusting, if you prefer. Wrap them in silver foil, and store them in a dry spot for about seven weeks.

Take the pomanders from the foil, remove the tape, and substitute a length of bright ribbon, tied in a bow, for hanging them in your closets.

Spiced Potpourri

Mix ½ ounce of each of the following in a bowl: allspice, borax, ground cinnamon, whole cloves, ground nutmeg, and ground orrisroot. Blend a cupful of lemon, orange, or tangerine peel with the spices.

Put the spicy mixture into an open china jar, or one with holes in its lid to allow the scent to escape.

Rose Potpourri

On a fair morning, collect unblemished rose petals. Spread them in single layers on paper in a dry, cool spot. Turn them daily for about two weeks until dry.

Put some of the petals in a glass jar to a depth of two inches, covering them lightly with salt. Continue to alternate layers of petals and salt until the jar is full. Close it tightly. Put it in a dark, cool spot for seven days.

Blend these ingredients: ½ teaspoon of ground cinnamon, ½ teaspoon of ground cloves, ½ teaspoon of ground mace, 1 ounce of orrisroot, 10 drops of oil of bergamot, 20 drops of oil of eucalyptus, and 6 drops of oil of geranium. Mix the petals thoroughly into this blend, and put the mixture back into the jar, closing the lid tightly. After a period of two weeks, the potpourri is ready for use.

Smelling Salts

To make smelling salts, put 8 ounces of true carbonate of ammonia (a volatile salt of lasting pungency) and 1 ounce of oil of lavender (or any other essential oil) in a glass bottle. Close the bottle tightly.

2 | RURAL REMEDIES

When the nearest doctor lived many miles away folks were forced to rely on their own knowledge to treat a wide variety of ailments. Most families had a "doctor book" of some fashion, often handwritten, that contained instructions for home treatment. The treatments and medications were handed down from family to family. This important book often took its place beside the family Bible. Ethel Rogers of South Carolina said years ago that "the Bible shows how to live and the doctor book shows how to *live*."

Here are some of the choice home remedies from Ethel's "doctor book" and from others over the country.

(Please note that these "health cures" are intended as a historical reference only. They are not recommended by the editors or publisher of this book.)

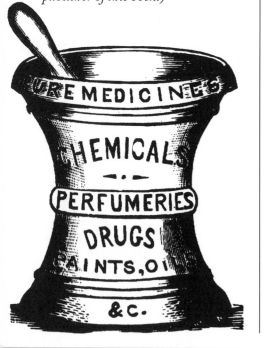

Abscess

• Dip a cabbage leaf into hot water and apply to the abscess.

• Cut open a fresh fig. Soak it for 1 minute in warm water. Apply it as a poultice to inflamed abscesses and boils.

Arthritis

• Take a teaspoon of chopped garlic twice a day with water for relief from the pain and swelling of arthritis.

• To cure arthritis, eat ½ pound of fresh cherries daily.

Asthma

• Simmer a bit of skunk cabbage root in ½ cup of hen's grease. Take 1 teaspoon three times each day to relieve asthma symptoms.

• For relief of asthma a muskrat skin should be worn over the lungs, the fur side against the body.

• Simmer 1 heaping teaspoon of dried, ground okra leaves in 1 quart of hot water until but 1½ pints of liquid remain. Add 1 teaspoon of freshly chopped onion. Cover and let stand until cool. Stir and strain. Drink equal portions during the day as an asthmatic remedy.

• Fasten a live frog on the throat of one suffering from asthma. When the frog dies, the patient will be cured.

Athlete's Foot

To remedy athlete's foot, anoint the feet with whale oil mixed with a little oil of cloves.

Baldness

• Blend ½ ounce of castor oil and 5 drops of oil of rosemary into ½ ounce of goose fat. Massage the scalp with this preparation three times daily to combat baldness.

• Pound peach kernels and boil them gently in vinegar until a thick paste forms. Apply three times a day to bald spots on the scalp to regenerate hair growth.

Bed-Wetting

• To cure bed-wetting use 1 spoon of corn silk every day to make a tea or in salad.

• Make a plaster of vinegar and the root of the herb tormentil. Apply it against the kidneys.

Bleeding

• Apply a mixture of flour and salt and wrap with cloth or common paper; or press cobwebs and brown sugar over the cut.

• To stop the bleeding from a cut, sprinkle the fungus spore of the puffball on it.

• Black tea in powdered form bandaged over a cut will stop the bleeding.

- To arrest bleeding and relieve the pain and swelling of a cut, pour lamp oil over it.
- Bleeding due to tooth extraction can be checked if the cavity is packed with cotton soaked in alum water.

Blisters

Boil the bark from an oak tree in a small amount of water and apply to blisters.

Blood

- To purify the blood, take a small glass of the following mixture three times daily: 1 quart of hard cider, ½ ounce of horseradish, 1 ounce of yellow dock.
- Combine equal amounts of blueberries, sassafras bark, thyme, and watercress. Make a tea of 1 spoonful of the mixture to 1 cup of hot water. Cover and let stand

until cool. Stir and strain. Take 1 cupful four times daily to purify the blood.

Bone Felon

Saturate a piece of turnip in turpentine and apply to the felon.

Breath

- To make the breath pleasing, rub the gums with wool coated with honey.
- In 1 cup of hot water, steep ⅓ teaspoon each of anise, mint, and rosemary. Cover and allow to stand for 10 minutes. Strain. Rinse the mouth daily with this solution to combat bad breath.

Bronchitis

- Mix ½ pint of cider vinegar; ½ pint of water; 1 ounce each of elecampane root, licorice extract, and coltsfoot; and ½ ounce of bloodroot. Steep in a covered pot in a warm place for 5 to 6 hours. Strain and sweeten with honey. Take 1 teaspoonful four times a day for bronchitis.
- Simmer 1 teaspoonful of each of the following spices in spirits of turpentine for ½ hour: cinnamon, cloves, mustard, pepper. Strain. Stir ¼ teaspoon of pure, powdered camphor into 1 ounce of the liquid. Blend into 4 ounces of goose grease. Rub on the chest to relieve congestion due to coughs and colds. Cover with flannel.

Bruises

- Wash with warm water and anoint with tallow or candle grease.

- Apply a paste of butter and chopped parsley to bruises.
- Use the skin of a freshly peeled banana to reduce the pain and discoloration of a bruise. Place the inner side of the peel on the bruise and hold in place with wet cold bandages.
- Make a brew of the roots of bouncing Bet. Use it in poultice form to relieve the discoloration of a bruised eye.
- Treat a bruise by applying brown paper coated with molasses.
- Mix 1 part oatmeal and 2 parts of flaxseed, blending in sufficient water to make a thick poultice for bruises.

Burns

- The juice from the succulent plant aloe vera applied often is very good. Apply ice directly to burn.
- Mix 4 ounces of lard with 1 ounce of powdered wood soot. Apply the mixture to burns and scalds on a dab of cotton.
- Honey applied to burns will relieve the pain and prevent blisters from forming.
- Thoroughly blend 1 egg yolk with 2 ounces of flaxseed oil. Apply to a burn.
- Soak soft linen in cod-liver oil and leave on a burn for 48 hours. Apply fresh oil as needed.
- Make a poultice of cold water and oatmeal to benefit a burn.
- Mix 2 portions of corn meal with 1 of powdered charcoal. Add milk to make a paste. Use this as a poultice for burns.

- Mix the freshly squeezed juice of pokeberries with a little glycerin as an application for burns.

Canker Sores

- Several times a day apply ashes from a burned corn cob to canker sores.
- Boil 2 tablespoons of dried pomegranate rind in 3 cups of water until the liquid is reduced to 2 cups. Strain and let cool. Use as a mouthwash for canker sores.

Chapped Hands and Lips

- Apply castor oil or equal parts of glycerin and lemon juice often to area. Ointment used on cows' teats is a fast cure for chapped hands. Rubbing hands regularly in sheep's wool will work, too.
- Boil flakes of tragacanth, 1 inch in size, with a few quince seeds. Strain when cool. Thin the solution with some glycerin. Use as a soothing lotion for chapped hands.
- To benefit chapped hands, wash them in sugar and water.

Chicken Pox

- Tie bran in a cheesecloth bag. Steep it in boiling water for 2 minutes before applying it to chicken pox sores.
- To treat chicken pox externally, apply witch hazel to the sores.

Chilblains

- As a cure for chilblains, mix ¼ ounce of each of the following: ammonia, turpentine, olive oil, oil of peppermint. Apply mornings and evenings.

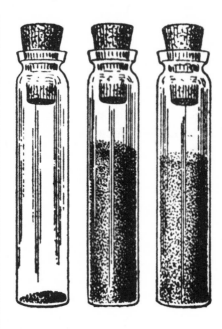

- Boil parsnips until soft, and bandage them on affected areas to treat chilblains.

Childbirth

- When labor is prolonged in childbirth, blow snuff, held on a goose feather, up the mother's nose. This will induce a sneezing fit, resulting in delivery.
- If complications occur during childbirth, give a strong tea of raspberry leaves.

Chills

- Mix ginger and pepper in very hot water and drink.
- Mix 1 teaspoon of grated jack-in-the-pulpit with milk and sugar. It causes sweating and will cure chills or a cold.
- Make a tea of smartweed. Drink it very hot. Go to bed and keep well covered when suffering from chills.

Choking

- Into a cup break an egg. Have the choking patient swallow it whole.
- When something is stuck in the throat causing choking, blow forcefully into the sufferer's ear.

Colds and Flu

- Mix and drink a mixture of cinnamon, sage, and bay leaves, and add a little lemon juice. Drink warm. Drink hot ginger tea freely. Take a dose of quinine every six hours. Drink juice of citrus fruits often.
- As a head-cold remedy, put 2 drops of spirits of camphor on a sugar cube; dissolve it in ½ glass of water. A teaspoonful should be taken every 2 hours. Grease the nostrils with a mixture of lard, mutton suet, and sweet oil.
- Eating a hot roasted onion before retiring can be helpful in curing a cold.
- To overcome a cold with its accompanying miseries of sore throat and fever, drink a tea made from the white flowers of the elderberry shrub.
- To relieve congestion due to a cold, rub throat and chest with skunk's oil.

Colic

- Put sliced green walnuts into enough whiskey to cover them. Let them soak for ten days. Take 1 teaspoonful of the liquid every ½ hour as a remedy for bilious colic.
- To cure colic in children, give a dose of 1 drop of camphor in 1 teaspoon of water.

Constipation

• Eat freely of preserves, drink plenty of water; eat garlic.

• Stir 2 teaspoons of flaxseed into 1 cup of cold water. Allow to stand for ½ hour. Drink both seeds and liquid to relieve constipation.

• Boil for 15 minutes 2 ounces each of barley, figs, and raisins. Put in ½ ounce of licorice root and let steep. Allow to cool, strain out the water, and mash together. Take a dose of 4 ounces, night and morning, as a laxative.

Convalescence

• A nourishing drink for those convalescing is barley coffee. Roast barley until brown. Boil 1 tablespoon of it in 2 cups of water for 5 minutes. Strain. If desired, add a bit of sugar.

• Put 1 tablespoon of grated garlic into ⅔ glass of red wine. Take 1 teaspoonful five times daily as a strengthening tonic following illness.

Corns

• To remove corns easily, bind on bread soaked in vinegar. Renew the application mornings and evenings.

• Burn willow bark. Mix the ashes with vinegar and apply to the corn.

• Mix and warm 1 teaspoon of brown sugar, 1 teaspoon of pine tar, and 1 teaspoon of saltpeter. Apply to corns on a plaster.

• Insert the toe in a lemon. Keep it on during the night. The corn can then be removed with ease. If not, repeat the procedure.

Cough

• Make a tea of wild cherry bark; mix with honey. Take a teaspoonful as needed.

• For a cough, chop 2 large turnip roots into small pieces, and boil them in 1 quart of water. Cool and strain the liquid. Add an amount of honey equal to whatever portion is taken.

• Simmer ⅜ ounce of senna leaf, ⅜ ounce of licorice root, and 1 ounce of anise seed in 2 cups of water until but 1 cup of liquid remains. Strain and cool. Add ½ pint of syrup. Take when necessary to relieve a cough.

• Beat together 3 egg yolks, 3 tablespoons of honey, and 1 teaspoon of pine tar, adding 2 ounces of wine. Take 1 teaspoonful three times daily before meals as a cough remedy.

• Scoop out a hollow in the middle of a good-sized beet; fill it with honey. Bake. Eat a little when needed to relieve a cough.

• Chew a piece of ginger root, swallowing the juice to benefit a cough.

• Mix 1 teaspoon of oil of sesame and 1 teaspoon of honey in 1 cup of warm milk. Slowly sip the beverage to relieve a cough.

Cramps

• Cramps in neck or legs can be relieved by an application of whiskey and red pepper.

• To 1 gallon of denatured alcohol add 1 ounce of monarda oil, 1 ounce of cajaput oil, 1 ounce of oil of thyme, ½ ounce of oil of peppermint, and 1 ounce of camphor gum. Shake thoroughly. Allow to stand for 24 hours. This is a good rub for cramps in the muscles of humans or animals.

Croup

• Administer 1 teaspoon of goose oil and 1 teaspoon of molasses to a child suffering from croup.

• Boil pig's feet in a vessel of water. Allow to stand overnight. Skim off the fat, put it in a pot, and boil until all moisture has evaporated. To cure croup, give a teaspoonful every fifteen minutes and also rub well on throat and chest.

Cuts and Scratches

• Rub with a sliced clove of garlic or apply raw honey.

• Crush the leaves of the blackberry bush between your fingers, and rub

them on a scratch to immediately check the bleeding.

• Remove the inside skin, or coating, from the shell of an uncooked egg. Place its moist side on a cut to promote healing with no scarring.

• Bathe the cut in a weak solution of water and baking soda. Sprinkle it, while still wet, with black pepper.

Dandruff

• Dissolve 1 ounce of borax in 1 pint of water. Wash the head with this mixture once a week to prevent dandruff.

• To cure dandruff make a mixture of 1 ounce of water, 2 ounces of bay rum, 2 ounces of glycerin, and 2½ ounces of tincture of cantharides. Rub this mixture into the scalp once a day.

• Make a tea from dried peach leaves and apply to the scalp as a treatment for dandruff.

Diarrhea

• Brown a little flour over the fire, add 2 teaspoons of vinegar and 1 teaspoon of salt, mix and drink. Mixing 1 tablespoon of warm vinegar and 1 teaspoon of salt will cure most severe cases. Do not eat fruit. A hot drink of ginger tea is often good. Repeat any of the above every few hours. Take sips of water often.

• For mild diarrhea eat burned rhubarb.

• Combine 3 tablespoons of vinegar with the same amount of hardwood ashes. Cover with hot water. Stir and allow to settle. Take 1 teaspoonful of the solution every now and then to check diarrhea.

Earache

• A piece of cotton sprinkled with pepper and moistened with oil or fat will give almost instant relief.

• Wash with warm water. Place small piece of garlic in ear.

• To alleviate the pain of an earache that is not too severe, blow pipe or cigarette smoke into the ear.

• For a very painful earache, drop mutton juice, as hot as can be tolerated, into the ear.

• Place a brass button in the mouth of one suffering from an earache. Surprise him by discharging a gun at his back. This will cure the pain.

Eye Inflammation

• Bind on hot tea leaves or raw fresh meat, leave on for several hours then wash well with warm water.

• Mix 3 whole eggs with 4 cups of cold rainwater. Bring to a boil, stirring frequently. Add ½ ounce of zinc sulfate and boil for 2 minutes more. Remove from heat. Take the curd that forms at the bottom of the vessel and apply it to inflamed eyes, using a bandage. Filter the liquid through cloth and use as an excellent eyewash.

• To soothe sore eyes, boil black mesquite gum. Dilute the liquid and apply to afflicted areas.

• Steep ⅛ teaspoon of eyebright and ⅛ teaspoon of fennel in 8 ounces of hot boiled water. Stir and strain through cloth. Use as an eyewash every 3 hours or when required.

• Chew ground ivy leaves, and apply the pulp to an inflamed eye.

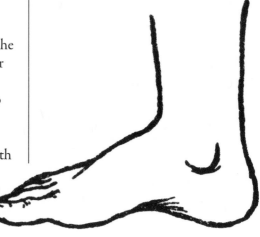

Feet

• To combat offensive odor of the feet, soak them in water in which the green bark of oak has been boiled.

• For excessive perspiration of the feet, put bran or oatmeal into the socks.

• Make a powder of equal amounts of powdered starch, fuller's earth, and powdered zinc. Sprinkle this mixture in the socks as a remedy for perspiring feet.

Fever

• Pound horseradish leaves until they are of the consistency of pulp. Apply them as a poultice to the soles of the feet to draw out fever.

- Simmer 4 cups of water containing a handful of cockleburs until 2 cups of liquid remain. Drink a small glassful of the solution every half hour until the fever dissipates.

Fits

- To arrest fits, throw a teaspoonful of salt as far back into the mouth as possible.
- Relieve fits by splashing water on the patient's hands and face. Plunging the feet into cold water will prove particularly beneficial.

Flatulence

- To alleviate wind in the stomach, chew saffron flowers and swallow the juice.
- Into 2 cups of boiling water put 1 teaspoon of dried orange or lemon peel, 1 teaspoon of coriander, and 1 teaspoon of gentian. Simmer for 10 minutes, strain when cool, and reserve the liquid. Slowly sip a small glassful three to four times a day to relieve flatulence.

Frozen Ears, Fingers, Nose, Etc.

Never rub snow on these tender members. Use warmth of hand to rub, thaw, and restore circulation. Dip affected areas in cold water, then add warm water gradually until water reaches blood heat, and massage area.

Hair

- Check hair from falling by washing the head each day with a strong sage tea. For best results use pure spring water.

- To make hair thicker, massage the juice of water cress into the scalp.

Hay Fever

- Use the following mixture as a snuff to cure hay fever: 10 grains of ammonium carbonate, 15 grains of capsicum, 20 grains of sodium borate.
- Steep several rose petals in a cup of hot water. Filter the liquid. To relieve eye irritation due to hay fever, apply 1 or 2 drops to each eye five times a day.
- Crush fresh milkweed in cheesecloth, and inhale it to combat hay fever.
- Mix the leaves and flowers of goldenrod and ragweed. Put ½ ounce of the herb mixture in 2 cups of boiling water and allow to steep for 10 minutes. Drink a small glassful four times a day to cure hay fever.

Headache

- Inhale fumes of boiling vinegar.
- Moisten a cloth with camphor spirits. Sprinkle black pepper on it and apply to the forehead to relieve a headache.
- Apply the fresh leaves of burdock or the fresh roots of pokeweed to the bottoms of the feet to assuage a headache.
- Mix 3 ounces of Castile soap, 1 ounce of camphor, and 2 ounces of ammonia in 2 quarts of alcohol. Bathe the forehead with this solution to relieve a sick headache.
- To dispel a headache, apply a poultice of grated uncooked potato to the forehead.
- For migraine headache, swallow a tablespoonful of honey.

Hearing Loss (Temporary)

- To cure deafness, drop a mixture of onion juice and ant eggs into the ear.
- Combine ½ ounce of olive oil, 15 drops of sassafras oil, and 1½ drams of glycerin. Put a few drops into the ear several times a day to reduce excess wax accumulation that is causing deafness.
- Melt hedgehog fat and drop a little into the ear to dissolve hard earwax that can cause temporary deafness.

Hemorrhoids

- Simmer 2 parts of fresh butter with 1 part of tobacco. Strain, and use as a poultice three times daily to relieve inflamed hemorrhoids.

- Remove the outer shell of 4 fresh horse chestnuts. Slice the chestnuts fine. Place them in a tin cup and cover with melted lard. Allow to steep for 1 hour in a warm place. Strain and squeeze out the lard. Apply the salve, when cool, twice daily to hemorrhoids.
- Mix equal amounts of horsemint oil, oil of fireweed, and pumpkin-seed oil. Apply twice a day to hemorrhoids.

Hiccups

- Eat a tablespoonful of peanut butter.
- Make a mint tea, adding 5 drops of oil of amber. Drink the brew every 10 minutes until the hiccups are arrested.
- To cure hiccups, eat a sugar cube that has been dunked in vinegar.
- Work the jaws as though chewing food while pressing the fingers in the ears. This procedure will speedily cure hiccups.

High Blood Pressure

- With mortar and pestle crush 2 teaspoons of dried watermelon seeds. Steep them for 1 hour in 1 cup of hot water. Stir and strain out the seeds. To relieve high blood pressure, drink 1 cupful four times each day.
- Forsake salty foods and partake of honey.

Hives

- Bathe with rubbing alcohol and follow with a strong solution of baking soda and water over the affected area. Do not drink anything cold.

- Cure hives by rubbing them with buckwheat flour.
- Make a tea of ground ivy, using 1 teaspoon of the herb to 1 cup of boiling water. Take 1 cupful three times daily to cure hives.

Hoarseness

- Dry nettle roots in the oven. Powder, and add them to the same amount of molasses. A dose of 1 teaspoon three times a day will cure hoarseness.
- Drink milk and red pepper every so often, and hoarseness will disappear.

Hunger

- To allay the feeling of hunger, chew beechnut leaves.
- Chewing elm leaves will quickly dissipate the sensation of hunger.

Indigestion

- Stir 1 teaspoon of each of the following into 1 cup of hot water: fennel seeds, peppermint, caraway seeds, spearmint. Cover and allow to stand for 10 minutes. Mix and strain. Take 1 cupful four times a day to counteract excess stomach acid and resulting indigestion.

- To prevent indigestion, take 1 teaspoon of whole white mustard seeds before meals.
- Take 1 ounce of Peruvian bark and the same amount of gentian root and ½ ounce each of coriander seed and orange peel. Steep them in 4 cups of brandy. Allow to stand for five days. An hour before eating take 1 teaspoonful in a wineglass of water to prevent indigestion.
- Stir ¼ teaspoon of ground cinnamon into 1 cup of hot water. Cover for 15 minutes and stir again. Strain. Take 1 tablespoonful for chronic indigestion. Repeat if necessary.
- Take an infusion of horehound to remedy stomach distress.
- Dry and powder peach leaves. Mix 1 teaspoon of this powder and the same amount of chalk into a glass of hot water. Take after meals to prevent stomach upset.

Ingrown Toenail

- Apply mutton tallow to an ingrown toenail for several days. The nail can then be cut without harm.
- Cut a notch in the center of the toenail's edge. In attempting to grow together, the nail will pull away from the skin on either side, providing relief from the pain and swelling of ingrown toenail.

Insect Bites

- Apply common mud, a slice of onion, garlic juice, lemon juice, baking soda, tobacco, or honey.
- Dissolve 1 heaping teaspoonful of sodium bicarbonate in 1 cup of cold

vinegar. Apply as a compress to insect bites.
- Apply a poultice of plantain leaves to insect bites.

Insomnia
- Drink a glass of warm milk; or mix equal parts of apple cider vinegar and honey, take 2 teaspoonfuls each hour.
- Make a medicinal tea of ¼ teaspoon of celery seed, ¼ teaspoon of valerian, ½ teaspoon of catnip, and ½ teaspoon of skullcap in 4 ounces of hot water. Keep the brew covered for 10 minutes. Mix and strain. Take the tea 1 hour before retiring.
- To overcome sleeplessness, eat a dish of baked onions before retiring.
- Mix lettuce juice with oil of roses and apply to the forehead and temples to induce sleep.

Irritable Infant
- Onion tea will cure a baby of fretfulness.
- To arrest postweaning restlessness, put molasses on the baby's hands. Give him chicken feathers to hold. During repeated attempts to remove them from first one hand and then the other, the babe will tire and fall asleep.

Itching
- Combat itching by bathing with hot water and soap, scrubbing with a corn cob. Follow this with an application of sulfur and lard.
- In a small amount of alcohol, dissolve ½ teaspoon of pure camphor. Add this to 4 ounces of calamine lotion and mix. Shake the solution thoroughly before applying to skin afflicted with itching.
- A blend of lard and the powdered root of pokeweed makes a good salve for itching.
- Apply mutton tallow to skin affected by itching.

Jaundice
Chop fine a handful of black alder. Boil it in 4 cups of old cider. Allow to cool. Drink it liberally to cure jaundice.

Kidney Disorders
- Steep fresh yellow corn silk, cut fine, in 1 cup of hot water. Cover, let stand until cold, and strain. Take 1 cupful four times each day for kidney complaints.
- Mix artichoke juice with an equal amount of white wine to increase the discharge of urine.
- Steep strawberry and mullein leaves with cleavers in water. Drink the solution to assuage kidney ailments.

Liver Ailments
Mix pure olive oil and lemon juice in warm water and drink once each day.

Lockjaw
To treat lockjaw, place moistened tobacco on the patient's stomach. Remove immediately when a cure is affected.

Measles
- Steep ⅓ teaspoon each of catnip, marjoram, and yarrow, adding a pinch of marigold or saffron. Give the warm tea each hour to one afflicted with measles to reduce the fever.
- Take a tea of elderberry flowers as a remedy for measles.

Mosquito Bites

Apply ammonia, camphor, tar soap, or crushed pennyroyal weed.

Mustache

For a fine, healthy mustache, apply a mixture of the following: 5 drops of oil of bergamot, 7 drops of tincture of cantharides, ½ ounce of simple cerate.

Nervousness

• Chew snakeroot or drink a tea made from dandelion leaf, passionflower, plantain leaf, peppermint, or snakeroot.

• Combine equal portions of the following: wood betony, root of valerian, skullcap herb, and mistletoe. Boil 1 ounce of this mixture in 2 cups of water for 5 minutes. Allow to cool, and strain. Take a small glassful three times daily for nervousness.

Nervous Stomach

Drink bottled mineral water or make your own mineral water by buying some powdered slaked lime (be sure it is slaked lime) at the drugstore. Add one teaspoonful to one quart water. Shake well. Put in refrigerator and leave until the lime has settled to the bottom of the jar. Pour off the clear, top liquid and drink a few swallows for stomach relief.

Nettle Sting

Rub the area that has been pricked by nettles with mint, sage leaves, or rosemary.

Neuralgia

• In 2 cups of boiling water, steep 1 ounce of burdock seeds for 1 hour. Strain. Take 1 tablespoonful before meals and retiring to relieve neuralgia.

• Bind wilted horseradish leaves on the area affected by pain of neuralgia.

Nosebleed

• To stop bleeding from the nose, chew paper.

• Blood flow from the nose can be stopped by insertion into the nostrils of wool saturated with rose oil.

• To arrest nosebleed put grated dried beef into the nostrils.

• In cases of nosebleed, soak cotton in nettle juice and insert it into the nostrils.

Overweight

Put 1 teaspoon each of fennel seed and chickweed with ½ teaspoon of sassafras bark, sweet flag root, kelp, and licorice in 1 quart of boiling water. Simmer for 5 minutes. Keep the liquid covered for 15 minutes. Strain. Drink ⅔ cupful, warmed, three times daily to reduce excess weight.

Pain

• Sprinkle brown sugar on a pan of burning coals. To alleviate the pain of a wound, hold the injured part over the smoke.

• To relieve pain in the back, mix vinegar and beef gall. Apply the solution to the affected area morning and evening.

Phlegm

• Dry the leaves of coltsfoot. Smoke them as you would tobacco to loosen phlegm in the chest.

• To remove phlegm from the stomach, make a tea of chicory leaves.

Pleurisy

• To cure pleurisy, ingest a tea of catnip or pennyroyal, and then apply a poultice of hot boiled nettles.

• Boil 1 ounce of pleurisy root in 2½ cups of water for 10 minutes. Strain. Take a small glassful three times daily to treat pleurisy.

Poison Ivy

• Wash area often with a cooling solution of baking soda and water and apply apple cider vinegar, or squeeze the juice from jimson weed and use as a lotion.

- Put 1 tablespoon of carbolic acid and 1 ounce of glycerin in 2 cups of boiling water. Bathe areas affected by poison ivy with this solution.
- Apply milk, heavily salted, to skin affected by poison ivy. Allow to dry.
- For protection all year from the rash of poison ivy, eat a small amount of either the leaves or roots of the plant at the onset of spring.

Poisoning

Give a strong emetic of warm water, mustard, and salt mixed. Cause vomiting by swallowing small piece of soap or tobacco.

Poultices

- Boil grape leaves with barley meal to make a soothing poultice for wounds and inflammations.
- Roast pokeweed root in hot ashes. Mash them and use in a poultice for felon.
- Thicken yeast with finely powdered elm bark and charcoal. Apply as a poultice to open sores.

Prickly Heat

- Dust the skin with browned cornstarch to cure prickly heat.
- As a remedy for prickly heat, keep a piece of alum in the pocket.
- Add 1 quart of alcohol, 1 ounce of borax in powdered form, and 2 ounces of cologne to 3 quarts of rainwater. Bathe with this mixture three times daily as a remedy for heat rash.

Quinsy

- Sprinkle densely with red pepper a rasher of salt pork. Bind it about

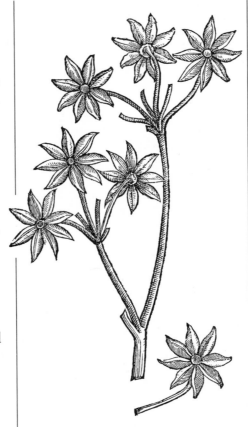

the throat upon retiring to alleviate quinsy.
- A good remedy for tonsillitis is a dose of rattlesnake oil.
- Boil 1 quart of water containing 1 tablespoon of tincture of benzoin. Inhale the vapors to soothe tonsillitis.
- Rub a combination of turpentine and oil of anise on the throat to relieve the soreness of tonsillitis.

Rheumatism

- Powder the following: bloodroot, blue flag root, sweet flag root, prickly ash. Steep in spirits. Take a dose of from 1 tablespoon to a small glassful three times daily for rheumatism.

- Heat a sadiron. Cover the iron with woolen cloth, and moisten it with vinegar. Apply as hot as can be tolerated to parts afflicted with pain of rheumatism.
- Put 4 eggs into 2 cups of cider vinegar, dropping in the shells as well. When the vinegar has eaten up the eggs, add 2 cups of turpentine. Bathe on parts affected by rheumatic pain.
- Combine 2 cups of bear or coon oil, 2 cups of spirits of turpentine, and 2 cups of spirits of camphor. Rub sore areas with this solution for 25 minutes to relieve the pain of rheumatism.
- Simmer 2 ounces of chamomile flowers and 3 ounces of celery seed in 2 quarts of water until the liquid is reduced to 3 pints. Strain. Take 1 small glassful before eating to cure rheumatism.
- Steep 1 tablespoon of sulphur and 2 cups of pokeberries in 4 cups of brandy. Let stand for 24 hours. Take 1 tablespoon three times daily as a remedy for rheumatism.
- Blend 1 ounce of cream of tartar, 1 ounce of sulfur, ½ ounce of rhubarb, and 1 teaspoon of guaiacum into 2 cups of honey. Stir 1 tablespoon of this into a glass of water and take in the morning and evening.
- The miseries of rheumatism can be eased by a massage with goose oil. Follow this with a drink of calomel mixed with cayenne pepper, gum camphor, and tartarized antimony.

Ringworms

- Apply juice from a green walnut hull to area three times each day until ring and redness disappear.
- Dissolve 1 teaspoon of borax in 2 ounces of warm cider vinegar. Apply on the scalp to combat ringworm.
- Mix vinegar and gunpowder. Apply the paste to ringworm.
- Drop a copper coin in vinegar. While it is still wet, place it in the area affected by ringworm.
- Wash the root of yellow dock, and chop it into small sections. Simmer in vinegar. Strain. Apply the solution three times daily to cure ringworm.

Scalds

Relieve instantly by using common baking soda applied thickly to wet rags and placed on scalded area. If baking soda is not available flour may be used.

Scalp

Steep ¾ ounce of nettles and ¾ ounce of sage in 2 cups of alcohol for 1 week. Strain, and gradually add 2½ ounces of castor oil. Apply to the scalp to heal irritation.

Scarlet Fever

Steep 1 teaspoon of yarrow, 1 teaspoon of catnip, and ¼ teaspoon of saffron in 1 cup of hot water. Drink 1 cupful each hour to treat scarlet fever.

Scrofula

Cover areas affected by scrofula with codfish skins.

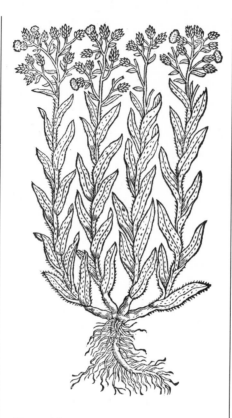

Seasickness

- To overcome seasickness, drink great quantities of strong green tea as frequently as possible.
- Chew several leaves of sage or mint until they reach the consistency of pulp and no longer have flavor. This is a good remedy for seasickness.

Sinus

To relieve the congestion and pain of sinus trouble, chew honeycomb.

Snake Bite

- Incise the snake bite, and apply a mixture of tobacco and salt.
- To treat snake bite, cut open a freshly killed chicken and place it on the wound.

Sores

- To heal sores apply a poultice of powdered comfrey root.
- Boil the following in weak lye: blue vervain, smart weed, wormwood herb. Apply with a feather to sores.
- Boil over a low flame for 30 minutes ½ pound of rosin, 1 pound of lard, and 10 ounces of elder bark. Strain and apply to sores.

Sore Breasts

- Roast turnips until soft. Mash them with oil of roses. Apply this mixture to sore breasts twice daily and cover them with flannel.
- Boil 1 pound each of spikenard root and tobacco and 12 pounds of comfrey root in 3 quarts of lye until nearly dry. Press out the juice, and add beeswax and pitch to it. Simmer over a medium flame. When it becomes salve-like, apply it to sore breasts.

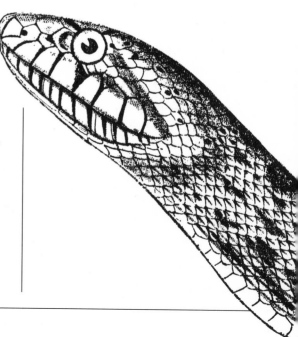

Sore Mouth

- Combine ½ teaspoon of tincture of myrrh, ½ teaspoon of borax, and 1 teaspoon of glycerin in sufficient boiled water to equal 1 ounce. Several times a day apply the solution on a camel's hair brush to the inside of the mouth.
- Mix the following with honey: burnt alum, burnt leather, powdered sage, roasted egg yolk. Use this mixture to cure a sore mouth.

Sore Throat

- Apply fat bacon or pork to outside of throat and hold in place by tying a rag around it. Keep in place until soreness is gone. Swab the throat with diluted tincture of iron. Gargle with warm salt water or apple cider vinegar, repeat often. Hold small piece of garlic in mouth for several minutes, several times during the day.
- Combine 1 ounce of honey and 2 teaspoons of borax in 2 cups of hot water. Use while it is yet warm as a gargle for a sore throat.
- Boil 2 ounces of apple cider, ½ red pepper pod, and 1 tablespoon each of honey and salt. Add to 1 cup of strong sage tea. Take a teaspoonful when required to relieve a sore throat.
- Make a strong brew of equal amounts of hyssop and sage. Add ¼ ounce of borax to each cupful. Gargle often with this solution to ease soreness of the throat.
- In 2 cups of water, steep a red pepper. Strain, and add 1 heaping teaspoon each of salt and of powdered alum and ½ cup of vinegar. Gargle with this mixture when necessary to soothe a sore throat.

Spasms of Muscles, Cramps

Eat two teaspoons of honey with each meal.

Speck in Eye

Place flaxseed in eye to absorb particle.

Spider Bite

- Combine the beaten white of 1 egg with alum powder. Apply as a poultice to relieve the pain and swelling of a spider's bite.
- Treat a spider bite by applying the juice of plantain leaves to the wound. Take 2 ounces of the juice internally.

Splinters

- To remove splinters or thorns, apply raw bacon as a poultice.
- Mash the freshly picked leaves of marsh mallow. Mix them with niter and apply to splinters and thorns for their easy removal.

Sprains

- Mix sea salt and cider vinegar into a paste and apply; or apply Epsom salts with a cloth wet in vinegar.
- For 2 hours continually beat a large spoonful of honey and the same amount of salt with 1 egg white. Allow this to stand for 1 hour. Apply to the sprained area the oil which comes from this mixture.
- Mix kerosene, cider vinegar, and salt to make a liniment for sprains.
- Make a poultice using 2 hen's eggs, 1 ounce of ginger, and 1 teaspoon of salt. Use it on sprains.

Stiff Joints

- Simmer 1 pound of hog's grease into which a handful of yellow clover has been dropped. Strain, and add 1 ounce of rattlesnake oil, 10 drops of oil of lavender, and 1 ounce of olive oil. Mix thoroughly. Use it three times daily to massage stiff joints.
- Massage stiff joints four times a day with olive oil in which camphor gum has been dissolved.

Stye

- Into a small cloth bag, put 1 teaspoon of black tea. Moisten it with boiling water. While the bag is yet warm, place it on the eye during the night. By morning the stye should be gone. Repeat the application if necessary.
- Make a poultice of milk and linseed meal. Apply it warm to a stye. Renew the poultice every 6 hours.

Sunburn

• Apply butter or buttermilk, boil tan oak or commercial wet ground tea and apply frequently. Wet dressings of Epsom salts or baking soda also help.

• Apply the following ointment for relief of sunburn: Mix 2 tablespoons of almond oil, 2 tablespoons of spermaceti, and ½ teaspoon of honey. Add attar of roses for a pleasant scent.

• Mix lime juice in Vaseline to make a soothing salve for sunburn.

Tapeworm

• Drink a tea made from pumpkin seeds to be rid of tapeworm.

• In 2½ cups of water, boil 1 ounce of fern root until 2 cups of liquid remain. Abstain from eating before going to bed. Upon arising, take a small glassful of the liquor to combat tapeworm.

• Make a tea of 2 ounces of pomegranate root in 2 cups of water. Drink this remedy for tapeworm in three doses before eating breakfast.

Teeth Coming Loose

Dissolve ¼ ounce of myrrh in 1 pint of port wine; add 1 ounce of oil of almonds. Wash the teeth each morning with this solution to make loose teeth more secure.

Toothache

• Mix warm vinegar and salt, hold in mouth until pain ceases. For cavities, plug with cotton doused with pepper and ginger.

• Mix 1 dram of powdered alum and 3 drams of nitrous spirits of ether. Apply on a dab of cotton to an aching tooth.

• Melt 16 parts of beeswax and 4 parts of lard. Cool. Then add 8 parts of oil of cloves and 8 parts of creosote. Thoroughly soak cotton in the mixture. Roll into small sticks and chew slowly when needed to alleviate a toothache.

• To relieve a toothache chew the leaves of catnip.

• Roast an onion. Cut it in two and place a half, while still hot, over the pulse of the wrist on the side opposite the painful tooth.

Vomiting

• Remove the peel from a good-sized onion and slice it in two. Put a half in each armpit to check vomiting.

• Brown field corn, but do not burn it. Immerse it in boiling water. Drink the liquid when necessary to arrest vomiting.

• Pound green wheat, and pour boiling water over it. Squeeze out the juice, and sweeten it with sugar. Take 1 tablespoon at 10-minute intervals to stop vomiting.

• Skin and clean the gizzard of a freshly dressed chicken. Simmer it in 1 pint of water for 30 minutes. Discard the gizzard. Sipping the broth cures most cases of vomiting.

Warts

• The juice from milkweed or castor oil will take away warts when applied regularly.

• To remove warts, rub them with green walnuts or bacon rind.

• Collect cobwebs to form a mass big enough to cover a wart but not touch the flesh around it. Place the wad of cobwebs on the wart, and ignite it. When the fire has consumed the cobwebs, the wart will turn white and disappear in several days.

• Remove warts by applying freshly crushed marigold leaves and their juice.

• Make a paste of vinegar and hickory-wood ashes. Use as an application to destroy warts.

- To be rid of warts, apply oil of cinnamon to them four times daily.

Whooping Cough

- Cook 2 ounces of garlic in 2 ounces of oil. Strain. Mix in 1 ounce of camphor and 2 ounces of honey. A dose of 1 teaspoon taken four times a day, or as required, will relieve whooping cough.
- Cut into pieces 3 prickly pear leaves, and boil them in 1 quart of water for 30 minutes. Filter the liquid through a cloth to strain out all prickles. Add a bit of sugar to sweeten, and boil for a short time. Take 2 teaspoonfuls to cure whooping cough.

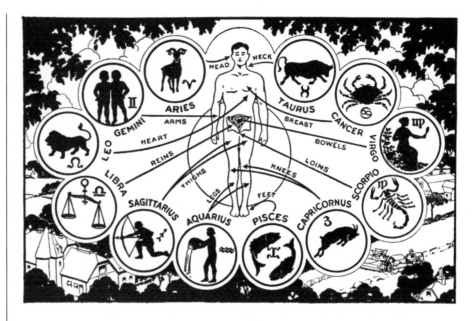

- Add sweet oil to brandy and simmer with a slice of onion. To treat whooping cough externally, spread the solution, morning and evening, on the soles of the feet, the spine, and the chest.
- Rub the spine with garlic to cure whooping cough.

Wounds

- To treat wounds apply a mixture of 1 tablespoon of crushed rosemary and a pinch of salt.
- Treat wounds with an application of fresh warm cow dung.
- Sprinkle the dried, powdered leaves of wild sunflowers on a wound to arrest blood flow.
- To treat the wound from a rusty nail, apply peach leaves that have been pounded into pulp.

Moon Sign Medicine

Followers of moon signs in the treatment of human and animal ailments say that all procedures should be in rhythm with the moon and its various phases. Most agree that proper timing should be as follows:

Dental Work

Cavities should be filled during a waning moon period of the third and fourth quarter and in a fixed sign of Aquarius, Taurus, Leo, or Scorpio. Teeth should be extracted during a waxing moon period of the first and second quarters, but only in the signs of Pisces, Gemini, Virgo, Sagittarius, or Capricorn.

Plates are best made under a decreasing moon of the third and fourth quarters and in a fixed sign of Aquarius, Taurus, Leo, or Scorpio.

Operations

The best time to have operations, pull teeth, remove tonsils, or remove any growth is when the signs are in the knees or feet (the best), such as Capricorn or Pisces.

Removal of Noxious Growths (this includes corns, calShared, superfluous hair, warts, any unwanted growths): Use a barren sign such as Aquarius, Aries, Gemini, Leo, Virgo, or Sagittarius with the moon in the fourth quarter.

Surgical procedures: Choose a time when the moon is on the increase in the first and second quarters. Vitality and thrifty conditions prevail and wounds tend to heal better and faster during this time. An exception is the cutting away of noxious growths, and this should be done on a decreasing moon, third and fourth quarters.

Do not have an operation during the period the moon is in a ruling sign of that part of the body on which the operation is to be performed. Heart operations, for example, should not be performed during the sign of Leo unless absolutely necessary, as Leo rules the heart. If at all possible do not allow an operation on the day the moon is in a ruling sign of that part of the body on which the operation is to be performed as the results are sometimes not good. It is better if the signs are going away from the affected part than approaching it. Consult the table in Chapter 2 for the body parts ruled by the different signs.

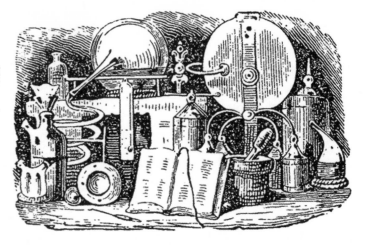

Babies and the Signs

To establish the sex of babies divide in half the time between the last day of menstruation to the first day of the next period. If copulation occurs when the moon is in the feminine signs of Pisces, Taurus, Cancer, Virgo, Scorpio, or Capricorn in the first half of the menstrual cycle as noted above, the child is most apt to be female. If copulation occurs when the moon is in the masculine signs of Aquarius, Aries, Gemini, Leo, Libra, or Sagittarius in the last half of the menstrual cycle, except for the last seventy-two hours before menstruation starts again, the child is most likely to be a boy. The seventy-two hours of the last half plus the first half of the new cycle again produces females.

Hazel Berry of Texas says she practically "cut her teeth" on moon signs. Her father farmed by them and her mother always raised her garden by the signs. Hazel believes babies are born "by the moon." For example, if a baby is thought to be due on April 23 and the next change of the moon phase is April 26 then that's when the baby will be born.

Proper weaning is done when the moon is in a zodiac sign that does not rule a vital organ. These signs are Aquarius, Pisces, Sagittarius, and Capricorn. Weaning should not be done when the moon is in any other sign. The last nursing of the child should be done in a fruitful sign.

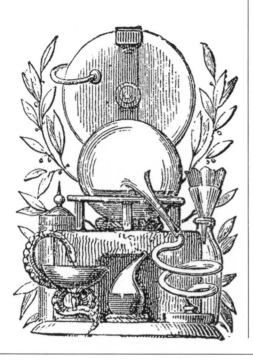

3 | SPIC-AND-SPAN

Cleaning Methods

Old-fashioned procedures for removing spots, stains, and odors are as effective today as they were in times gone by. Here are some cleaning methods that were used generations ago to maintain spic-and-span households.

Acid Stains

Wrap the stained area around some pearlash (potash) and tie with twine. Boil the cloth in soapy water until the stain is gone.

Baked-on Foods

Scour baked-on foods from pans by using a paste of ½ flour moistened with a little vinegar and ½ salt.

Barrels

Dissolve 2 pounds of baking soda in 4 quarts of hot water. Pour this into a barrel of water and let stand for 12 hours. Empty the liquid and let the barrel stand for 2 hours, and it will be free of odor. All wooden vessels can be treated in this way.

Beds

A good way to shine unvarnished brass beds is to rub them with half a lemon dipped in table salt. After washing them in hot water and drying them well, rub the brass with rottenstone.

Boots and Shoes

For a fast shine, cut a lemon and rub it over your leather boots or shoes; wipe off quickly with a soft cloth.

Bottles and Jars

To remove odor from bottles and jars, fill them with a solution of water and dry mustard. Let stand for several hours and rinse in hot water.

Brasses

Crush onion with a little damp earth for cleaning brasses.

Breadboard

Using a piece of pumice, scrub breadboards and carving boards clean with a mixture of borax and salt.

Carpets

Cut the heart of a cabbage in half. Using it like a brush, go over the entire carpet to clean and renovate it.

Cocoa Stains

Soak the article stained with cocoa in a mixture of water and borax to remove discoloration.

Copper

To remove the tarnish from copperware, clean it with half a lemon dipped in a mixture of 1 tablespoon of salt and 1 tablespoon of vinegar.

Crust

To prevent a crust from forming in water kettles, keep a large marble or an oyster shell in them.

Dust Mop

Clean a dust mop by boiling it in water to which have been added 2 tablespoons of paraffin and 1 tablespoon of baking soda.

Faucets

Lime deposits around faucets can be removed by rubbing with a cloth dipped in vinegar.

Feather Beds

To satisfactorily clean feather beds, spread them on tall grass during a heavy shower. Be sure to turn them so that both sides will be soaked. Place them on slats across chairs in the full sun to dry. Beat them with a stick to fluff up the feathers.

Fireplace

When the fire is burning strongly, toss in a handful of salt. It will act as a cleaning agent and aid in preventing chimney fires.

Flatiron

Wrap a piece of beeswax in a coarse rag. When the iron is almost hot enough to use, rub it with the beeswax cloth to remove starch or rust.

Floors

Clean varnished floors and woodwork with cold tea to bring out their shine.

Flyspecks

Soak a bunch of chopped leeks in a half bucket of water for a week. Strain the resulting infusion and use for washing paintings, mirrors, lampshades, etc. to protect them from being dirtied by flies. To remove flyspecks from varnished furniture, clean with a mixture of half cold water and half skimmed milk.

Fruit Stains

Hold cloth stained by fruit over a piece of burning sulphur. Wash thoroughly.

Glue

Use a cloth dipped in vinegar to remove glue from fabrics.

Gold Articles

Make a paste of cigar ashes and water to polish gold articles.

Grease Spots

Stale grease can best be removed with wood alcohol. Rinse the garment, scrub it with yellow soap, then give it a thorough rinsing in hot water.

Greasy Pots and Pans

Wipe out greasy pots and pans with paper; then scour them with corn meal.

Grindstone

When your grindstone gets coated with dirt and oil and will barely sharpen an axe or knife, clean it easily by holding a piece of ice to the stone while you slowly turn it.

Ink on Cloth

To remove ink stains from white cloth, rub them with freshly picked sorrel. Wash with soap and water, and if necessary repeat the procedure.

Ink on Paper

To remove writing in ink from paper, add 2½ drams of muriate of tin to 4 drams of water and apply with a camel's-hair brush. When the writing has disappeared, dip the paper in water and allow to dry.

Iron Stains

Soak the cloth with iron stains in buttermilk. Dry it in the hot sun. Then launder in cold water.

Kid Gloves

Clean kid gloves by rubbing them with cream of tartar.

Knives

To clean rusty knives, insert the blades in an onion and let stand for a half hour. Rust will quickly disappear when this is followed by washing and polishing.

Lace

Put 1 rounded teaspoon of borax in 1 pint of warm soapsuds. Let soiled lace soak in this for 1 hour. Rinse 3 times, adding 1 teaspoon of sugar to the last rinse water.

Lamp Globes

To remove smoke stain from lamp globes, soak them in hot water in which washing soda has been dissolved. Then wash the globes with a good stiff brush in a pan of warm water to which has been added 1 teaspoon of powdered carbonate of ammonia. Rinse them in cold water and dry.

Lamps

To prevent a lamp from smoking, soak the wick in vinegar; allow it to dry thoroughly before using it.

Leather Articles

Clean leather articles by rubbing them with equal parts of vinegar

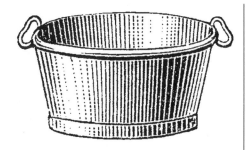

and boiled linseed oil. Then polish with a soft cloth.

Leather Bookbindings

Brighten leather bookbindings by rubbing them with egg white.

Linoleum

To clean and preserve new linoleum, wash it with beer, and wipe it dry. Do this daily for the first week. Then clean it weekly with warm, clear water. When it is dry, sponge with beer. Washing linoleum with milk will also help to preserve it.

Mildew

Rub soap on mildew; then apply salt and lemon juice to both sides of the material. Wash and hang in the open air to dry.

Mud Stains

Remove mud stains from black cloth by first brushing the garment well and then rubbing the stains with half of a raw potato.

Odor

If clothing has a musty odor, restore it to freshness by placing charcoal in the folds.

Paint Brushes

To soften and clean hardened paint brushes, insert them for a few minutes into boiling vinegar. Then wash them in warm soapy water.

Paint Odor

A pailful of water placed in a freshly painted room will eliminate the offensive paint smell.

Piano Keys

Clean piano keys by using a piece of silk cloth barely moistened with alcohol.

Picture Frames

To bring luster to the gold leaf of picture frames, rub them with boiled onion juice and wipe dry. Gilt frames can be cleaned and brightened by washing with a mixture of 2 egg whites and 1 ounce of soda.

Pots and Pans

Boil apple peelings in aluminum pots and pans to brighten the metal.

Privies

Three spoonfuls of spirits of turpentine in a pail of water is an effective cleaner for eliminating odors in privies.

Rugs

Sprinkle a generous amount of corn meal on a rug where there are grease spots. Gently brush it into· the rug, and leave it for 24 hours before removal.

Rust on Cloth

To remove rust stains from white cloth, put a slice of lemon between two layers of cloth on the stain; apply a very hot iron. Repeat until the stain has disappeared.

Rusty Pots

Remove rust stains from iron pots by boiling water and clean hay in them. Allow to stand for 10 hours and boil again with fresh water.

Saucepans

Boil a few pieces of rhubarb in water to remove lime in saucepans.

Scorches

Clothing that has been scorched during ironing should be laid in the bright sunshine.

Shades

Dirty window shades can be cleaned with a piece of rough flannel dipped in flour.

Shawls

Spread a clean cloth on the table and sift dry white corn meal over it. Place the soiled shawl on this and sprinkle more corn meal on top. Roll it up tight. After seven days dust away the meal, and the shawl will be clean.

Silver

Clean tarnished silver by soaking it in potato water for 2 hours. Use a soft brush and silver polish to remove any lingering tarnish.

Sink Drains

To keep sink drains free of unpleasant odors, pour into them 1 gallon of water to which has been added ⅓ pound of calcium chloride.

Skunk Odor

Soak clothing in milk, vinegar, or tomato juice to remove the odor of skunk. If this fails, bury the garments.

Smoke

Put vinegar in an open vessel to eliminate the odor of smoke.

Stains

Apply glycerin to wine and fruit stains. Let it remain for 5 minutes and rinse.

Steel Machinery

Heat 1 pound of lard. Dissolve 12 ounces of powdered gum in it. Add enough black lead to make the mixture the color of iron. Rub this on steel or iron machinery, and leave it for 24 hours. Then rub with a soft rag. This method will prevent rust from forming on sewing machines, coffee grinders, etc.

Sticky Iron

Run a hot iron over salt sprinkled on a piece of paper to remove sticky spots from its sole.

Stovepipes

The best way to clean stovepipes is to put a piece of zinc on the coals in the fire.

Tar on Clothing

To remove tar, rub the clothing with lard, and leave it for an hour or more. Scrape off the lard, and scrub the garment with hot water and soap. If this is not completely successful, apply turpentine.

Tar on Skin

Take tar from your hands by rubbing them with lemon or orange peel and then wiping them off.

Tea Stains

Mix 1 tablespoon of salt with 1 cup of soft soap. Use it to rub the tea stains. Spread the cloth on the grass in a sunny spot. Leave it for two days and then launder.

Vases

Put soapy water and crushed eggshells into vases or bottles that are difficult to clean because of narrow openings. Shake well and rinse.

Wallpaper

To remove grease spots from wallpaper, rub them lightly with a piece of flannel dampened with spirits of wine.

Wax

To remove candle-wax drippings, place a blotter on the spot and hold a hot iron over the blotter.

Windows

Add 1 tablespoon of kerosene to 1 gallon of water for washing windows. This solution will prevent the glass from streaking. To make windows shine, add a little vinegar, or rub them with newspaper.

Wood

Remove stains from wood surfaces with ½ ounce of vitriol in 4 ounces of water. Use a cork instead of a cloth for rubbing.

Woodwork

To clean oak woodwork, wash it with warm beer. Next boil 2 quarts of beer, 1 tablespoon of sugar, and a piece of beeswax about the size of a walnut. Brush the wainscoting with this mixture. When it is dry, polish it with flannel.

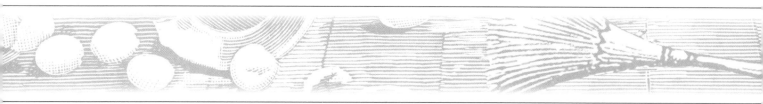

Woolens

Remove stains from black or colored woolens by soaking them in water in which a handful of ivy leaves has been boiled for 15 minutes.

Wrought Iron

Clean wrought iron with a drop of paraffin on a soft cloth.

Cleaning Aids

Laundry Soap

Put 1 pound of quicklime into 1 gallon of very hot water. Stir occasionally over the next 2 hours. Allow it to settle. Pour off the clear liquid into a large vessel, and add

5 gallons of soft water, 4 pounds of bar soap, and 3 pounds of washing soda. When the soap and soda are dissolved, stir in 2 ounces of salt. After the mixture has cooled a bit, pour it into jars or half-barrels. Store covered for use. This amount of half-solid soap will wash four times as much laundry as the bar soap alone would do.

Hard Soap

Put 6 pounds of washing soda, 3½ pounds of quicklime, and 4 gallons of soft water into a kettle. Boil. Stir until the soda is dissolved and the quicklime slaked. Allow it to settle; then pour off the clear liquid. Rinse the kettle, and boil in it 6 pounds

of liquid grease (during the winter save drippings from ham, mutton, etc. for soapmaking) and ½ pound of borax until soap begins to form. Empty it into a tub to cool.

When hard enough, it can be cut into bars and placed on boards to dry. This is a good laundry soap; with the addition of a little perfume, it becomes a nice complexion soap. Scent it with oil of sassafras or oil of caraway, using 1 ounce to 10 gallons of soap. Stir it in well when the soap is fairly cool.

Scouring Soap

Put 1 pound of borax and 3 pounds of washing soda into 3 gallons of soft water. When they are dissolved, add 10 pounds of yellow soap shaved fine and 1 pound of tallow. Heat to melt. Then sift a quantity of lime to remove the lumps, slake it, and add as much to the mixture as you can stir in well. This soap is good for difficult cleaning jobs, such as removing grease or tar from the hands.

Renovation Soap

Put 3 drams of camphor gum into 1 ounce of alcohol and reserve. Put 1 dram of powdered pipe clay into 2 ounces of beef gall and reserve. Reduce ¼ ounce of saltpeter and ¼ ounce of borax to powder; mix them and 1 teaspoon of common salt with ¼ ounce of honey and reserve. After 3 hours shave ¼ pound of good soap (such as used by barbers) into a porcelain vessel. Add the gall mixture and stir over a low fire until the soap is dissolved.

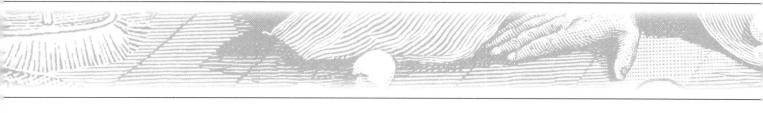

Remove from the stove and allow to cool somewhat. Put in the other ingredients, stirring well. Quickly pour the mixture into glass jars, where it will harden. Store them covered in a dark closet until needed for renovating soiled garments. To use, spoon out ½ ounce, and dissolve it in 1 quart of boiling soft water. Scrub soiled areas of jackets, trousers, etc. with a scouring brush dipped in this solution.

Washing Fluid

Dissolve concentrated lye (potash) in 1 gallon of rainwater. Put 2 ounces each of muriate of ammonia and salts of tartar into another gallon of soft water. Combine both solutions in a 2-gallon stone jug. Cork and shake. Use ½ cup of the fluid for each boiler of dirty clothes.

Washing Powder

Pulverize 1 pound of borax, 2 pounds of washing soda, and 2 ounces of salts of tartar. Mix them, and add 1½ ounces of muriate of ammonia. Bottle and cork. Use 1 rounded tablespoon of the powder in each boiler of laundry.

Homemade Lye

Here is how to make lye the old-fashioned way. Save fireplace ashes from hickory or oak logs. Find a fallen hardwood tree trunk, and burn it out hollow. Put in the ashes, and set it over an inclined wooden trough, with a bucket at its lower end. Due to the corrosive effect of lye, the bucket should be of enamel,

pottery, or iron. Pour a considerable amount of water on the ashes. It will filter through them, run down the trough, and drip into the bucket as a lye solution.

Soap

The making of soap is thought to have developed accidentally through early Roman sacrifices. After animals were burned to appease a god or win divine favor, ashes and a little fat remained. Rain added the final ingredient that produced suds.

Homemade soap is very inexpensive and will efficiently whiten your laundry. Here are the requirements for making 9 pounds of soap:

> 6 pounds grease (drippings or drippings mixed with half suet for a whiter soap)
> 1 can lye (13 ounces)
> 5 cups cold water

Whenever you trim meat, save the fat. Keep bacon fat, beef fat, or

pork fat in the refrigerator. After several cupfuls have accumulated, cook it slowly, rendering out the liquid fat. Strain the grease through cheesecloth. You will need 6 pounds of drippings to make a good batch of white soap.

If you failed to strain the drippings after rendering the fat, prepare the grease the day before making soap. Melt each 3 pounds of grease in 2 quarts of water. While it is heating, stir. Allow it to cool. The following day, remove the cold grease from the surface of the water. The salt and cracklings should remain at the bottom of the vessel.

Put a large stainless-steel pan or glass jar in the sink. Fill it with 5 cups of water. Wearing rubber gloves (remember that lye is caustic), carefully and slowly stir in 1 can of lye with a steel or wooden spoon. Reheat the grease, and cool it until tepid (130°F). Stir it into the lye and water. Continue stirring for twenty minutes, when the soap should have the consistency of honey. Pour it into a granite or heavy metal pan. Allow to set overnight.

The next day, cut the soap into large practical bars or small, personal-sized cakes. However, do not remove them from the pan for several more days. After that, let them season from six weeks to two months.

One-quart milk cartons provide good soap forms. After fourteen to eighteen hours, cut away the cardboard and slice the blocks. Allow the soap to dry further.

You may shave and melt down larger bars for such household tasks as washing woodwork.

If you like, scent the personal-sized soap by adding a few drops of any essential oils before it becomes cool enough to set. Should perfume be added while the soap is too hot, it will escape with the steam; if the soap is too cold, the fragrance cannot be easily incorporated. Try almond oil, attar of roses, lemon, wintergreen, or whatever you prefer. Another method is to wait until the soap hardens, run it through a meat grinder, and melt it in a double boiler with orange-flower water, rose water, or various other scented waters and common salt. Use 1 pint of scented water and 2 ounces of salt to each 6 pounds of soap. After boiling it, let the mixture cool. Cut it into small cakes with a wire, and dry them away from direct sunlight. Allow to season.

A small bottle of inexpensive hand lotion can be added to hand or bath soap as both emollient and perfume. To make floating bath soap, fold in air (as you would eggs into batter) when the mixture thickens.

Glycerin soap can be made by adding 6 ounces of glycerin to the soap mixture after pouring in the lye solution. This is a good complexion soap.

For saddle soap, use 1 can of lye, 2¾ pints of water, and 6 pounds of tallow. It is excellent for cleaning and preserving leather.

To make tar soap, prepare tallow soap and let it stand, stirring now and then until thickening occurs. Then work in 8 ounces of wood tar. Stir the mixture thoroughly to prevent lumps. Use the soap for shampooing hair.

Water Softener

Thoroughly mix 4 cups of soda ash (found in hardware stores) with 8 cups of waterglass (sodium silicate, available in drugstores). Store the mixture in glass containers.

To soften 5 gallons of water, stir in approximately ½ teaspoon of the concentrate. This ratio is a general recommendation and subject to adjustment according to the water hardness in your particular locale.

Bluing

In 1 quart of soft water, dissolve 1 ounce of Prussian blue powder and ½ ounce of powdered oxalic acid to make a good bluing. It should be added to the last rinse water.

Cleaners for Carpets, Tile, Copper, Glass, and Leather

Carpet Cleaner

Blend equal amounts of salt and baking soda. Add several drops of white vinegar to each 8 ounces of the dry mixture. Stir in sufficient water to form a paste.

Spread the paste on the soiled area, and let it dry completely. Then brush away the powdery cleanser along with the dirt. In the case of stubborn stains, gently scrub the rug when the cleanser is first applied.

Ceramic Tile Cleaner

An inexpensive cleaner for ceramic tile can be made by dissolving 1 tablespoon of trisodium phosphate (found in hardware stores) in ½ gallon of water. Store in a glass container.

To use, moisten a sponge with the cleaner. Always wear rubber gloves when preparing or applying the solution.

Copper Cleaner

Combine vinegar and salt. Apply the mixture to copper surfaces with a rag, and rub clean.

Glass Cleaners

Mix a handful of cornstarch in a pail of lukewarm water. Wash windows and mirrors with the solution, and wipe them dry. They will be clean and shiny.

Or mix 1 cup of isopropyl alcohol in 2 cups of water. Add

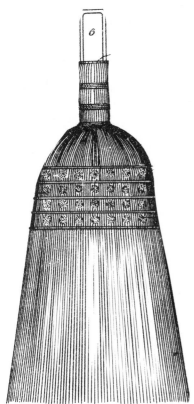

5 drops of lactic acid (found in paint and hardware stores). Transfer the mixture to a spray bottle for cleaning glass and windows.

Another excellent window cleaner is made by stirring 2 tablespoons of ethylene glycol into 3 cups of water. (Ethylene glycol can be bought at service stations.) Put the solution in a spray bottle for use.

Leather Cleaner

To maintain leather articles in a clean, supple condition, combine these ingredients: ¾ cup of isopropyl alcohol, ½ cup of white vinegar, and 1½ cups of water. Stir to blend. Keep the cleaner in a glass container. Rub it on leather with a damp sponge or cloth.

Air Deodorants

Air Deodorant Spray

Mix 4 teaspoons of baking soda in 4 cups of water. Fill a convenient-sized spray bottle. To dissipate offensive odors, spray the solution in a fine mist.

Herbal Deodorant Vinegar

Fill a 1-pint jar with an aromatic material (flower blossoms, leaves, dried herbs, etc.). Heat 2 cups of white vinegar. When it reaches the boiling point, add it to the jar. Put on the lid, and allow the mixture to stand for several weeks, shaking it daily.

After two weeks, check the scent. If it is satisfactory, strain the jar's contents into a decorative container. Set it wherever odors are a problem.

Refurbishing Aids

Creamy Furniture Polish

Grate 2½ ounces of beeswax into a tin can. Melt the wax by placing the can in a pan of preheated water. Blend 1 cup of turpentine with the melted wax. Using a separate vessel, dissolve 2 tablespoons of powdered rosin and 1 ounce of Castile soap in 2 cups of water. Add this to the turpentine mixture. Store the creamy polish in a glass jar.

For use, rub a little at a time on furniture and polish with a dry, soft cloth.

Lemon Oil Furniture Polish

In 1 quart of mineral oil, mix 1 tablespoon of lemon oil (available at drugstores). Use a spray bottle to apply the polish. Wipe clean.

Rust Preventive

Combine raw linseed oil and about 30 percent turpentine. Coat steel tools—spades, chisels, etc.—with the mixture. It will dry quickly, forming a long-lasting, waterproof finish. When the coating eventually wears off, smear on another. Make sure that the steel is completely dry before applying the mixture, which should never be used on wood.

Whitewash

In 3 gallons of water, soak 25 pounds of slaked lime until a paste forms. You will have roughly 4 gallons of lime paste.

Dissolve 3 pounds of salt in 1½ gallons of boiling water. Allow the solution to cool. Then add it to the lime paste, and stir in 1½ pounds of white Portland cement.

Apply the whitewash to a slightly damp wall for best results.

Another good whitewash can be made by adding ½ pound of salt, dissolved in 3 gallons water, and 1 pound of sulphate of zinc to 8 quarts of slaked lime. This combination produces a firm, hard wash that will not crack. The salt makes the whitewash stick better. For a clearer white, add a little bluing.

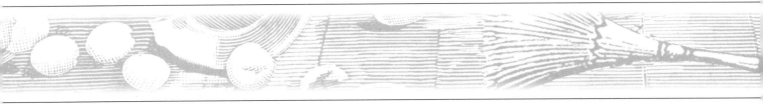

Adhesives

Ordinary paste is made by mixing rice flour or wheat flour in water, with or without boiling. To improve it, various adhesives, such as glue, gum arabic, and rosin, may be added along with alum.

Simple Flour Paste

Make simple cold flour paste by mixing 1 tablespoon of flour with 1 cup of cold water. Add several drops of carbolic acid as a preservative.

Library Paste

Dissolve ½ ounce of alum in 2 cups of warm water. Stir in flour until the consistency of cream is reached. Break up all lumps. Add a few drops of oil of cloves and 1 teaspoon of powdered resin. Boil until thick. If the mixture becomes too thick, thin it with a small amount of hot water. Put it in a glass jar and close it tightly. Keep it in a cool place. When necessary, soften the paste with several drops of warm water, and melt it over very low heat.

Gum Arabic Paste

Dissolve 2 ounces of gum arabic in 2 cups of water in the top of a double boiler. Combine ½ ounce of white sugar and ½ ounce of laundry starch. Stir the mixture into a little cold water until it reaches the consistency of thick paste, free of lumps. Add this to the contents of the double boiler and boil until the starch is clear. Put in several whole cloves or a few drops of any essential oils, such as oil of cloves, lavender, etc., for a preservative. A little alcohol will also serve as a preservative.

Isinglass Glue

Isinglass—not to be confused with mica, which is often so named—is an animal tissue mainly derived from the air bladders of some fish. It dissolves easily in water and is a strong adhesive.

Dissolve 1 pound of isinglass in 2 cups of soft water in a double boiler. Slowly add ¼ cup of nitric acid, and stir continuously. Bottle the liquid glue and close tightly to prevent evaporation. It is excellent for paper, leather, wood, and many other materials.

Cement for Broken China and Glass

Beat egg whites until frothy. When they have settled, beat in quicklime and grated cheese. Mend china

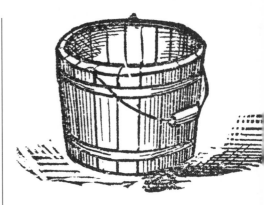

or crockery by applying it to the broken edges.

In boiling water (enough to fill a wineglass) dissolve gum acacia. Add sufficient plaster of Paris to produce a thick paste. Use this almost-colorless mixture to cement broken china.

Combine 1 pint each of vinegar and milk. Remove the whey, and beat it well with 5 egg whites. Add enough finely powdered quicklime (you may substitute burned oyster shells for the lime) to form a thick paste. It is excellent for mending glass or china.

Cement for Labels on Tins

Boil glue in vinegar. Thicken the liquid with flour to make a paste for sticking labels on tin boxes.

Cement for Paper

To make a white, almost transparent paste for fancy paper work that calls for a strong but colorless cement, mix a little cold water into powdered rice. While stirring constantly, slowly add boiling water until the proper consistency is reached. Then boil for 1 minute.

Cement for Boots and Shoes

Combine 1½ ounces of sulphide of carbon and ¼ ounce of gutta-percha. Bottle it for use in applying patches to boots and shoes.

Paste for Stamps, Labels, etc.

Put 5 ounces of glue into 20 ounces of water to soak for 1 day. Dissolve 9 ounces of rock candy and 3 ounces of gum arabic in this liquid. It makes a particularly good mucilage for the labeling on bottles to be stored in damp cellars.

Wallpaper Paste

Add enough water to 2 cups of flour to make a thin dough, without lumps. Stir it into 1 gallon of boiling water. When it again reaches the boiling point, pour the hot batter into a tin bucket. Let it stand for 24 hours. Strain it through some coarse muslin. Use the paste as an adhesive for wallpaper.

Fire Control

Fire-Extinguishing Powder

Make a low-cost, effective fire-extinguishing powder by combining 6 pounds of fine silica mason sand (available from a dealer in building supplies) and 2 pounds of sodium bicarbonate (available at grocery stores). Mix them thoroughly, and keep the powder in 1-pound glass or metal containers. Locate them in strategic places.

When extinguishing flames, scatter the mixture on the base of the fire.

Pest Control

Here are some old-time means, passed on from generation to generation, for ridding both house and garden of various pests.

Ants

• Save cucumber peelings and mix them with salt. Place the mixture wherever ants are a problem.

• Place small sponges soaked in sweetened water wherever in the house ants have been seen; the ant-covered sponges can be collected periodically and plunged into hot water.

• Paint the floor with paraffin oil in areas that ants most frequent.

• Mix 3 ounces of powdered fennel, 3 ounces of chrysanthemums, and 1 ounce of powdered sassafras bark with equal parts of red pepper and borax. Spread where ants have been seen.

• Boil 1 cup of tar in 1 quart of water. Put this in shallow containers to destroy ants.

• To rid the home of red ants, put slices of raw onion in the closets.

• If you can locate ants' nests outside the home, put quicklime into the openings and wash it in with boiling water.

• Dissolve camphor in spirits of wine, mix it with water, and pour it into the nests of ants.

• Pouring a solution strong with tobacco into their holes is an effective means of destroying ants.

• A little carbolic acid in boiling water washed down their holes will kill ants.

Aphids

Dissolve 1 ounce of shaved soap in 1 quart of water. Separately, boil 3 pounds of elder leaves in 3 quarts of water for 30 minutes. Cool and strain. Blend this solution with the soapy water and pour or spray on plants to combat aphids in your garden.

Bedbugs

- To exterminate bedbugs apply kerosene, benzine, or corrosive sublimate and turpentine on a small brush to the crevices of a bedstead.
- Fill a quart bottle with equal amounts of spirits of turpentine and alcohol; add 1 ounce of camphor gum. Shake well before using. Apply the solution with a feather to all recesses in the bedstead to rid it of bedbugs.
- Tansy leaves sprinkled between sheets and mattresses will keep bedbugs away.

Centipedes

Though useful for keeping households free of insects, centipedes are not very welcome in most homes. Use pyrethrum powder (made from certain chrysanthemums) to drive them away, putting it freely around pipes.

Cockroaches

- Mash ⅔ pound of plaster of Paris, add a little sugar, and mix with 1 pound of oatmeal. Place in areas most frequented by cockroaches.
- Fill jars partly full of stale beer. Prop sticks against their sides. The roaches, attracted to the beer, will mount the sticks and fall into the jars.
- To rid the premises of cockroaches, mix equal amounts of borax and brown sugar in a dish. Place it where they are most frequently seen.
- Bruise the roots of freshly dug black hellebore. Put them where cockroaches have been observed. Hellebore is poisonous, and they will eat it greedily. The plant can be found growing in marshy places.

Crawling Insects

- Add ½ pound of alum to a pail of hot water. Sprinkle it boiling hot in areas of the house where crawling insects have been seen. This solution is effective against roaches, ants, chintz bugs, and other pests.
- To discourage crawling insects, spread walls and cracks with a solution of 2 pounds of alum boiled in 3 quarts of water.
- Cayenne pepper will keep your pantry free of roaches, ants, and other pests.

Crickets

To destroy crickets, put Scotch snuff into their holes.

Fleas

- Tansy leaves, fresh or dried, will keep away fleas.
- You can eradicate fleas in the kennel by mixing dried walnut leaves with the straw.
- To free your cat or dog from fleas, saturate a string with oil of pennyroyal, and tie it about the animal's neck.

Flies

- To keep the house free of flies, put dishes containing oil of bay leaves on window sills. Alternatively, mix equal amounts of bay leaf pieces, coarsely ground cloves, broken eucalyptus leaves, and clover blossoms. Put this blend in small bags of mesh or some loosely woven material. Hang them just inside entrance doors to repel flies. Or, paint door and window casings with paint to which 4 percent of bay oil has been added.
- Melt 6 ounces of rosin, and add 2 ounces of shortening. When cold, this mixture will have the consistency of molasses. Spread it on small pieces of wood, and place them about the house. Flies are attracted to it and will be held fast.
- To make flypaper, mix equal amounts of castor oil and melted

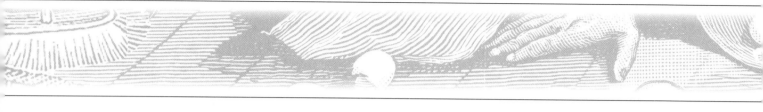

resin. Spread the gooey mixture on nonporous paper (for example, magazine and catalog covers) with a warm knife. Leave the edges clear so that you can fasten the paper down wherever flies are a nuisance.

Garden Insects

• Steep ¾ pound of tobacco leaves in 1 gallon of boiling water. Strain it after 15 minutes. Pour this solution over your garden plants to drive away harmful insects.

• Several bugs that are attracted to roses and some vegetable plants can be lured away to marigolds planted near them.

• If you have a little kitchen garden in the back yard, plant hot peppers among tomatoes and other vine crops to protect them against insects.

Grasshoppers

Make traps for destructive garden grasshoppers by half-filling deep jars with a solution of water and molasses.

House-Plant Parasites

To effectively destroy parasites on house plants, place containers of steaming soapsuds close to them 3 times a week. Once a week wash the leaves to keep them free of insects.

Insect Eggs

Wash corners of drawers and closets with scalding potash water, 1 teaspoon of potash to 12 gallon of water, to destroy insect eggs.

Lice

Sprinkle sulfur under the wings of your chickens and pet canary to rid them of lice.

Mice

• Mix tartar emetic with any favorite mouse food. After eating it, mice will sicken and leave.

• Mint, particularly pennyroyal, strewn on floors and placed in beds, in sacks, and near cheeses will keep mice away because of its odor.

• Mix corn meal and cement, half-and-half. Place in shallow containers where mice run.

Mites

To rid a pantry of mites, empty it and fumigate it with sulfur. Afterward, scrub it thoroughly with kerosene emulsion.

Mosquitoes

• To keep mosquitoes off your person, apply hemlock oil to the hands and face.

• Burning pyrethrum powder in the house will discourage mosquitoes.

• Make traps for mosquitoes in the form of boxes that can be easily closed. Line them with black or dark blue cloth, to which these insects will be attracted.

• A freshly cut sprig of pennyroyal placed in the room will keep away mosquitoes.

Moths

• Clean garments before storing, and wrap them in linen with lumps of camphor to protect them from moths.

• Combine cloves, lavender, tansy, and wormwood as a substitute for camphor to discourage moths.

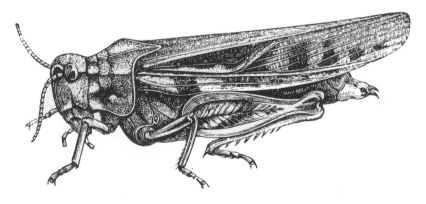

- To protect clothes from moths, hang bunches of woodruff in closets. The herb will also serve to scent the linens.
- Steep walnut leaves in cold water for 2 hours. Bring gently to a boil and continue boiling for 2 minutes. Then allow the leaves to steep for 15 minutes. Wash cupboards with this solution, and moths will stay away.
- As protection against moths place small muslin bags filled with cedar shavings or camphorwood shavings among the clothing, or sprinkle the clothes with allspice berries.
- Hang sachets of dried lemon peel inside cupboards and closets to keep moths away.
- To safely store fur or hair wraps against moths, add a quantity of black pepper to powdered camphor.
- Thoroughly mix 1 dram of flour of hops, 4 ounces of cedar sawdust, 2 ounces of Scotch snuff, and 1 ounce each of black pepper and powdered gum camphor. When scattered among stored woolens and furs, it will keep moths away.
- Grind the following to a fine powder: 3 ounces of orrisroot and ½ ounce each of tanguine leaves, caraway seeds, cinnamon, cloves, mace, and nutmeg. Blend them thoroughly, and put the powdered mixture into small cloth bags. Place these among clothing to protect them from moths.
- Sprinkle salt around the edges and over the entire surface of the rug while sweeping as a preventive against moths.

Rats

- Put powdered potash near the holes of rats. It will encourage them to go elsewhere.
- To exterminate rats, mix 2½ ounces of carbonate of barites with 1 pound of grease. Since this mixture produces intense thirst, put some water close by. (It is a deadly poison; be sure all other animals are kept away from it.)
- Spread slices of bread and butter, and sprinkle them with arsenic and sugar. Press the arsenic and sugar into the bread with a knife to prevent their falling off. Cut the bread into small squares, and put them in rat holes. As soon as some rats begin to die, others will depart.
- Lure rats to one particular spot by leaving quantities of cheese there for some days. When they are accustomed to gathering at this place, affix a piece of cheese to a fishhook suspended about 12 inches from the floor. The first rat to leap at it will be left hanging; his example will put the other rodents to flight.
- Mix well equal amounts of unslaked powdered lime and rye meal. Put this on pieces of board where rats are most frequently seen. Place containers of water close by. When they have eaten the mixture, thirst will drive them to the water, which slakes the lime. The resulting gas will kill them.
- Add 2 parts of bruised squills (squill is the dried bulb of a plant belonging to the lily family) and 3 parts of chopped bacon to enough meal to make a firm mass. Form into small cakes and bake. Put them about the premises as food to exterminate rats. It is thought that the action of the squills is responsible for their death.
- Using a piece of lead pipe as a conduit, introduce 2 ounces of sulphite of potassium into holes occupied by rats outside the house.

Roaches

Place shallow pans or fruit jar lids containing powdered borax in dark corners of the house, especially around the kitchen sink and cabinets. Replace with fresh borax once a week. Do not allow any food waste or pet food to accumulate in infested areas.

Silverfish

Mix boric acid and sugar. Sprinkle it in areas affected by silverfish.

Slugs and Snails

Pour several inches of stale beer into a shallow vessel. Place it where slugs and snails are damaging garden plants. These pests will be attracted to the beer and drown.

4 | WAYS WITH FIBERS AND FABRIC

Plant Dyes and Dyeing Fibers

Plants offer an almost infinite source of pigments for dyeing fibers, yarns, and fabrics. Wool has traditionally been the most common textile in Europe and North America, where large areas are suited to sheep raising. Thus, over the centuries, plant dyes were developed chiefly for that fiber.

You should first experiment with wool, which is easier to color than other natural fibers because of its greater compatibility with plant dyes. However, you can toss samples of any kinds of material into the dye bath along with the wool in order to observe their reaction to a specific dye.

The beginner should start by dyeing fibers or yarns, not cloth. Dyeing a quantity of cloth requires greater skill. Through the use of fibers and yarns, you will learn which plants give dye and amass a repertory of colors.

For initial experiments, we recommend unraveling some discarded, white knitted garment, washing the wool well, and winding it into skeins. If no such garment is available, a hank of white wool from the five-and-ten-cent store will do. Check to see that no man-made fibers have been incorporated.

General Information for Dyeing

• Use steel or unchipped enamel vessels of 1½-gallon capacity for dyeing and plastic pails for rinsing.

• Use soft water for the dye bath and rinses.

• Stir with a glass or stainless-steel rod. A peeled stick (be sure it is smooth) may be used. Since wood absorbs some dye, use a different stick for each color.

• You may want to wear rubber gloves while working.

• Wash all plants before use to eliminate dirt or chemical sprays.

• Loosely tie the wool in skeins with string so that the dye can reach all areas.

• Thoroughly wet yarn or wool fibers before immersing them in the dye bath lest the dye take unevenly.

• Use a dairy thermometer to check the temperature of the dye bath.

• Never dry fibers or yarn in direct sunshine.

Dye Sources and Shades

Certain plants will dye well only in the presence of a mordant—metallic salts that fix the coloring. The following dye recipes for beginners use substances generally available in any locality and in any season. They all produce dyes that do not require mordants. However,

Strain the vessel's contents into a plastic pail, discarding the berries. Pour the liquor back into the dye pot. When it is comfortable to the touch (100°–120°F), immerse the clean and completely wetted wool. Bring to a simmer and continue simmering for thirty minutes, gently moving the wool around with a peeled stick.

Lift a skein from the pot, and allow it to drip into the bath for a few seconds. First rinse it in hot water and gently squeeze out excess water. Then give it a cooler rinse, again squeezing gently. Dry it on a rod suspended on hooks. Now and then turn the skein during drying, and give it a gentle pull to stretch it. Clip or tie on a label indicating the dye source, number of the recipe, and the mordant used, if any. This skein will probably be pink.

Simmer the wool remaining in the pot for thirty minutes longer. Remove another skein. Rinse, label, and hang to dry.

Simmer the rest of the skeins for another hour. Take out a skein. It will be considerably darker than the previous two.

Continue the same procedure until all skeins have been dyed.

you probably have some mordants on hand in your home—vinegar, salt, and cream of tartar. Though not essential to the success of these dyes, a very small pinch of cream of tartar added to the dye pot before introducing the wool will enliven the color.

Dye Source: Blueberries
Shades: Pink to Purple

    1 ounce wool, separated into 5
       skeins and tied with string
    ¾ pound blueberries
    ½ gallon soft water

Crush about ¾ pound of blueberries (they may be fresh, dried, or canned) in an unchipped enamel pan or one of steel. Since the berries will yield juice, add something less than ½ gallon of soft water. Rainwater is preferable, but hard water can be softened with 1 tablespoon of vinegar or a commercial water softener. Bring to a simmer; continue simmering for thirty minutes.

Dye Source: Yellow Onionskins
Shades: Gradations of Yellow

  1 ounce wool, divided
      into 5 skeins
  2 handfuls yellow onionskins
      (outer skins)
  ½ to 1 gallon soft water

Put 2 handfuls of yellow onionskins in ½ to 1 gallon of soft water. Bring to a simmer; simmer for thirty to sixty minutes. Cover to confine the odor. Add water to compensate for whatever amount boils away.

Strain the dye bath, discarding the onionskins. Return the liquid to the vessel. When it is cool enough to touch comfortably, put in the clean, completely wetted wool. Slowly bring to a simmer. Gently stirring the wool about, simmer for fifteen minutes.

Remove a skein and allow it to drain over the pot for a few seconds. Rinse it in hot water and squeeze. Then give it a cooler rinse and squeeze again. Label and hang to dry.

Simmer the remaining wool for fifteen minutes more. Remove another skein. Rinse, label, and hang to dry.

Simmer the rest of the wool for an additional fifteen minutes. Remove a skein. It should be much stronger in color than the other two.

Continue as already directed until all the skeins have been dyed.

Dye Source: Turmeric Powder
Shades: Yellow to Brilliant
      Yellow

  1 ounce wool, separated
      into 5 skeins
  1½ teaspoons turmeric powder
  ½ to 1 gallon soft water

To develop a yellow to brilliant yellow color, accompanied by less aroma than the previous recipe, use 1½ teaspoons of turmeric powder, commonly found on most kitchen spice shelves. Bring ½ to 1 gallon of soft water to hand heat (100°–120°F.) as you stir in the powder. Introduce the completely wetted wool. Gradually bring to a simmer. Simmering for two minutes, gently stir the wool around.

Lift out a skein, and let it drip over the pot a few seconds.

Rinse the wool in hot water and gently squeeze it. Then squeeze it again in cooler water. Label and dry the skein.

Simmer the wool remaining in the pot for two minutes more. Remove another skein. Rinse, label, and hang to dry.

Continue simmering the rest of the wool for a few minutes more, and follow the same procedure. A brilliant yellow can be achieved in ten minutes.

Uses for Dyed Fibers

After a number of dyed skeins have accumulated, they can be used in many interesting ways: for decorative embroidery, for crocheting small individual squares that can be sewed or crocheted together, in appliqué, patchwork, samplers, free hangings, cushions, clothes, and in macramé.

The experienced dyer will probably wish to plan a project in advance and dye the necessary quantity of yarn.

Perhaps these first attempts at dyeing yarn will instill you with the desire to try your hand at dyeing cloth and to experiment further with dyes requiring mordants.

An intriguing number of substances provide dyes—bark, pine cones and needles, nut hulls, berries, flowers, roots, cactus fruit, leaves, lichens, mollusk shells, and even insects. To learn more about natural dyes and the process of dyeing, enjoy the thrill of experimentation with these substances or any others that are available to you.

Quilts

A quilt is a bedcover consisting of two layers of cloth with a filler of batting in between. The three layers are stitched together in patterns or lines.

Simple Quilt Frame

For a finished quilt to lie smoothly, it should be stretched on a wooden frame while its layers are being stitched together.

Construct a simple frame with the following materials:

  4 boards suggested dimensions:
      1 inch by 4 inches by about
          8½ feet in length
  4 C-clamps
  4 chairs of the same height

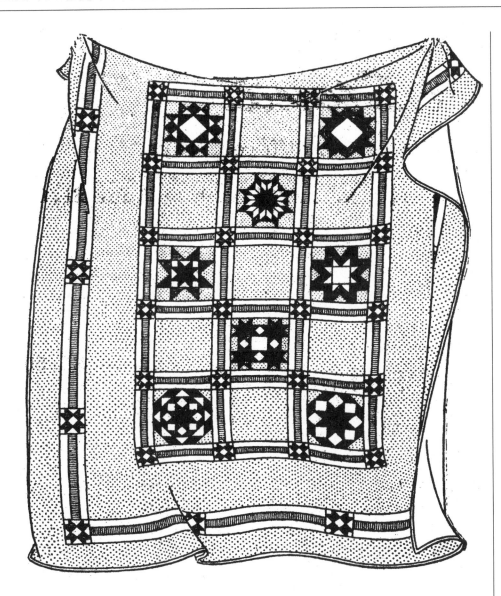

Scrap lumber would be suitable for this project, since the thickness and width of the wood are not crucial. Sand the boards until smooth to avoid splinters during quilting.

Place two boards parallel to one another on the floor. Lay the remaining two across them to form a square. Use the C-clamps to hold the frame together. Raise the frame and rest it on the tops of the chair backs at each corner. Securely fasten the corners to their supports with strips of cloth or rope.

In the middle of each board, make a permanent ink mark to use as a guide when attaching quilting material. Use thumbtacks to fasten the quilt fabric to the frame.

Tied Quilt

Covers with an underside of satin, nylon, or other slick fabrics tend to slide from the bed. Choose a non-slippery, closely woven material for the backing of a tied quilt. Sheets, cottons, and flannels are appropriate for the purpose. An old blanket (if it is thin, use two) provides a good filler. Scraps of fabric sewn together as patchwork or a colored sheet can be used for the top.

Check to see that the measurements of the top and backing are identical. Indicate the center of all four edges with a straight pin.

Now, match the center points on the fabric edges with those on the boards and fasten the backing to the frame. Working from the middle of the edges to their ends, tack the material to the stretcher.

Spread the filler smoothly on the taut backing. Then lay the top over the filler, and pin it to the backing. Adjust the C-clamps to keep the quilt taut.

Now begin tying. Space the ties evenly, with no more than two inches between each. Either stagger them or arrange them in rows. If the fabric pattern is geometric, it can serve as a guide for spacing your ties. To space them evenly on a scattered print, make a 9- by 12-inch grid of cardboard. Punch holes in it at regular intervals. Place the grid on the fabric, and through each hole put a pencil dot to indicate the spot for tying.

Thread your needle with a 3-foot length of string or yarn.

Adjust the ends evenly to form a double strand, but do not make a knot.

Begin at the first pencil mark in an end row. When tying, work through the top of the quilt; have one hand beneath to ensure that the needle penetrates all layers. Make a stitch as small as possible down and back up through the thicknesses of cloth, and leave a tail of thread 2 inches in length on the quilt's surface. Take another stitch directly over the first one. Then tie a firm square knot. Do not snip the thread. Continue to the next pencil mark and repeat the tying method until all the needle's yarn is used. Now go back and cut the thread midway between the pairs of ties. Leave the tails, which should be the same length if you have snipped the thread precisely halfway between ties. Trim any that are uneven.

After you have tied as far as you can reach from one end, work from the other as far as possible. Then free an end of the wooden stretcher. Removing tacks as necessary, roll the tied section around that board until you arrive at the untied area. Replace the clamps and be sure that the material is again pulled taut. Continue in this manner until the tying is completed.

Finish your tied quilt by turning raw edges of both top and bottom to the inside and blind-stitching all sides.

Crazy Quilt

To make a crazy quilt, empty all the fabric scraps from your ragbag. The scraps may be of any color or size. If you prefer that your quilt be washable, choose pieces that are colorfast and will shrink minimally. Iron them so that they are smooth and wrinkle free. Then group the scraps as to light and dark shades.

From some soft, loosely woven material, like muslin or cambric, cut a block sixteen inches square for a foundation. A full-sized

quilt will require twenty such foundation blocks.

For sewing, use a short needle 1⅛ inches in length and white thread (#50 or #60), which is stronger than colored thread and tends to knot less.

Baste a 16-inch-square block of cotton or dacron batting to the foundation block. Dacron will make a fluffy quilt filling. Bulky to work with when fine stitching is required, it is particularly suitable for a crazy quilt, which does not call for delicate sewing. Batting can be bought in sheets.

Start by laying a fabric scrap on the batting in one corner. Fold under the edges on the sides bordering the edges of the block, and baste them in place. Repeat this procedure in the other three corners. Complete the block by placing patches with two basted edges on the unbasted edges of those patches already in the block. Begin in a corner. Working from left to right, use a hemming stitch to sew the patches in place. Produce a pleasing effect by choosing colors that harmonize or make an interesting contrast of light and dark hues. When the entire block is filled in, cover all patch seams with yarn. Use a simple embroidery stitch.

After all twenty blocks have been completed with patches of varying shapes and colors, it is time to "set" your quilt. First, sew the blocks in rows. Since your quilt will be four blocks wide and five long, you may make either four rows of five blocks each or five rows of four blocks each. Now sew the rows together. Make sure that all seams match. Tack the backing in the middle of alternate blocks with decorative stitches.

Finish your quilt by binding the three layers—patches, batting, and foundation—with bias tape purchased in a store or with bias strips you have cut yourself. You may make the bias strips from material that contrasts with the quilt or repeats a predominant color in it. Homemade binding is usually sturdier than store-bought tape.

Puffed Quilt

Making a puffed quilt is simple. Each puff is a square of velvet (you will find cotton velvet easier to use than slippery rayon velvet) or silk sewn to a muslin square and stuffed with batting. The puffs are then sewn together. A quilt of any size can be made by this method.

Cut 3-inch squares of velvet or silk (here's a chance to put those discarded or out-of-date silk ties to use) and 2¼-inch squares of muslin. Putting the wrong sides of the material together, pin the corners of the velvet or silk squares to those of the muslin squares. Pleat the excess velvet or silk on three of the square's sides and pin in place to the muslin. Through the fourth side, fill the puff with batting. Pleat this side and pin it in place.

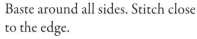

Baste around all sides. Stitch close to the edge.

Keeping the velvet-silk sides facing, and allowing for a ¼-inch seam, sew the puffs together. Then iron the seams open and make rows of either the desired width or length of the quilt.

Line the puffed quilt with some plain soft material. Finally, tack it on the back at regular intervals and catch the seams under the squares so that no tacking shows on top.

Rugs

Braided Cloth Rug

Before attempting to make a braided cloth rug, try a small sample one. In this way you will learn to do even work and to properly calculate the amount of needed materials. A larger rug may then be designed more accurately, ensuring satisfactory results.

Assemble the following equipment and materials:

- 12 (or more) straight pins
- a few large safety pins
- 1 large needle for stitching braids or a bodkin—a thick, blunt needle—for lacing them
- 1 smaller needle for splicing strips
- scissors
- cloth strips, from 1 to 6 inches wide, the width depending upon the weight of the material and the intended rug design

Be sure all cloth is clean and well ironed. Roughly nine ounces of fabric are needed for each square foot of a braided rug. Do not mix materials that have different degrees of shrinkage or varying rates of wear. If you are using old cloth, remove any weak areas.

Cut the material into even strips. When the material is of different weights, the width of strips should be relative to the thickness of the cloth. (Best results are obtained, however, when all the cloth is of uniform weight.) Cut thin cloth in 6-inch widths, medium cloth in 3-inch widths, and heavy cloth in 2½-inch widths. It is wise to use woven, rather than knitted, material. Because the warp is sturdier than the weft, strips should be cut lengthwise on the material. For easy handling, make the strips between 1 and 1½ yards long. Fold the strips in half lengthwise, and

iron them with their raw edges turned in.

To obtain a pleasing proportion of colors in a rug, arrange and rearrange the bundles of materials on the floor until the desired effect is reached.

Put three or more cloth strips on a safety pin—or fasten them to something stationary—for braiding. You could anchor the strips by closing a window on them. Begin with the left-hand strip. Bring it over the second one and under the third. If your braid is composed of more than three strips, continue in the same manner, placing the strip over the fourth strand and under the fifth. Eventually, you will learn to braid from both sides. Maintain an even braid by folding the outer strip as it is brought back rather than pulling it around as you would with a round cord. When nearly at the end of a strand, attach another by opening it out, cutting a bias at its end and the end of the new one, and sewing a smooth seam. Avoid having two joinings parallel to each other in the same braid.

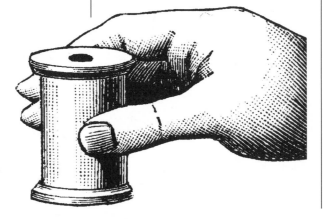

Your first braid is the central one. Its length should equal the difference between the width and length of the completed rug. For example, a rug that's 36 inches by 48 inches would have a central braid of 12 inches. Indicate the center of your rug by attaching a safety pin at the starting point. In this way you can gauge whether you have an identical number of braided rows on each side and at each end.

In an oval rug, turn the end of the central braiding by easing it around and along its side. Avoid cupping. You can do this by pulling the inside strip a bit at the turn and stretching the outside one. When the opposite end is arrived at, the tips of the braid should be fastened in place with pins. The lengths of the parallel braids may then be sewed together.

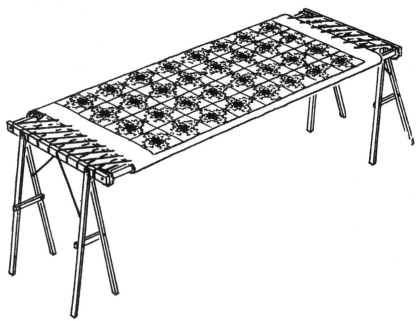

In an oblong rug, the corners must be turned at each round. When flat strips are used, a good corner can be made by bringing the last strip of a braid to the point of turning back, over, and then under the other strips parallel to it. Follow the same procedure with the other strips; then commence braiding as for the straight braid. In the case of round strips, turn corners by easing the tension of the outside ones and drawing up the inside ones.

Sew the contiguous sides of the braids together with a slip stitch or blind stitch; the stitching should not be visible on either side. While sewing, keep the rug flat on a table top to maintain its proper shape. After sewing one side of the rug, braid as far as the next turn. Then sew the braid in place. By alternately sewing and braiding for only short distances, you'll find it easier to prevent cupping and make the braids fit smoothly together.

Add new color while working by fastening a new color, one strip at a time, to the braid. The most favorable effect is achieved when each series of a braid color forms a complete circle in an oval rug and a complete, rectangular stripe in an oblong rug. The border may be composed of colors located in the middle of the rug, but will be more interesting if they are of either brighter or darker hues. The size of the border will vary in proportion to the size of the rug's center according to the vividness of its color.

As your rug nears completion, especially when it is a large one, you may want to transfer it to the floor to keep it perfectly flat as you work.

When the rug has reached its planned dimensions, check for an even number of braids on all sides. Now snip the final braid at the rug's curve. Insert the ends of the braid beneath the last braiding row and pull it into shape, making the two oval rug ends match. Cut the ends of the last braid at uneven lengths so that they terminate at different places.

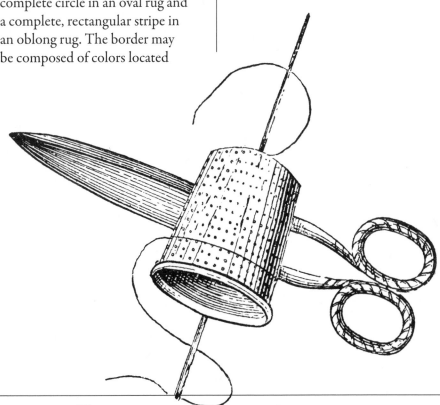

Sew the ends of the strands firmly to the rug's edge.

For a stronger rug, you may fasten the braids together by lacing instead of stitching. Use a bodkin or safety pin for lacing. Thread the bodkin with a strip of material, or fasten the strip to a safety pin. Starting at the turn, lace the braids together. Do this by first sewing the tip of the lacing material to the braid. Now push the threaded bodkin or safety pin through the first loop on the side of the braid on the left, then over to the adjacent braid, and through the first loop on its side. Keep the lacing strand flat by folding it as it turns from loop to loop.

After aligning the braid loops, push the bodkin downward through the left loop, fold it back, and push it up through the right loop. Fold back once more and again pass the bodkin down through the left and up through the right side, thus lacing the two braid lengths together. Continue to braid and lace until the rug is completed. At the turns, extra lacing stitches will be required to avoid cupping. Instead of a strip of material for lacing, you may use a strong thin cord for a different effect.

Crocheted Rug

Crochet a low-cost rug quickly and easily by using fabric from cheap, secondhand clothing and a large crochet needle.

Explore re-sell shops and rummage sales for bathrobes, coats, and wide-skirted dresses with plenty of material in them. Whittle your crochet needle from a ¾-inch-thick wooden dowel, and smooth it with sandpaper.

Rip the garments into strips. Avoid having to sew short strips together by tearing the cloth one way to within ½ inch of the end; then reverse your direction and tear the opposite way. The kind of cloth determines the width of the strips. Those of cotton should be at least 2 inches wide; wool strips can be 1 inch in width. You won't need to hem them if you turn under the raw edges as you work.

Begin the rug with three chain stitches, and continue with a single crochet stitch in concentric circles. Occasionally, when the rug's edges start to curl up, make two single crochets in one stitch. When the end of one strip is reached, sew or tie on another. Keep loose ends on the underside.

5 | WAYS WITH LEATHER

Tanning Hides and Fur Skins

Time and patience are the initial requirements for tanning hides and furs. Choose the hide and fur of deer and squirrel for your first attempts. They are more easily readied for tanning than those of some other animals having thin skins, which require greater skill in preparation to avoid damage.

For all soaking and tanning operations, use a wooden, earthenware, or plastic container. Metal containers react with the salt and tanning chemicals.

Preparations

After skinning the animal, flesh the hide; that is, remove all meat remaining on it. Be sure it is also free of blood and mud. Cutting from the skin side, trim any ragged edges.

The hide is now ready for the tanning process, unless you plan to tan a deerskin into buckskin. In that case, the hair must first be removed. In 5 gallons of water, mix 5 quarts of hydrated lime. Leave the hide in this solution until the hair is easily pushed from the skin with your hand, generally between six and ten days. Spread the hide on a board, and push off the remaining hair with the blunt side of a knife. Then work over both sides of the skin with the back edge of a knife. Hold it nearly flat to remove any fleshy material, grease, or lime. (This is known as *cudding*.)

The remains of the liming process—fleshings, limewater sludge, and lime—can be put to good use as fertilizer because they are particularly suitable for acid soil.

The hair, collected as it is removed from the hide and rinsed several times, can be utilized in plastering. After being washed thoroughly in repeated changes of water and dried completely, it is useful in padding, upholstery, and in the insulation of pipes. The body hair of deer is valuable for making the bodies of fishing flies. By adding a water-repellent dressing to the already naturally buoyant deer hair, dry flies can be fashioned that will remain afloat almost indefinitely. Without the protective dressing, a fly of deer hair will become soaked after a time and will serve only as a wet fly.

Now soak the hide in clean water for five hours. Scud again. Fill a 10-gallon container with water. Stir in 1 pint of vinegar with a wooden

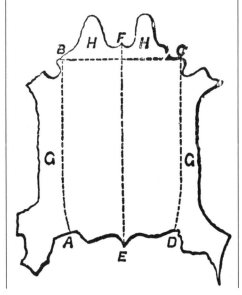

paddle. (You may substitute 1 ounce of lactic acid for the vinegar.) Leave the hide in this mixture for twenty-four hours to halt the action of the lime. Then proceed with tanning.

Tannage Procedures

Salt and Alum Tannage: Prepare the salt-alum solution by dissolving 1 pound of ammonia alum (or potash alum) in 1 gallon of water. In another container, dissolve 8 ounces of salt and 4 ounces of washing soda in ½ gallon of water. Slowly empty the salt-soda solution into the alum solution, while stirring rapidly. Immerse a clean skin in this solution for two to five days, according to its thickness.

Due to the effect of alum on certain furs, it might be advisable, in general, to apply the tanning solution in paste form, and only on the flesh side. Gradually, add flour mixed with a little water to the tanning solution until a thin paste forms. Blend well to avoid lumps.

Spread the skin smoothly and tack it, flesh side out. Completely coat the skin with the paste to a thickness of approximately ⅛ inch. The following day, scrape off the paste. Apply a second coat. Thick skins will require an additional coating on the third day. The final coating should be left on for four days. Then scrape away the paste, wash the skin in 1 gallon of water with 1 ounce of borax, and rinse in fresh water.

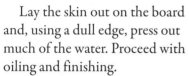

Lay the skin out on the board and, using a dull edge, press out much of the water. Proceed with oiling and finishing.

Alcohol and Turpentine Tannage: Tannage with alcohol and turpentine is easiest for a small fur skin. Mix ½ pint each of wood alcohol and turpentine in a wide-mouthed gallon jar having a screw-on lid. Put in the small fur skin. Since alcohol and turpentine tend to separate, shake or stir the solution daily.

After a week to ten days, take out the skin. Wash it in detergent water, removing grease, alcohol, and turpentine. Rinse thoroughly several times to get rid of the detergent. Squeeze water from the skin without wringing. When it is partially dry, begin the oiling and finishing operation.

Oiling and Finishing

Allow the tanned, wet leather to dry somewhat. While it is yet fairly damp, apply a coat of sulfated neat's-foot oil. The amount of oil will vary according to the natural oiliness of the skin. For example, a raccoon skin, being normally more fatty than a deerskin, would require less oil. For a 10-pound deer-hide, the following solution is recommended: In 3½ ounces of warm water, mix a like amount of sulfated neat's-foot oil with 1 ounce of ammonia.

Lay the skin, hair side down, on a smooth surface. Evenly spread one half of the mixture over the hide with your hand or a paint brush.

Wait thirty minutes. Then apply the remainder in the same manner. Cover the hide with a plastic sheet. Keep it covered overnight. If several skins have been coated, stack them, flesh sides together, overnight.

The next morning hang the skin, fur side out, over a sawhorse to permit drying of the hair. Then nail the skin, hair side down, on a plywood board and stretch it slightly. Hammer the nails (no. 6 finish) ½ inch in from the edge, spaced about 6 inches apart. The flesh side should be dried at room temperature.

While the skin is still slightly damp, stretch it from corner to corner. Work the flesh side over some wooden edge, such as a chair back. Achieving a soft skin depends on repeatedly working it while it is in the process of drying.

When softening and drying are complete, give the skin a quick bath in unleaded or white gasoline to deodorize it and remove any excess grease. (Do this outdoors, away from flame or fire.)

Clean and brighten the pelt by tumbling it again and again in warm, dry, hardwood sawdust.

Shaking, beating, and brushing will clean sawdust particles from the fur.

If need be, you may smooth the flesh side with a sandpaper block. Also, this will further soften the skin.

Preservation of Pelts

Unless tanning is to take place within twenty-four hours, hides or pelts should be treated or cured to avoid deterioration.

Preserve a small animal pelt by air-drying it. Tack it flat, hair side down, on a board.

A large pelt must be salted immediately. Place it, flesh side up, on a smooth surface. Sprinkle the hide thoroughly with salt and work it into wrinkles, neck, legs, and cut edges. For every pound of hide, use 1 pound of salt. If you are curing more than one hide, lay one on top of another, hair side down, and thoroughly salt the flesh side of each. The surface on which the pelts are stacked should have a slight incline to aid drainage of any liquid from the pile.

In two weeks you may hang the hides for complete drying. If salted a second time, they may be stored as late as May, but no longer.

A cured skin must be softened prior to tanning by soaking it several times in a 5- to 10-gallon container of cool water. Renew the water for each soaking. The soaking time is relative to the skin's condition. Some may require two hours; others, more.

As the skin starts to soften, spread it on a flat board. Begin

scraping
the flesh side with
an old hacksaw blade to break up
tissue and fat. To do a thorough job
of removing the adhering tissue, you
may need to alternately scrape and
soak the hides. While scraping, take
care not to damage the true skin.

Now mix a solution of 1 ounce
of borax or soda to every gallon of
lukewarm water. You may also add
soap. Put in the skin when it is just
short of being soft. Stir it about
with a paddle. This procedure
cleanses the skin, cuts grease, and
induces the final softening.

Again place the skin on a board,
and scud it. Then rinse it well in
lukewarm water. Press out the water
without wringing the skin. Unless
you intend to de-hair it, proceed
with the tanning operation as
previously described.

Making Rawhide

Hide that has been taken as quickly
as possible after the death of an
animal is called "green hide"; from
it the best rawhide is made.

First, stake out a green hide on
the ground in some shaded spot
for roughly two hours. To stake it
properly, pull outward from the
center before fastening it down.

After two hours Nature will
have changed it from green hide
to rawhide, which should be
sufficiently stiff to work with. Cut
off any bits of hanging flesh. Using
heavy shears, cut the hide in an oval
or round shape, and remove legs,
neck, and other projecting portions.

Now cut the oval or disc into one
continuous strip about 2½ inches
in width by scissoring around the
circle until you reach its center. In
thinner areas (such as the belly),
cut the strip a bit wider, for after it

has thoroughly dried it will shrink
to approximately two-thirds of its
original width. When rawhide is
neither too dry nor too damp, it
can be cut with ease. If the strip
becomes difficult to cut due to
excess dryness, dampen the hide
somewhat.

Attach one end of the long strip
to a post, pull taut a section at a
time, and grain off the hair with
a keen-edged knife. Hold the
blade almost flat. Guard against
cutting the top skin (scarf skin),
which gives strength to the rawhide
string.

Once the hair has been removed,
stretch the rawhide strip between
posts or trees in complete shade.
Leave it for five days to dry
thoroughly. Then it will be ready
for cutting into strings.

Bevel rawhide strings on the
hair side to prevent the sharp edges
from curling up. If the rawhide strip
or strings are to be softened, rub
them well with saddle soap (yellow
laundry soap is also effective) and
work them back and forth against
a piece of wood, such as a post or
sawhorse.

Sewing Needle for Leathers

Fabricate a needle for sewing leather
articles from the "key" used to open
sardine cans. Straighten the handle
end, and hammer and file—or
grind—it to a point. Thread sewing
material through the slot at the
opposite end.

Preserving and Mounting Snakeskins

Carefully skin the snake by centrally slitting the underside of the skin from top to bottom. If the snake is a rattler, take care not to disjoin the rattles. Using steel wool and borax, scrub the skin to remove all meat.

Leave the skin overnight. The following day, paint both sides with a mixture of one-half wood alcohol and one-half glycerin. After twenty-four hours, paint on a second coat. The skin will now be pliable as well as durable.

Select a board of interesting grain, saw it to the correct length, and finish it. Fasten the snakeskin on the board with any good glue.

Shoe Repairs

In olden times the shoemaker was itinerant, as were tinkers and other tradesmen. His kit consisted of a leather apron, a lap stone on which to work, an awl, knives, pincers, hand-forged nails, a hammer, wax filched from beehives along the way, and sturdy, bark-tanned leather heavily impregnated with whale oil.

The shoemaker was welcome in every home not only for his craft, but also for the "news" he dispensed. Ensconced in a chimney corner with his last, he would fashion new boots and shoes or repair old ones.

However, a good many rural folks were often obliged to tan hides and make their own rough footwear, either for the sake of frugality or because the shoemaker's calls were too infrequent. Whether for purposes of economy or the pure satisfaction involved, you can repair your own boots and shoes by using these guidelines.

Ripped Seams

The repairing of ripped seams in shoe and boot uppers requires a very small outlay for tools and materials. You will need a kit of hand-sewing needles, which can be purchased inexpensively at any dime store or shop selling sewing supplies. The packet contains five different needles, each about 4 inches in length and designed for a specific purpose. You will also need extra-strong thread, either the kind used over the years for sewing carpets and buttons or the more recently manufactured polyester-cotton-wrapped thread.

Follow these steps to repair the seams in footwear:

Pull apart the seam until you meet with resistance. Stop at this point. Remove all old stitching with the help of a penknife.

Choose the proper needle from the kit. If your hand will fit behind the seam, a straight needle will be appropriate. If the seam is located close to the shoe's toe, select the curved needle.

To sew a fine seam, use single thread. Use double or even triple strands of thread when the original holes in the leather are large enough. For a more water-resistant seam, first coat the thread with the wax from a beeswax candle. If beeswax is unavailable, ordinary candle wax will do.

Close the seam by sewing through the original holes. Take care not to enlarge them. Make the stitching taut.

Secure the finished seam by repeating the final stitch several times; a knot is unnecessary. To achieve a smooth finish, pound or rub the stitching into the leather.

Attaching Leather Half Soles

Sewing on new half soles will require a last, an item not as easily come by today as in the 1930s and 1940s, but nonetheless available to the adventurous of spirit. Search secondhand stores and you may find one for a dollar or two. Antique shops are sometimes a source, but there a last would sell for considerably more. Made of metal, it resembles an inverted leg with a foot (for holding a shoe) and is attached to a wooden base.

In addition to a last, you will need clinching nails and an awl for making new holes in leather. Fashion one from a hardwood dowel of a size that fits comfortably in your grip. Drive a long, heavy nail perpendicularly through the center of the dowel, allowing a portion of the point to extend beyond the wood. Hammer this extension flat against the wood to secure the spike in the dowel. Flatten the nail head with a hammer, and grind it to a smooth point with a coarse file.

Follow this procedure for stitching on leather half soles:

Buy precut half soles, or purchase leather and cut your own.

Soak the half sole or leather piece for ten minutes in tepid water. This step will make cutting and sewing easier. Then wrap newspaper around the leather to absorb excess water.

If you're making a sole, place the sole of the shoe on the new leather and trace around it. Carefully cut along the outline with a sharp knife.

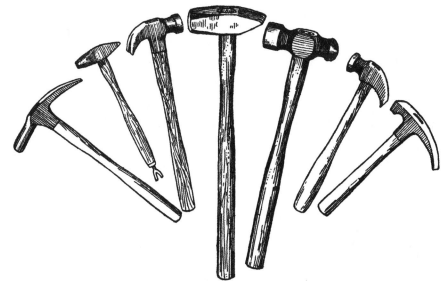

Place the shoe on the last. With a penknife or razor blade, cut the old threads on the original half sole. Lift the sole and separate it from the shoe with a somewhat diagonal cut at the arch.

Bevel the half sole so that it slightly extends over what remains of the old sole.

Clinching-shoe nails range from ⅜ inch to ⅞ inch in length. Choose one a half size longer than the total thickness of both new sole and shoe. Hammer in about nine nails along the juncture of the new and old half soles. Next nail down the tip and sides of the half sole.

Using a sharp knife, trim the edge of the sole for neatness.

Cut a shallow depression or trough on the sole's bottom where the stitching will be. Having the stitches slightly recessed protects them from wear.

With the old holes of the shoe welt (a strip of leather sewn in the seam between the upper of a shoe and the sole to reinforce their joining) to guide you, use the awl to make holes from the topside in the half sole. Every other hole will be enough.

Take a waxed strand of thread 3 feet long and thread two needles, one at each end of the thread. Begin at the first hole closest to the arch. Run the needles consecutively through the same opening, one needle in one direction and the second needle in the other direction. Sew such opposing stitches all around the sole. To secure the final stitch, either sew the last stitch several times or make a knot. Snip off excess thread.

Complete your work by pounding down the depression made for the stitches in the sole. Rub all the needle holes, stitches, and cracks with beeswax or shoe polish.

6 | WAYS WITH PAINT AND PAPER

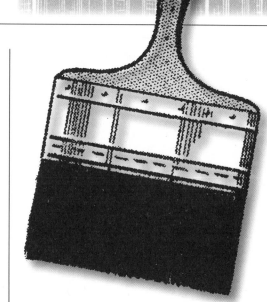

House Painting

Main Tasks

Painting a house consists of four main tasks:

Surface Preparation: Some scraping, sanding, caulking, and priming may be necessary. For paint to adhere properly, underlying areas must be free of dirt and loose paint. Start by hosing down the outside walls of the house to remove soil; then scrape any cracked, chipped, or peeling places. Areas where the bare wood has been exposed need primer. If the patch is not large, however, two coats of paint will suffice. Recaulk doors, window frames, and chimneys when necessary.

Window and Trim: Save time by painting windows with care to avoid the job of scraping panes later. When doing trim on a house with overhanging eaves, you will be painting overhead, so wear a hat.

Main Body of House: Using a wide brush, take long strokes, but don't overextend your reach when standing on a ladder.

Cleaning Up: Pick up and dispose of any old caulking material, putty, or paint chips. Look over your work, and touch up places you have missed or failed to cover well.

Requirements for House Painting

Paint: Buy the best quality paint you can afford. The results of your labor will last longer and look better than when a cheaper product is used. Available types of paint are oil-based and water-based (latex). Water-based paint dries in roughly one hour so that two coats can be applied on the same day. Brushes can be cleaned with soap and water. Allow a drying time of forty-eight hours between coats of oil-based paint. Clean the brushes in spirits of oleum.

Brushes: Some painters like a wide brush because of its extensive coverage. Others prefer one 2½ inches in width with a rounded handle. It easily covers narrow siding while its length permits reaching a wide swath. As time wears on, brushes of larger width tend to feel heavy. The better the brush, the better the results. One of nylon retains its shape and is easy to clean.

Spirits of Oleum: Use it for cleaning brushes and thinning paint.

Ladders: Generally a 6- to 8-foot ladder and a 12- to 14-foot extension are sufficient.

Dropcloths: Protect shrubs and bushes from paint by draping them with old sheets or dropcloths of light canvas or plastic.

Scrapers: Prepare surfaces with a 2-inch scraper that's been maintained in sharp condition with a file. A razor-blade scraper and putty knife will also come in handy.

Rags: For cleanup.

Nylon Stockings: Paint that becomes scummy can be satisfactorily filtered through a piece of old nylon stocking. To prevent this condition in the first place, splash a small amount of oleum on the contents of the paint can before covering it at day's end.

Wire: Hang paint buckets on the ladder with the aid of coat hanger wire. Suspend the pail on the side nearest your painting arm.

Painting Clothes: Hat, shirt, and overalls (or pants) can be purchased cheaply at thrift stores. Overalls provide room for stowing cloths and tools. When working in warm weather, choose white garb to minimize the heat.

Shoes: Footwear with steel shanks will make perching on a ladder more comfortable. Your feet won't tend to wrap around the rungs.

Massage (optional): At the end of a day's painting, you may welcome a massage to assuage aching muscles.

Paint Estimate

Here are some guidelines for estimating the amount of paint needed for a house:

Figure the number of square feet of surface to be painted by finding the distance, in feet, around the outside of your house. Next, determine the average height to the eaves. (If there are gables, add 2 feet to this number.) Now multiply the first number (the distance around the house) by the second (the height to the eaves).

Ask your paint dealer for the approximate coverage in square feet of each gallon of undercoat. Divide the total surface area by this number.

Ascertain how many square feet are covered by 1 gallon of top coat; divide as indicated above.

If the surface condition is uncommonly dry, porous, rough, or heavily textured, 20 percent more paint may be needed for the first coat.

Application of Paint

Begin painting under the eaves at the highest point and work downward. Guard against lap marks, the buildups where ending and beginning areas meet. Whenever possible, avoid painting in direct sunlight, which dries the coat too rapidly and can cause lap marks. If you do encounter a sunny spot, feather the ends of your brush strokes and draw the paint out to a thin, gradually fading streak.

When approached by flying, stinging insects (bees, hornets, etc.), yield ground. If the creature persists, have a knotted rag handy to flick at it in self-defense. The insect will be dazed long enough for you to make a safe retreat. It may be of some solace to know that you are less likely to be bothered by such pests in the morning. During the early hours of the day, flying insects are more sluggish in their activities.

Making Paper

Paper from Plants

Paper can be made from all fibrous vegetation. One can prepare a wide assortment of paper, differing in texture and quality, from the various plants that grow in woods and meadows.

The most favorable time to gather your plants is toward summer's end or at the beginning of fall.

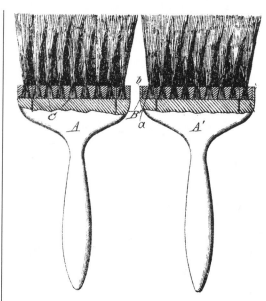

Place them on a floor of stone, and keep them moist until they decompose.

Chop the rotted material into ½-inch-long pieces. Put them into a large vessel filled with water and add a good amount of caustic soda. Rub a thumb and forefinger together in the water. If enough soda is present, the water should feel greasy. Immediately after this test, wash your hand well, or the caustic soda can cause burns.

Paper intended for writing or painting has to be sized. Slowly heat the pulp. Use a thermometer to check the temperature. When it reaches 98°F, add gelatin for sizing. (Sizing—any thin, viscous substance—serves as a filler for porous materials, such as paper.) Boil for a minimum of three hours; be careful that the container does not boil dry.

Transfer the pulp to a pail. Wash the material until the water is clear, and pound it with your hands to press out the water. Put bleaching powder (chlorinated lime, available through building supply and hardware stores) into a large jug for mixing; then add water and stir. Allow to settle. Pour the bleach solution on the fibrous pulp. Let it stand for twelve hours, and stir now and then with a stick. When the material has become a pale fawn color, it has bleached sufficiently.

Once more, wash the material well and squeeze out the water. Cut the fibrous pulp into ½-inch pieces with scissors. In a large mortar, crush the pulp with a pestle until the fibers split lengthwise. You may pound the pulp on a stone slab with a heavy mallet if mortar and pestle are not available. Continue this procedure until the desired consistency is achieved. The longer the pulp is crushed, the smoother the paper will be.

To make but one sheet of paper at a time, put a nylon sieve, 10 inches in diameter, into a shallow pan of warm water. Place 3 cups of pulp in the sieve. Using your hand, spread it evenly on the sieve. Take the sieve from the pan and let any water drain off. Place it in a warm spot to dry.

Lift the dry sheet by slipping the tip of a knife beneath the edges of the paper. Its thickness will depend on the amount of pulp used. Repeat the process to make more sheets.

To prepare a greater number of sheets in a shorter time, make a wooden frame and nail a sheet of perforated zinc to it. Spread pulp evenly on the piece of zinc. Have some old blankets handy. Invert the frame and press the paper onto a wet blanket. Place another wet blanket on top in readiness to receive the next sheet. Continue alternating layers of blankets and paper sheets. Finally, place large, heavy stones atop the pile to press out the water. Now unstack the blankets, letting each sheet of paper dry on its blanket.

Paper from Paper Scraps

Paper can also be made from odds and ends of gift-wrapping paper, old magazines, junk mail, and newspaper. For equipment you will need an electric blender, a 5- by 7-inch picture frame (one that's 8 by 10 inches may also be used, but no larger), window screening the size of the frame, thumbtacks, a pile of newspapers, a 14½- by 10½- by 2-inch glass baking pan, two desk-sized white blotters, one wooden spoon, paper towels, and an iron.

Tear or cut the old paper in slender strips; loosely fill one-third of the blender with them. Pour water into the machine until it is two-thirds full. Blend the contents for four or five seconds. In the next step you can control the shade of your paper by introducing a preferred color; for example, if pink paper is desired, add strips of red. Blend once more. Produce texture by mixing in bits of colored thread, parsley, or even chili-pepper flakes.

Fashion a sieve by tacking the piece of screening to the frame. Place three stacks of newspapers in a row. Set the baking pan on one and a desk blotter on the next.

Pour the pulp into the baking pan, and add about 1 inch of water. Mix thoroughly with the wooden spoon. Holding the screen side of the frame uppermost and over the pan at a slight angle, spoon the pulp evenly on the sieve. Let excess water drip back into the pan.

Put a long edge of the sieve on the blotter, and quickly flip it over, pulp side down. With paper towels, blot up excess moisture, particularly at the edges of the frame, and carefully lift away the sieve. Immediately cover the soggy paper with the remaining blotter. Transfer the blotters protecting the moist paper to the last stack of newspapers.

Heat the iron at its wool setting, and press the blotter "sandwich" on both sides. Take away the top blotter; peel off the sheet of paper. If difficult to remove, it is still too

damp. Iron directly on the paper until it is dry. Then lift it from the blotter.

Your tinted paper is ready for use.

Wallpaper and Wall Stenciling

Preparing Walls for Paper

Stretched on his deathbed, Oscar Wilde quipped, "My wallpaper is killing me—one of us must go!" If you have long felt that your wallpaper "must go," but have postponed replacing it to avoid the cost, consider making and hanging your own paper. The job is not difficult or expensive and the results are rewarding.

First, judge whether it is necessary to remove old paper before putting up new. Your decision depends on whether the present covering is firmly attached to the wall. Examine it closely. If no bulges exist and the seams are securely in place, new paper quite probably will adhere well. Should there be a few pieces of loose paper, snip them off and sand the edges. Unanchored seams can often be re-glued.

When old paper is in an overall loose condition, it must be removed. Heavy types of wallpaper generally peel away with ease. Other kinds require sufficient moistening to soften the glue beneath. At that moment, scraping (use a wide-blade putty knife, large case knife, or hand scraper) or stripping should commence immediately, for it will quickly dry. Wetting and stripping but one section at a time is the most efficient procedure. To permeate the paper and soften the glue, use a wet sponge. You can also use a liquid wallpaper remover (available at paint dealers and hardware stores).

Once the paper has been taken off, wash the walls with vinegar and water or soda and water applied with a brush or large sponge. Then let the walls dry thoroughly. Prepare whitewashed walls by wetting them with a solution of 1 pound of alum to 2 gallons of water. Allow them to dry before papering.

Fill any holes or seams in the plaster or wallboard with patching plaster. When patching wallboard, it is advisable to use a primer-sealer over repaired places. The walls are now ready to receive your homemade paper.

Making Wallpaper

Wallpaper is believed to have been a Chinese invention. Europeans next adopted it, and by the

seventeenth century the practice of covering walls with decorative paper became popular in North America.

Early wallpapers were designed by woodblock printing, handstamping, and the letterpress method. They were sometimes made to resemble fabrics that were the valuable wall coverings of the period.

To decorate your wallpaper with the simplest or the more complicated designs, use the rubbing technique described under "Gravestone Rubbings." Produce them on lining paper, which comes in the same width and length as ordinary wallpaper. Detail paper (used in architectural firms) will also serve. The motifs can overlap or be spaced in a chessboard, stripe, or diamond arrangement.

For your design to be most effective, rub it with varying amounts of pressure—lightly in some areas, heavily in others, sometimes using a mixture of the two. By such selective rubbing, you can develop certain areas of the design to greater prominence. Either one color or a pleasing combination of colors may be employed throughout.

Preparing Papering Paste

Prepare papering paste the day before it is needed so that it will be cold when applied. For fourteen rolls of wallpaper, 5 quarts of paste are required. Mix a bit more than 2 cups of wheat flour (rice flour or cornstarch can be substituted) with enough water to form a thin dough. Thin it down to avoid lumps. Heat 4 quarts of water. At the boiling point, pour in the thin hot batter. Stir constantly to prevent burning until the boiling point is reached once more. Then empty the vessel into a tin pail, and allow the paste to stand until the following day. To insure a lump-free paste, strain and press it through coarse muslin.

Hanging Wallpaper

Hang your wallpaper in the customary manner. Climb a ladder, and hold plain lining paper up to the ceiling while a helper below marks it along the baseboard with any blunt instrument. Cut along this mark. Use it as a pattern, cutting a sufficient number of decorated strips for walls that have no doors or windows.

Lay some boards, a sheet of scrap plywood, or an old door across widely spaced sawhorses, chair backs, or barrels. Place a wallpaper strip face down on this work surface, and evenly apply the papering paste with a whitewash brush. When the paper is sticky rather than wet, press the upper end just up to the ceiling, beginning at a corner, and work downward. Smooth out any wrinkles and large bubbles by moving a clean cloth from the center outward to the sides. Don't be concerned about smaller bubbles; they will dry smooth. Place the next strip so that its edge abuts on the first piece but does not overlap it.

Do not attempt to cut paper to fit around windows and doors prior to putting it up. Hang it in the usual way, and upon reaching the obstruction, paper right over the edge. Then trim around doors and windows by cutting diagonally up to and a little beyond their corners, which you can indicate with your finger as you feel them through the paper. Fold back the excess paper, mark the edge, and cut it off.

Remove light fixtures, switch plates, thermostat covers, etc. Papering under instead of around them makes a much simpler and neater job. Mark the paper in these areas; then trim out the holes and replace the items.

Old-time paperhangers advise brushing an even coat of paste on walls instead of wallpaper, moistening the backs of strips with a water-soaked sponge, and then hanging them.

Preparing Walls for Stenciling

If you prefer painted walls to wallpaper but want them decorated, employ the technique of stenciling.

First, prepare walls with a coat of latex paint. Those that have been whitewashed will require scraping with a blunt-edged tool to remove any loose lime. You will find a hoe handy for this job. Next, go over the walls with sandpaper tacked to a large piece of wood that has a handle attached to it. Wash them down with a sponge. After they are dry, fill all cracks and breaks with plaster of Paris. Then apply the latex in white or in some pastel shade as the background for your stenciled pattern. Latex is preferable to oil-based paint. With its use, any necessary touching up will not be as evident as it would be with oil-based paint.

Stencil Designs

Select your stencil designs. You will find books containing patterns at the library or in art supply stores. You may enjoy creating original designs of your own. Using carbon paper, trace your motifs on waxed stencil paper or yellow stencil paper (available at paint and art stores).

Cut the stencils with a single-edged razor blade. Work on a glass surface. This step requires great care, for any errors will show up when you apply pigments to the wall.

Plan the layout of your stencils by measuring the design and the wall space it will occupy. Position it

according to the number of times it will occur in that area.

More than one color may be incorporated in a design. Use oil-based, semi-gloss paints for the stenciling work. If you intend to mix your own paints, be sure to prepare enough for the whole room, thus insuring uniformity of tone.

Methods for Applying Stencils

Choose either of the following methods for applying wall stencils:

Stencil-Brush Method: Cut your stencils from waxed stencil paper. As they must be cleaned with turpentine between each application of pigments, it is convenient to make more than one set. Hold the stencil on the wall with masking tape. Apply pigments

with round stencil brushes. Dip the brush into the paint; wipe off any excess on a rag or newspaper. Very little paint is needed. More can be added if necessary, but too much cannot be removed. Painting from the outside of the hole toward the center, rub the paint on the wall through each stencil opening. Make certain that the opening is completely filled with color before going on to another. Smudges, fuzzy edges, or other imperfections should be corrected with the background paint with a watercolor brush. Old-time stencilers generally used this method.

Watercolor-Brush Method: Cut stencils from inexpensive yellow stencil paper. This method will require no more than one set of stencils, and you won't need to tape them on the wall. Using one as a guide, hold it in place as you lightly but clearly outline the design with a hard lead pencil. You may want to sketch the designs throughout the room before beginning to paint. Set the stencils aside, and carefully paint in the drawn motifs with small watercolor brushes. This simplified method of stenciling was used during the fifteenth and sixteenth centuries in France.

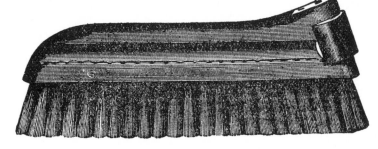

Wall stenciling adapts to any decor, from Early American to modern.

If you intend to cover plaster walls in oil-based paint without stenciling, first brush them with a thin glue sizing (prepared by dissolving 4 ounces of glue in 1 gallon of boiling water over low heat). When wall surfaces are covered with several coats of whitewash, make and apply the following glue sizing:

In 2½ gallons of water, dissolve 10 ounces of glue. In another vessel, mix 9 pounds of bole—a reddish-colored, easily pulverized clay available in paint stores—with sufficient water to produce a creamlike consistency, and strain it through cheesecloth. Add the moist bole to the glue sizing, and stir in 2 pounds of gypsum. Strain the mixture through cheesecloth. Dilute it with water for brushing on walls. When it is dry, apply the oil-based paint.

Gravestone Rubbings

History of Rubbing Technique

The technique of rubbing is thought to have originated in China around 300 B.C. The practice spread throughout the Chinese empire and eventually the entire Far East. In the beginning, it served as a means to disseminate the written word prior to the invention of the printing press.

Literature and edicts of emperors were incised on stone tablets and then reproduced on paper by rubbing. Eventually, pictures were carved in stone expressly for the purpose of being copied in this way. Later, archaeologists employed the method to record early tomb carvings.

Choice of Gravestones

You can use this ancient technique to create decorative pictures for your walls. Surfaces or objects to rub are almost limitless: brasses, architectural reliefs, medals, coins, any incised designs, bark, leaves, flowers, etc.

Perhaps some of the most unusual and interesting rubbings can be made on gravestones in old burial grounds. Those dating before 1800 are hand carved and represent the first sculpture of colonial settlers. As such, they are a unique expression of primitive American art. The stone slabs with their carved motifs and religious symbols were intended for instruction of the generally illiterate public in matters of man's mortality, his relation to God, and the blessings of heaven, thus reflecting religious attitudes of the times. Gradually, as Puritan faith became less strict, religious symbols were replaced by stylized portraiture. Details of dress currently in vogue and often the occupation or social status of the deceased were depicted by the stonecutter. These early craftsmen displayed an instinctive sense of design and expert workmanship. So, rubbings of tombstones several centuries old are both historically and artistically valuable.

While the philosophy of Puritans was revealed in symbols, views of the Old West were expressed in pithy epitaphs, always informative and sometimes amusing. Epitaphs in southern burial grounds often exceeded a single statement; they related a complete story of the circumstances leading to death in colorful local dialect, many times with primitive spellings.

Stonecutters, much in demand in more densely populated areas of colonial life, were master craftsmen. However, smaller towns throughout the country had to depend on woodcarvers or even shoemakers for tombstone carving. Their inexperience left us markers with entire words deleted or letters squeezed in at the end of a line, giving them a quaint appeal.

If you want to create and display such samples of your national heritage, follow these guidelines.

Essential Materials

The essential materials for making rubbings are few:

Cleaning Aid: piece of Styrofoam, a soft hairbrush, or a rubber school eraser

Paper: butcher paper (long sheets are available at meat markets), detail paper (used by architects), rice paper, or any kind of thin, strong, linen-base paper

Masking Tape

Rubbing Medium: black lumber-marking crayon or primary crayons (used in primary grades, they have a flat side to prevent their rolling off desks)

Kneeling Pad (optional): carpet sample or foam-rubber pad

Surface Preparation

The time of year when you can work most comfortably and efficiently is early spring. By then winter has killed the weeds, and the sun and showers of a warmer season have not yet prodded the growth of grasses, briars, and branches, or roused snakes from their hibernation. The rains and snow of winter will have removed at least some moss from the surface of old gravestones.

If you find a heavy accumulation of moss or lichen on the stone's face, clean the surface gently but effectively with a small block of Styrofoam, a child's nylon hairbrush, or a rubber eraser. (Never use a wire brush or harsh abrasives; old, weather-beaten markers are soft in texture and will erode easily.) By gently rubbing across the stone, most of the moss or other foreign matter will be removed. Where moss clings

stubbornly, rub the area with a rag or sponge saturated with vinegar.

Rubbing Technique

After preparing the stone's surface, attach a large sheet of white or light-colored paper with masking tape in the center of all four sides, smoothing the paper from the middle outward before applying each strip. If more pieces are needed to make the sheet adhere tightly, position them midway between the original tape.

Remove the paper wrapper from the crayon (brown or black is most effective) and, using the flat side, work from the center outward. Establish the entire design lightly. The inscription and decorative motifs will spring into relief on your paper. Raised areas beneath the sheet will be registered by the crayon; depressed areas will remain white. Then, using firmer pressure and working from the edges inward, repeat the procedure.

Check your reproduction at a distance for uniformity of color. Correct weaker areas.

Now that your print is complete, remove it by peeling the tape from the paper toward the stone. To reproduce other surfaces, from coins to manhole covers, follow essentially the same method.

Framing the Rubbing

Set off your rubbing to best advantage with a rustic picture frame. An abandoned, weather-beaten farm building will provide appropriate material (with the owner's permission, of course). Usually, you can have a few rough-textured boards for very little or nothing at all. Select boards that are relatively straight. Don't be concerned about nail holes; they will only enhance the rustic look of the finished product.

Before making the frame, dry any wet wood for several days or more. You may want to add to the frame's weather-beaten appearance with the application of a light gray, semi-transparent shingle stain. Brush in the direction of the grain.

7 | WAYS WITH WAX

Candles

Materials and Equipment

For simple candlemaking, assemble the following materials and equipment:

Paraffin Flakes: They can be bought in bags by the pound from a candlemakers' supply shop. Paraffin wax is quite hard and makes a smooth-burning candle.

Beeswax: When a small amount of beeswax is added to the paraffin, the candle has a smooth finish, gives off the aroma of honey while burning, and drips only minimally. Small beeswax discs can be purchased as an addition.

Stearin (sometimes known as sterene or stearic acid): This flaky white substance, when melted separately and added to the melted paraffin, facilitates the removal of the candle from the mold, gives it a harder finish, and prevents guttering. As a general rule, you should use 10 percent stearin to 90 percent paraffin-beeswax mixture. It can be bought by weight at a candlemakers' supply shop.

Common White String: Use ordinary white string to make your wicks. Closely braid it in two or more strands according to the thickness desired. To achieve a smoothly burning wick, it is necessary to correlate the wick size with the candle size, particularly with its diameter. The bigger the candle, the bigger the wick. Experience will teach you to gauge the wick size correctly.

Now make a solution of 8 ounces of water, 1 tablespoon of salt, and 2 tablespoons of borax. Soak the wicks in this mixture for about six hours. Then hang them up. Once they are completely dry, they will be ready for use. (You may purchase ready-made wicks very reasonably. Most have a label indicating the diameter of the candle for which they are suited.)

Wax-Based Dye: If you care to color your candles, use commercial wax dyes. Buy them in either powder or liquid form.

Wax Perfume: Scenting your candles is optional. Oil-based perfumes for wax are available at your supplier.

Two Old Saucepans: One pan should be small enough to fit into the other.

Sugar Thermometer: Measure the temperature of the wax with it.

Scissors: You will need a pair of scissors to cut and trim wicks.

Plasticine: Use this to keep melted wax from leaking through the wick hole in the bottom of the candle mold and to attach bases on bottomless molds.

Knife: Have a sharp one handy for evening the bottoms of candles and doing other small jobs.

Candle Mold: Almost any container can serve as a candle mold as long as it has straight sides and a mouth with at least the same width as its base. You can probably find many appropriate containers in your kitchen vases, cups, mugs, and jugs. By exploring secondhand stores, you can often turn up interesting and inexpensive containers to use as candle molds, and various types can be bought at a candlemakers' supply shop.

Be sure that the molds will allow for easy removal of the finished candle. Check this by oiling their interior and compactly filling them with Plasticine. If the "candle" of Plasticine slips out easily, the chosen container is acceptable as a mold.

Copper and plastic piping provide excellent molds. Purchase off-cuts from a builders' supply center. Making certain that they are perfectly level when standing on end, saw them to the desired length. Smooth the edges with fine sandpaper. Make notches opposite one another on the rim of the top to hold a skewer or pencil from which to hang the wick. Find a jar lid the size of the mold's bottom (or cut one from cardboard, plastic, etc.). Make a central hole

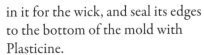

in it for the wick, and seal its edges to the bottom of the mold with Plasticine.

Wick Retainers: These are metal discs for candle molds lacking wick holes. Fasten the wick to one and lower it into the bottom of the container. Wick retainers can be bought at a candlemakers' supply shop.

Procedure

Fill the larger of your saucepans one quarter full of water, and place it on a lighted stove burner. Bring the water to the boiling point. Put the required amount of paraffin wax in the smaller saucepan, and lower it into the hot water. Reduce the heat so that the water barely simmers, and let the wax melt.

Cut wicking to correct lengths, somewhat longer than the molds' height, and knot one end of each. Dip them in the melted wax and hang them until dry.

Make sure your molds are absolutely clean. Then insert wicks in their bases, pulling the unknotted ends through the holes until the knot is firmly against the bottom. Carefully seal the hole with Plasticine. For molds without wick holes, use a wick retainer by attaching the wick to it and lowering it into the middle of the bottom.

Now tie or tape the free end of a wick around a metal skewer or pencil placed horizontally and centrally across the opening of the mold. Be sure that the wick is taut and precisely centered.

If the base of the mold is not recessed, the wick knot will cause imbalance. Remedy this by placing your mold on an improvised platform made of two slightly spaced wood blocks, bricks, or any objects of exactly the same height.

When the paraffin has melted, add a small amount of the beeswax. Gently introduce it into the molten paraffin; let it melt. In a separate pan, melt stearin in an amount equaling 10 percent of the total of the paraffin wax plus beeswax. Add the dye immediately if you desire tinted candles. When melted simultaneously with the wax dye, stearin imparts a more vivid color to the finished product. Tint the mixture a slightly lighter shade than is desired, since the finished candle, being denser, will be darker in color. Carefully spoon the tinted stearin into the paraffin-beeswax mixture.

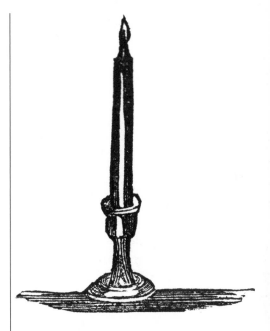

Insert the sugar thermometer into the saucepan of wax. Check for the temperature to reach 180°F. At this point, take the container from the stove.

Using a spoon or soup ladle (you may prefer to empty the wax mixture into a warm metal jug with a long spout), pour the wax very carefully into the candle mold at its center. Be sure to avoid wax drips on inner side surfaces. Then tap the mold to release air, thus preventing air bubbles from forming on the surface.

Now let your candle set. Depending upon its size, this may require as many as twenty-four hours. During the setting period, "top up" the candle. As the candle sets, the wax will contract and a depression will appear around the wick. Fill in this hollow with leftover wax from the batch made up for your candles.

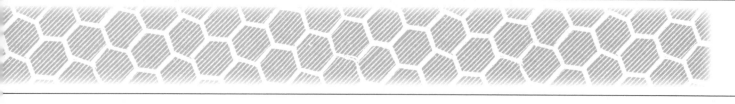

At the first appearance of the depressed area, make several holes in the surface of the wax. As the candle firms up, pierce more holes and pour in melted wax until level with the surface. You may need to repeat this procedure three times before the surface hardens without forming a hollow.

When your candle has shrunk from the mold's sides, it is set and ready for removal. First, free the wick from the skewer or pencil. Then, holding your hand over its mouth, invert the mold. Remove the Plasticine seal around the wicking knot. Cut off the knot with a sharp knife. Handling the candle delicately in order not to mar its surface, gently shake the candle from the mold. If the surface does not appear sufficiently smooth and shiny, hold on to the wick and dip the candle in boiling water and then ice water.

Stand your candle upright. You may need to trim the wick with scissors. It should be about ¼ inch in height.

Cure the finished candle in a cool, dry place for three days before using it.

Candle in a Glass

To make a candle that will remain in its glass container requires but one item in addition to the supplies already mentioned—glue.

Select some transparent glass container that is eye-catching. Make sure it is thoroughly clean.

Wax a wick somewhat beyond the usual size appropriate for the container's diameter. (The whole surface of a candle in a permanent holder becomes molten; therefore, a too-small wick would fall over and be extinguished.) Turn a short span of the wick at a right angle, and glue it in the middle of the container's bottom. Fasten it at the top in the customary way.

Pour in melted wax that does not exceed 180°F, or you will risk cracking the glass.

Let the candle set, and top up in the usual manner. Try to achieve as smooth a surface as possible. Trim the wick to ¼ inch.

Your dripless candle in glass will need no other holder.

Dipped Candles

Fill a vessel with a prepared candle-wax mixture. Choose one that is somewhat taller than the length of candle intended.

Cut a wick about 3 inches longer than necessary. Completely soak the wick in the melted wax, and hang it to dry, keeping it as straight as possible. Tie the dry wick on the horizontal bar of a wooden coat hanger.

Now add stearin to the wax—about 20 percent for dipped candles—along with dye (optional). When the temperature of the wax is 160°F, dip the suspended wick slowly into the wax. Be careful to hold the coat hanger as nearly on a level as possible. Leave the wick in the wax for approximately five seconds; then slowly lift it out. Suspend the hanger from a hook located away from a wall, and

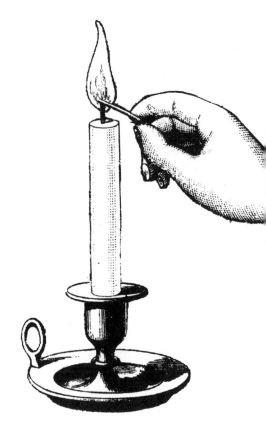

let the taper dry for roughly two minutes.

Continue dipping and drying until the taper reaches the desired thickness. Allow the candle to set hard, an hour or more, before cutting it from the hanger. Trim the base evenly with a sharp knife.

More than one taper can be made at a time by using a vessel with a wider mouth to hold the wax and by hanging more wicks on a longer rod which, after the dipping process, can be suspended across the backs of spaced chairs. Remember to place newspapers beneath the tapers to catch drips.

8 | WAYS WITH CLAY

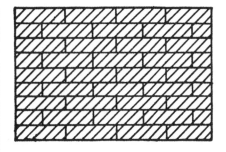

Adobe Bricks

Adobe is derived from a wide variety of clay soils, heavy in texture and composed of very fine grained material. The name designates the sun-dried bricks, the clay of which they are composed, and structures built of the stuff.

The word adobe comes from the Spanish *adobar*, to plaster. Its use as building material is said to have originated in northern Africa centuries ago. The indigenous peoples of Southwestern United States and Central and South America used adobe for thousands of years, and when the Spanish arrived, they began making adobe bricks.

Adobe making is an uncomplicated procedure. Put simply, correct proportions of sand and suitable clay are combined and wet down, a small quantity of some fibrous material is added, and the whole is mixed thoroughly either in a machine or with bare feet.

Ingredients of Adobe Brick Mix

The chief components of adobe bricks are sand, clay, and a waterproofing substance. The sand acts as filler; the clay is the binder. Adobe brick mix generally contains more sand than clay. Clay content should be greater than 25 percent but less than 45 percent. Too little clay makes the dry bricks weak and crumbly; too much clay causes cracking as the bricks dry.

Sand: Use sharp, coarse sand. If no natural sources of such sand are available, it can be purchased from a building supply company. (Avoid sand from ocean shores because of its salt content.)

Clay: Although many types of clay are usable in making adobe, one of high kaolin content is preferable. Such material not only is less sticky to handle than others, but also results in stronger bricks. To learn the location of kaolin clay deposits, consult local geologists or those connected with government offices, such as the Division of Mines and Geology.

Straw: The incorporation of straw in the mix causes the drying brick to shrink as a unit, thus

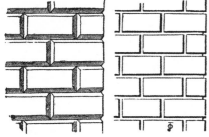

preventing a considerable amount of cracking in the finished product. Cut the material in four-inch lengths. Straw can be bought at feed stores. Avoid using hay, if possible.

Stabilizer (waterproofing substance): Use emulsified asphalt as a waterproofing agent, or stabilizer, so that the bricks will absorb only a small, safe percentage of water. (A stabilizer is required by the Uniform Building Code when adobe bricks are intended for construction of any type of building.) The liquid is available from road-paving companies or oil dealers.

If your bricks are to be used for outdoor walkways, garden walls, porch floors, and the like, Portland cement added to soil will produce strong bricks that will not be harmed by water. They will be very hard but not waterproof. (Bricks of this type would not comply with building code requirements and must not be used for inhabited structures.) Use 15 percent cement, and insure that it cures properly by keeping the bricks damp for several days.

Soil Testing

Test the suitability of soil for adobe-brick making in the following manner:

Shovel away leaf mold, sod, and other organic matter from a small area of the test site.

Dig a hole as deeply as you intend to go when excavating for soil. Mix the dirt removed from the hole so that all layers of earth are well blended.

Put 8 ounces of the soil sample in a one-quart jar, and fill it with water. Add a teaspoon of table salt to speed settling of the clay. Shake the jar well, and let the contents settle for one hour or until the water is clear.

Examine the jar's solid contents. You will see successive layers: lowermost will be small bits of rock; next will be sand, varying from coarse at the bottom to particles of silt size; the top layer will be clay, characterized by no perceptible particles. Rub some clay between your fingers. It should feel rather like soap and be free of grit.

To determine clay-sand proportions, measure the height of the clay layer and estimate its percentage of the combined layers and the percentage occupied by the coarser layers. Clay material must range between 25 and 45 percent. When the soil test indicates an excess in either clay or sand, you can procure high-clay soil or sand at a building materials outlet. Mix in the proper amount to correct whichever is deficient.

Making Test Bricks

If the soil tests properly, make a stiff mud with some of it and form several bricks of full size. Dry a few in the sun; dry others in shade.

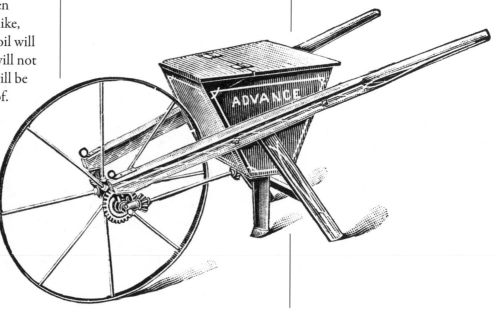

By so doing, you can determine which drying conditions are most favorable. Cracks will appear within the first few days if they are going to occur. A high degree of cracking can be remedied by shading the bricks or by adding more straw or sand.

Once the adobe drying test proves satisfactory, shape bricks that include emulsified asphalt to judge how much of it will be required.

Testing to Stabilize Bricks

Fill a 1-cubic-foot box with loose soil that has already been tested and found acceptable for use. Record the number of shovelfuls required to fill the box.

Empty the soil into a wheelbarrow. Hoe in sufficient water to form stiff mud.

Gradually pour in ½ gallon of emulsified asphalt while continually blending it with the mud. Mix the whole thoroughly until you can no longer discern any asphalt. (A half-gallon of asphalt to 1 cubic foot of soil is a good ratio.)

Shape the test bricks from the mud by hand. Make them some convenient size, perhaps 2 x 3 x 4 inches.

Dry these bricks in a warm oven to shorten the drying time, which would be much longer in the sun.

Immerse one of the dry bricks in water for a few hours. No softening should result, even at the edges. If softening does occur, repeat the test but this time use more stabilizer. Even though test results

are good, follow the procedure again to determine if using less emulsified asphalt will bring equally satisfactory results.

After determining the stabilizer-soil ratio, you can estimate what amount is needed for each mixer load according to the soil capacity of the machine in cubic feet. It's a good idea to use a bit more emulsified asphalt than the minimum required in testing, since conditions may alter somewhat during production. Always allow sufficient time for the stabilizer to thoroughly mix with the mud.

Molds

Make your molds from Douglas fir lumber. Besides being a strong wood, it holds screws and nails better than redwood or pine. Use fine-grained, finished wood. Rough lumber is difficult to separate from the wet bricks.

Molds range in size from 8 inches square and 2 inches thick to 2 yards long, 1 foot wide, and 6 to 8 inches thick. However, the standard dimensions for an adobe brick are 4 by 7½ by 16 inches. So that the finished brick will be 4 inches thick, make the mold depth 4¼ inches to compensate for slight sagging of the mud as the mold is removed and to allow for some shrinkage during drying.

Cut four boards of the proper size and waterproof them.

For a stronger mold, fasten the boards with wood screws instead of nails. Reinforce each mold with two corner braces located diagonally from one another. Countersink them so that they are flush with the wood's surface.

At each end of the form, add wooden rectangles of a convenient size to serve as handles.

Tack a thin metal strip on the top edges of the form to prevent wear as your trowel scrapes away excess mud after the mold has been filled. For ease in separating the mold from the mud, either line the form with a thin sheet of tin or make the mold's bottom 1/16 inch wider on each side.

Making Adobe Bricks
Necessary Equipment:
- rectangular mason's trowel
- wooden molds
- pick (for hard earth)
- two shovels: a pointed one for digging soil; a square one for shoveling mud
- deep wheelbarrow

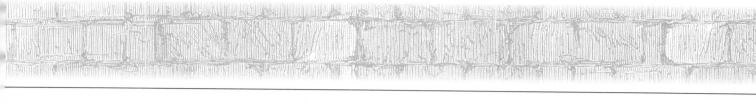

- containers for the stabilizer
- buckets
- large drum for storing water
- mechanical mud mixer equipped with paddles (A dough, plaster, or pug mixer works well; a concrete mixer is not satisfactory.) This piece of equipment is essential if your bricks are intended for any type of building and will, therefore, require emulsified asphalt. For other purposes not requiring a stabilizer, the ingredients can be deposited in a pit and trampled and mixed with your bare feet.

Casting surfaces: You can cast bricks on flat ground, but a smooth surface is preferable. Use boards or scrap plywood supported on a framework of two-by-fours.

Shading material: If you plan to dry bricks out of the sun, provide shade with plywood supported several inches above the bricks.

Mixing

Break up any dirt chunks, and thoroughly mix the soil during excavation to create a homogeneous blend of the various layers of earth. Speed the breakdown of hard, stubborn clay masses by wetting the soil and keeping it covered with a sheet of plastic.

Now multiply the previously noted shovelfuls (required to fill the l-cubic-foot box) by the cubic-foot capacity of the mixer. This quantity will be shoveled into the machine as you charge it.

To mix the mud, turn on the mixer and add most of the estimated amount of water required. Put in the soil and only enough additional water to form a stiff mud. After the paddles have beaten all lumps from the mud, gradually add the correct quantity of emulsified asphalt. Allow several minutes for this to be thoroughly mixed in. Lastly, add the straw. When it has been introduced, the mixer will labor due to the mud clotting and creating more resistance to the paddles. If left in too long, the straw tends to wrap about the paddles; therefore, just as soon as it is evenly dispersed throughout the mud, discharge the mixer's contents into a wheelbarrow.

Casting

Sprinkle the casting surface with sand or straw to keep the mud from adhering to it. Immerse the mold in water to avoid sticking; place it on the prepared casting surface. Fill the form with mud, making sure the corners are completely filled. Press the mud in with your hands. Using your trowel, strike the mold's contents even with its top. Now slowly and evenly lift the form from the fresh adobe brick. It is not necessary to let the mud set in the form before lifting it away.

After creating each adobe brick, plunge the mold into a tub of water to clear off any bits of clinging mud. Then proceed with making the next brick.

Drying and Curing Bricks

Freshly created adobe bricks must be allowed to dry evenly. During the initial four days, protect them from rain or foggy, cold weather with a sheet of scrap plywood supported several inches over them. Leave the ends open to the wind for further drying. Mild spring days are most favorable for the drying process. When the weather is hot, dry, and windy, however, hang burlap bags over the edges of the plywood protectors to avoid cracking caused by dry winds.

After four days set the bricks on one side to promote rapid, even drying. From this time on, the plywood protector will not be needed. Let the bricks dry in the sun for six weeks.

The molds, when not in use, should be kept in a container of water to prevent their drying out, warping, and separating at the joints.

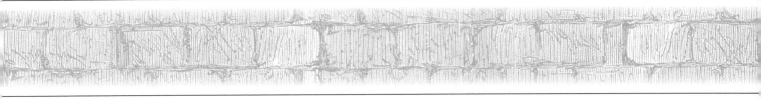

External Treatment of Adobe Bricks

A good protective covering for adobe walls, both inside and out, is linseed oil. Apply three brush coats. These may be followed by two coats of household paint for interior walls.

Inside walls can also be treated by first applying waterproof glue. Make it of one part quicklime, six parts cottage cheese, and enough water to create a smooth-flowing mixture. Over this primer coat of glue, apply buttermilk paint: 1 gallon of buttermilk to 4½ pounds of white cement.

Pottery

Clay Sources

The amateur potter may buy commercial clay directly from a pottery supplier. He will advise you on the clay best suited to your purpose. It will have proper consistency and texture and already have been subjected to necessary tests, particularly firing.

An alternative is to dig and prepare the clay yourself. Clay so obtained will be just as good as commercial clay, cost nothing, and provide you with adventure while seeking it plus satisfaction in literally creating your pottery from start to finish. Likely sources are pond or stream banks, road or railway cuttings, excavation sites, and brick or pottery works. If you fail to find clay through your own efforts, consult a surveyor or local builder. In most states a published geological survey is available that offers tips on locations of clays.

Preparation of Clay

Two kinds of commercial clay may be bought, either of dry body or plastic body. Clay of dry body comes in powder form and has to be mixed with water for a very considerable time. Clay of plastic body has already been prepared and is ready for use.

Clay you have dug yourself will probably require preparation, though some can be used as is. Others, being too soft, too hard, or full of vegetable matter, stones, and other impurities, will require special treatment:

First, let the clay dry thoroughly.

Then break it into walnut-sized pieces.

Soak them in a pail of water.

Let the clay soak for one to two days until it becomes a thick slop. The slop will remain as a sediment on the bottom of the pail, with the water on top.

Blend the clay and water in the pail to make a thin slop.

With your hands or a stiff brush, pass the material through a fine garden sieve into a second pail to eliminate undesirable impurities.

Let the slop settle once more. During the settling, water can be poured off little by little, and the thickening clay will stay on the pail's bottom. If the clay is needed urgently, it can be spread on a cloth to dry more quickly outdoors. When clay is not needed immediately, however, the ideal way is to let it dry naturally through evaporation until the proper consistency for modeling is reached. This would require several weeks. If the clay lacks sufficient plasticity, combine it with some bought clay by making alternate layers of both and kneading them together.

Storing Clay

Clay of ideal consistency, neither so soft as to stick to the hands nor so hard as to be unyielding to the touch, should be stored to maintain it in this condition. Keep it in airtight containers. Plastic ones are preferable to those of metal, which develop rust, although the rust has no adverse effect on the clay. To ensure that the clay is kept free from air, cover it with a plastic sheet or damp sack. Check it often for drying. If suitable containers are not available, closely wrap the clay in a plastic sheet. Unfinished clay work must also be kept free from air to prevent hardening. Wrap objects in plastic bags or sheets.

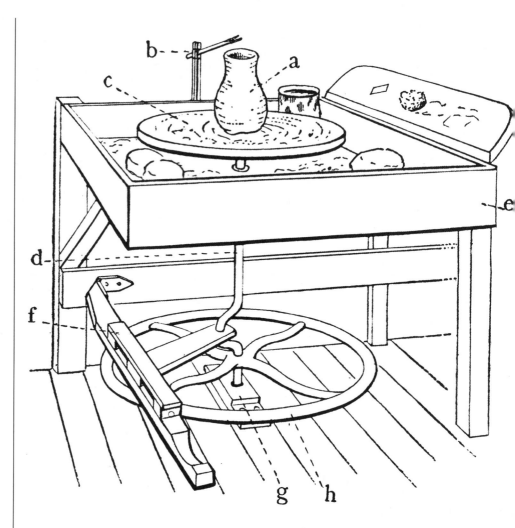

Slip

Slip is clay thinned to the consistency of cream. It is used for binding sections or coils of clay together. Make it by soaking pieces of clay in water until they become refined slop. Sieve it through an 80- or 100-mesh sieve, obtainable from a pottery supplier or lumberyard.

Wedging and Kneading

To prevent the explosion of clay articles during firing, trapped air must be expelled from the clay.

This is done through wedging and kneading home-prepared clay. Bought clay will not require such treatment.

Wedge the clay by cutting it into thick slices and forcefully slamming them down on your work table, one after the other. Form them into a mass again, and repeat the procedure ten to twenty times.

Knead the clay by pressing down on it with the base of your palms and pushing it from the body. Lifting the farthest edge of the clay, bring it over and toward you, and then press down again with the palms. The clay has been sufficiently kneaded when a cross section, cut by a wire, shows close, even texture without air pockets.

Clay that is to be fired in a primitive kiln must be strengthened with sand. Slice the clay, and make alternate layers of it and the sand. Then knead them together. Since sand tends to dry clay, you may need to put a thin layer of slop between each clay slice. Use one part sand to two or three of clay.

Techniques of Pottery Making

Pinch Technique: Shape a chunk of clay (the size of a small orange) in your hands as if shaping a snowball. When a smooth ball is formed, cup it in one hand while pressing the thumb of your other hand into its center, thus making a deep hole. Now you have the beginnings of a pot with thick walls. Still cupping the clay in your palm, pinch the wall between thumb and fingers, with the thumb inside and the fingers outside. Slowly rotating the pot in your hand, very gradually pinch out all sides of the pot and gently ease the clay. If cracks begin to appear as you are working, smooth over them with a wet finger.

Coil Technique: Roll clay backward and forward beneath your fingers to form long coils. A beginner should make the coils

somewhat thick—approximately the diameter of a fountain pen. Although it is not essential, try to keep them fairly uniform in length and thickness.

Flatten a sphere of clay into a disc roughly as thick as the coils. This is the pot's base. Now start the coiling. Shape the first coil around the inner edge of the disc, and press the coil's inner edge down on the base. When the coil completes the circle, guide it around on the top of the primary coil, pressing it firmly in place by smearing the inner edge down on the coil under it. Continue this procedure, coil upon coil, until the pot is finished. Control its shape

by the placement of the coils. If you want the pot to swell out, place the coils on the outer edge of the coil below. If the pot is to be narrower, place the coils on the inner circumference. To join the ends of coils, simply smear one against the other.

After a wall of seven to ten coils has been built up, permit the clay to become a bit firm in order to prevent sagging when the weight of more coils is added. Generally, one hour is needed for the clay to firm up sufficiently. If the clay overhardens, soften the top coil by scoring it and applying thick slip until it acquires the same consistency as the new coils.

Slab Technique: With the slab technique, the object is constructed from sheets of clay. Using a rolling pin (or a section of broom handle, a bottle, or a metal pipe), roll out a lump of clay into a flat sheet or slab of the desired thickness. Rolling should be done on a piece of cloth or paper to keep the clay from sticking to the work surface. Clay for the slab technique should be just a bit firmer than that for pinch or coiling work. If it is too soft, allow time for it to harden slightly.

Slabs can be cut into tiles with a knife and decorated with pictures that are incised or impressed on their surfaces. Containers can also be made. For example, to make a round pot, first cut out the base. Then mark it by outlining on the clay some circular object of suitable size. Holding a table knife vertically, cut around the outline. Then cut a long, narrow strip to form the side. Score all edges to be joined with a matchstick or modeling tool. Paint the scored edges with thick slip. Very soft clay can be bonded together securely without scoring and slipping. Stand the narrow strip on its side around the inside circumference of the base; attach it by firmly pressing the pieces together and smoothing over the joinings with a tool. Clay slabs may be wrapped around cardboard tubes of various lengths. Remove the tube as soon as feasible. A disc of appropriate size cut from a slab forms the base.

Make a simple dish by pinching up the edge of a circular slab. Any

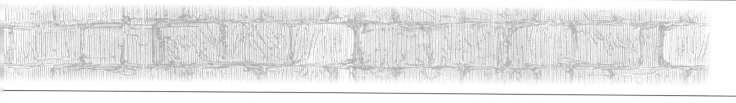

number of articles found about the house—plates, bowls, cardboard boxes, etc.—can be utilized as molds in slab work. Roll out a slab of clay a little larger than the selected mold. Using a damp sponge, gently press the clay, still on its cloth (to prevent sticking), into the mold. Cut away excess clay. Hold the clay down in the mold while cutting in case it should stick to the knife and be pulled out. With a damp sponge, smooth off the rim of the receptacle. Remove it when the clay is hard and pull away the cloth.

Decorating

While a finished clay article is yet in its soft, plastic stage, it can be decorated by impressing. Experiment by pressing small objects on the clay to make interesting patterns. In slab work, the design may be pressed on with the clay still in sheet form, prior to building up the final shape.

Relief decorations—small clay pieces applied to the object's surface—are pressed on while the clay is soft. If the clay is not soft enough, score and coat the surfaces to be bonded together with slip (a small brush is handy for this).

Clay surfaces can be decorated by incising. The clay should be almost completely dry. Experiment with simple tools to scratch, score, or carve.

Kilns and Firing

The beginner can fire his pots in a simple, homemade sawdust kiln. Select a kiln site where the ground is free of vegetation and well away from buildings. Collect dry fuel—wood shavings, twigs, wood—the amount depending on the kiln's size.

For the kiln floor, lay a groundwork of shavings and twigs.

Cover this with a 3- to 4-inch layer of sawdust.

Fill the articles to be fired with sawdust. Place a layer of pots, 2 inches apart, in the bed of sawdust. Be sure the articles do not touch each other and are not too close to the edge of the foundation. Cover the pots with a layer of sawdust. Continue to build alternating layers of pots and sawdust.

The complete mound should then be thickly covered with sawdust, followed by shavings, twigs, and wood. The purpose of the foundation of shavings and twigs and the outer layer of the same materials is to ignite the sawdust. The firewood will burn strongly for about ten minutes and then die out. The sawdust, once lit, will smolder for quite some time. Sudden changes in temperature would cause the pots to explode. However, the temperature within your kiln will rise gradually because of the slowly burning covering of sawdust.

As the sawdust is consumed, more can be added. Leave the kiln until thoroughly burnt out. Depending on the kiln's size, firing time will last anywhere from twelve to twenty-four hours.

When the pots are cool enough to be lifted from the kiln, wash or brush them clean.

Firing of clay articles can also be done in a metal drum with holes pierced around its sides. Fill it completely with dry sawdust. The articles should be dispersed throughout the sawdust. Light the fire from the top. It will slowly smolder downward and require no additional attention.

There are small electric kilns on the market that have been designed for testing purposes. If firing out of doors is not feasible, small objects can be fired indoors in such a kiln.

Should these first attempts at pottery-making spur you to work on a larger scale, a more sophisticated kiln may be constructed.

9 | ONE THING AND ANOTHER

In the old days few wants were "store bought." Country people supplied themselves with life's essentials by tediously making at home everything from blackboards to shoe polish. Here are some homemade items of the past and their methods of production.

Blackboard

You can make a large blackboard in no time from a sheet of hardboard, which is a thin sheet composed of pressed fibers, one side being hard and glossy brown. One 4 by 8 feet would be a good size. Coat it with blackboard paint. When the paint is dry, nail up your homemade blackboard.

Corncob Pipe

Self-sufficient old-timers seldom spent money for things they could produce themselves. The corncob pipe is an example of such thrift.

To try your hand at making one, select a firm ear of corn having sufficient pith to be properly hollowed out. You will need to break several ears and examine their cross section. In addition, choose one with ends that fit comfortably in your hand. When you have found the right cob, dry it.

Now decide which of the ends better suits your hand. Some people prefer the pointed end. Snap off an appropriate length for the size of bowl you favor. A bowl of 1¾ to 2 inches should be satisfactory. You may trim the break evenly, but this step is not essential.

Using the bigger blade of your pocketknife, dig out the pith to an approximate depth of 2 inches. The next layer will be woody and hard. Because it will give strength to your pipe, be careful not to remove too much of it. The completed hole should have a diameter of ½ to ¾ inch, depending on the cob's size.

Whether or not you believe the claim that a thicker bowl means a cooler smoking pipe, don't shave its outside walls. You'll like the rustic appearance and cushiony feel.

The pipestem can be made from the cornstalk by cutting the most slender part that's close to the top of the plant. An elder twig makes a good pipestem too. Either can be hollowed out with a hot coat-hanger wire. After piercing the stems, blow through them to force out any loose debris. A section of wild rice stalk, being naturally hollow, can provide a convenient stem. Cut the mouthpiece end directly above a joint in the reed. This strong area can be gripped between the teeth without concern about splitting the pipestem. Cut the opposite end directly above a joint in the stalk. The solid joint at the mouthpiece end is the only place you will need to ream out. Prepare the bowl end of the stem by cutting a flat slice, roughly ⅓ inch in length, from one side, forming a U-shaped opening.

Make a hole in the wall of the bowl just above the bottom of the hollowed-out area. This job can best be done with a twist drill having a diameter slightly smaller than that of the prepared pipestem. Maintain the bit at a right angle to the pipe bowl; bore a full twist in one direction followed by a half twist the opposite way. Work cautiously to keep the opening from becoming too large for the stem. After you have drilled clean through the bowl wall, insert the stem with the U-shaped opening uppermost. Firmly press in the pipestem for a snug fit.

Be patient with your pipe for the first few smokes. Any pith remaining in the bowl will have to burn away, and the woody part will need to season a little. Then, too, it's always difficult to keep a new pipe lit. After two or three smokes, however, you should be able to settle back and puff with satisfaction on your homemade corncob pipe.

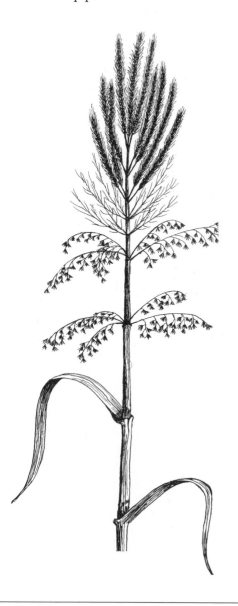

Crystal Garden

If the weather is too cold for outdoor gardening, make a garden indoors—of crystals.

A beautiful crystal garden can be created inexpensively and easily in any glass container, such as a jar or glass bowl. In addition, you will need enough coarse sand to layer the bottom of your container; some water glass, which is a stony powder that forms a colorless, syrupy liquid when dissolved in water (in times past, housewives preserved eggs by coating them with it); and packages of different crystals. The most satisfactory crystals to use are cadmium nitrate, cobalt nitrate, Epsom salts, ferrous sulfate, manganese sulfate, and zinc sulfate. The water glass and crystals can be bought at most drugstores or hobby shops.

Before starting your crystal garden, place the container in its intended location; otherwise, the delicate growths might be damaged in moving. Layer the floor of the container with coarse sand, which can be obtained from a building supply company or from the beach. From Plasticine, available at craft shops, create miniature trees and shrubs, garden seats, and birds, positioning them in the sandy bottom. You might add a few small shells and pebbles. If you want the crystals to grow in specific areas only, put them in place now. For a beautiful effect, try slightly embedding some (not too deeply or they will not grow)

in the branches of the Plasticine shrubs and trees.

Mix the water glass by dissolving 3 tablespoons of it in 2 cups of hot water. Prepare sufficient solution to fill the container. Pour it slowly into the glass receptacle until full. The crystals will immediately begin growing.

If you prefer a wild, unplanned garden, pour in the water glass and then drop in enough crystals to cover the bottom of the container.

The crystals will develop into beautiful plantlike forms within about ten minutes.

A crystal garden can also be made with some common household items, but it will require considerably more patience than the first one described.

Assemble these materials: ammonia, liquid bluing, food coloring, table salt (not iodized), water, a 6-inch container, and several lumps of soft coal or a brick.

Wrap the coal or brick in a rag, and pound it with a hammer into chunks about the size of a walnut. Arrange the pieces in the middle of the container.

Mix the following ingredients in the order in which they are mentioned: 4 tablespoons of salt (noniodized), 4 tablespoons of liquid bluing, 4 tablespoons of water, and 1 tablespoon of ammonia. Blend them until the salt liquefies.

Pour the mixture on the chunks of coal or brick. Using an eyedropper, spot the wet pieces with various shades of food coloring.

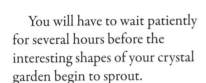

Drinking Glasses

The conversion of tall glass bottles into drinking tumblers requires a small amount of new, standard-weight motor oil, a ⅝-inch steel rod about 12 inches long, pliers, and a source of heat.

Decide at what level you want the bottle to break, and mark the spot. Pour in the oil to within ⅛ inch of that mark to allow for a slight rise in fluid when the rod is introduced. Before cutting the glass, let the liquid settle and be sure that none adheres to the bottle's sides above the intended cleavage line. The colder the container and oil, the more successful the operation. Fill bottles, and set them outdoors on a cool night. Complete the task the following morning.

Gripping the rod with pliers, heat the first 3 or 4 inches of the metal until they are visibly red hot. Immediately immerse it about 2 inches into the oil, keeping it there for at least thirty seconds. In approximately that amount of time, the majority of glass will snap off clean. If the method is unsuccessful, however, it may be that the glass is too thin. In that case, try a thicker-walled container, such as a wine or soda bottle.

Don't touch your newly created drinking tumbler until the oil has

cooled. Empty it into a jar to keep for future use. Wash the glass in hot, soapy water. After rinsing and drying it, smooth the cut edges with sandpaper or emery cloth.

Another method for cutting glass containers involves wrapping ordinary cotton cord several times around a bottle at a slightly lower level than the planned severance line. Thoroughly saturate the string

with alcohol; light it with a match. After the flame has subsided, pour ice-cold water over the jar or bottle. The glass will separate easily.

Gourd Uses

Gourds, with their variety of colors, shapes, and textures, make an attractive table decoration; hollowed out, they become objects for daily use.

If you are raising your own gourds, train the vines on trellises or fences to prevent the fruit from growing lopsided or rotting on the bottom. Discourage bug attacks by sowing a few radish seeds among the plants.

Soft-shelled gourds serve for ornamentation; the more durable thick-shelled gourds are good for utilitarian purposes.

After harvesting, clean them in warm, soapy water containing a

You will have to wait patiently for several hours before the interesting shapes of your crystal garden begin to sprout.

household disinfectant. Dry the gourds with a cloth, and spread them on newspaper in a warm, dry place. At the end of a week, wipe them with a cloth moistened only in disinfectant. Again spread the gourds to dry in a warm, dark, damp-free spot for about one month. Every other day, turn them. When seeds rattle about inside them, they are properly seasoned. Some thick-shelled gourds may require as much as a six-month drying period.

Now is the time to varnish or shellac thin-shelled gourds to prevent their fading and decaying. Waxing and polishing them will accentuate their lustrous hues.

Select large thick-shelled gourds for making containers.

Using a sharp knife, cut the shell to suit its intended function as bottle, bowl, water dipper, etc. Smooth rough edges with sandpaper or a file. Remove seeds and fiber from the interior.

When creating a bottle, slice a nub from the narrow end of a gourd. In it, wedge a cork long enough to extend into the bottle's neck when stoppered. A bowl can be fashioned quickly from the bottom half of a gourd. You might like to glue on wooden feet. For a dipper, lay the gourd

horizontally, and cut a slice from the top side, leaving the neck to serve as a handle.

If you want to attract birds to your yard, with the added advantage of keeping down the mosquito population, convert gourds into birdhouses. The purple martin likes both mosquitoes and a gourd home.

Choose large, round gourds having short necks. If you are growing your own, let them dry right on the vine until January. After picking them, cut a hole 2 inches in diameter on one side. Sand or file the doorway's edges smooth. Clean out the inside. To permit drainage, drill a few small holes in the gourd's bottom. Bore two more on opposite sides of the neck, and run a thong or nylon cord through them.

In February, suspend a number of gourd birdhouses 1 foot apart on wooden cross pieces

fastened to a 20-foot pole. Locate the pole in an area no closer to trees or buildings than 15 feet. A teaspoon of sulfur in each residence will discourage mites and ensure satisfied tenants.

Gourds can also be used for Christmas tree ornaments, flowerpots, napkin rings, toys— anything that your ingenuity might suggest.

Even the contents of a gourd are useful. They can provide you with a treatment that enhances well-being.

In Europe, dry bathing has long been famous for its favorable effect on one's skin. The bath, involving not water but a friction glove, stimulates blood circulation while removing any dead skin particles. The French claim that the dry bath is a remedy for insomnia.

The textured fabric of a friction glove is such that the slightest massaging movement tones the body. Friction gloves are fabricated from various materials: hemp,

horsehair, wool, coarse cotton, plastic. You can produce one of the finest kinds of dry bath gloves in your garden by planting old-fashioned dishcloth gourds. Harvest them when they are ripe, and carefully cut the shell away, revealing the web-like interior. Lay it in the sun for seven days to eliminate all moisture. Once completely dry, the web will be stiff and just a few shakes will rid it of seeds. Your friction glove is now ready for use.

Gently massage your body in an upward movement with the glove. This type of bathing should be indulged in no more than once each week. If you find the dry bath a little too severe, accustom yourself to it gradually by using the glove in your water bath the first few times. Its effect will be softened by the water.

Oatmeal-Box Radio

Anyone can build a crystal set with a few simple components: headphones, a crystal, coil, a variable condenser, and a long wire for an antenna. Having no tubes, no transistors, and no amplification, a crystal set has almost no distortion; music and voices are pure in tone.

Cut a rectangle 14 inches long and 12 inches wide from a well-seasoned board to serve as a base for the crystal set.

Use a cylindrical oatmeal or salt box for the coil form. Cut off one

end to a depth of 4 inches; immerse it in melted wax.

The wax coating will prevent it from absorbing moisture. The coil consists of about 150 feet of insulated copper wire (of a size ranging between numbers 22 and 28) or enameled wire (A WG number 24). Either fasten on the wire by running it in and out of three pinholes punctured about ¼ inch from one end of the cardboard cylinder, or secure the wire in place with cellophane tape. Wind on 166 turns. Every seventh turn, twist a small loop for a tap until you have a total of eight loops. Then wind forty turns with no taps. After that, make a loop on every tenth turn. Wind the coil tightly so that no space exists between turns. On each tap, scrape away any insulation to ensure a good connection

with the short wires leading to the switch points. When all the turns have been wound, attach the wire end with cellophane tape or thread it through pinholes in the cardboard. Bring down the various taps, and secure them beneath screws or brass-headed tacks on the baseboard. When the coil assembly is completed and working satisfactorily, you may give it a coat of varnish or paint it with melted candle wax.

Purchase a variable tuning condenser with the standard value of approximately 365 pF (picofarads). Position it on the board.

Headphones should be the high-impedance kind (at least 2000 ohms). Do not use hi-fi headphones.

In the old days the detector was an open crystal of galena (a lead-gray mineral), lightly touched by a delicate wire known as a "cat's whisker." Since such crystals are not easily found today, buy, instead, a germanium diode (for example, 1 N 34), costing about a quarter.

The longer the antenna the better. One about 200 feet long will give the best results. String it between trees or buildings, and bring a lead-in to your set. To be on the safe side, provide a lightning arrester. When the set is not in use, the lead-in wire can be ground to a water pipe.

A satisfactory ground connection is also necessary. Fasten the ground to a water pipe or radiator, making the lead as short as feasible.

Your crystal set uses no power and will cost nothing beyond the original small expense of constructing it.

Sawdust Stove

To make a cheap stove that burns either free or low-cost fuel, find a large empty paint can. Remove the top. In the center of the bottom, cut a hole 2 inches in diameter. Place the can on three improvised legs and your stove is finished.

For steady heat over a long period of time without refueling and without smoke, burn sawdust in your stove. Since powdered wood is generally discarded as a waste product, it can often be had for the asking at lumber yards and sawmills. When there is a charge, it is nominal.

Before loading your stove, be sure the sawdust is absolutely dry. To fuel the burner, you have a piece of water pipe or a smooth,

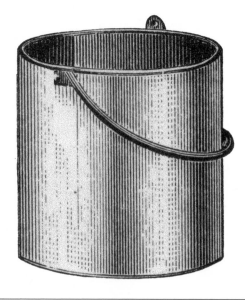

round stick of sufficient length protrude above the can's rim when it has been inserted through the hole in the bottom and rests on the floor. After positioning the pipe or stick in the hole, keep it vertical while pouring sawdust around it. Every so often, press the fuel down firmly as you load the can. Make the sawdust as compact as possible. When the stove is just about full, spread a thin layer of ashes or sand over the sawdust. Then, carefully twisting the pipe and pulling upward, remove it from the packed sawdust. There will be a neat hole directly through the mass.

To light your stove, fold a piece of newspaper accordion style and gently push it through the hole until it appears underneath. Ignite the lower end with a match. The burner will need no further attention until all the fuel has been consumed. Because some fumes are given off by the stove, ventilate the room where it is used.

The rate of burning is approximately 1½ to 2 inches an hour. A sawdust stove 12 inches in diameter will burn for roughly six hours. The degree of heat generated is controlled by the can's depth. The longer the central hole, the greater the heat. A tall, narrow container will be very hot for a relatively short period of time; a squat, wide container produces gentler heat for longer time; a tall, broad drum burns hot and long. Select a container to meet your requirements.

A sawdust stove is an inexpensive, efficient means of both cooking and heating.

Pet Food

Save all leftover food—meat, vegetables, etc.—and refrigerate it. When about 2 quarts have accumulated, put the scraps in a pot with enough water to cover them. Bring to a boil. Add 1 envelope of active dry yeast, 2 cups of dry beans (any kind), and 3 cups of oats. Cook the mixture over low heat for two hours. Refrigerate. Freeze the excess in containers.

Quill Pen

The use of large, stiff, tailor wing feathers as pens was first recorded in the sixth century; however, quills may well have served as writing

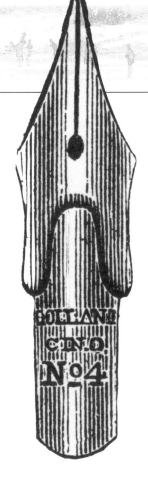

Grafting Wax

Melt 1 pound of rosin, and blend in 4 ounces of mutton tallow and 6 ounces of beeswax. Cool the mixture a bit in cold water; then work it until it is pliable. It not only makes a good grafting wax, but also serves as a salve for cuts you may sustain while climbing and sawing among tree branches.

Sealing Wax for Fruit Jars

Melt 1 pound of beeswax, 4 pounds of rosin, and 1 pound of orange shellac. Dip a brush into this mixture and paint the corks of fruit jars to seal them effectively.

implements at a more remote time. They continued in use until the early nineteenth century, when steel pens were introduced.

Pens have been most commonly fashioned from goose feathers. Only the five outer wing feathers are utilized, the second and third being considered best; left-wing quills are more prized than those from the right because they curve outward, away from the writer.

Crow, eagle, hawk, owl, turkey, and swan have also contributed quills for writing instruments. A swan quill is ranked superior to that of a goose, and crow quills are favored when a fine line is required.

The choicest quills are obtained from live birds during the spring. To make a pen, clean an appropriate quill until it is free of fat and oil. Thoroughly dry it in a warm spot to induce brittleness. Then, using a keen-edged knife, slit the tip and sharpen it to a point.

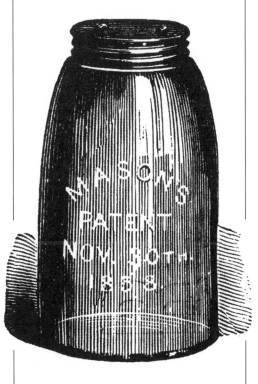

Black Copying Ink

Mix thoroughly ⅛ pound of soft brown sugar, ⅛ pound of gum arabic, ⅜ pound of powdered nutgalls (nut-shaped tumors found on oaks and other trees, formed by irritation due to insects), and ⅛ pound of copperas. Let the mixture steep in 1 gallon of rainwater for 2 weeks, shaking it occasionally. This procedure will result in a good black copying ink.

Indelible Ink

Dissolve a strong solution of Prussian blue in water. Add it to a quantity of gall ink. While being used in writing, the ink is green. When dry, it will be black and indelible.

Permanent Black Ink

Boil 1 ounce of logwood chips in 1 gallon of soft water. Cool and strain. Add more hot water to compensate for evaporation, and bring it to a boil. Pound ¾ pound of blue nutgalls into a coarse mash. Put them into the kettle with 3 ounces of purified copperas, ½ ounce of verdigris (acetate of copper), ½ ounce of pulverized sugar, and 4 ounces of gum arabic. Remove the mixture from the fire, and let it stand until it attains the desired blackness. Strain and bottle. This ink will not fade and consequently is excellent for keeping records.

School Ink

Dissolve 10 grams of bichromate of potash and ½ ounce of extract of logwood in 1 quart of hot rainwater. When it is cold, bottle it. Leave it uncorked for seven days; it will then be ready for use. It is a good black ink for school purposes, one that will not leave a permanent stain on clothing.

Copying Pad

Soak 2 ounces of glue in a dish of water. When it is soft, drain off the water. Put the dish into a pan of hot water and let stand until the glue melts. Mix in 1½ ounces of hot glycerin. Add a few drops of carbolic acid. Pour the mixture into a shallow square pan to cool. It can be used as a copying pad after 12 hours. Write what you want to reproduce on a sheet of paper with a sharp pen and aniline ink. When the ink dries, put the paper, writing down, on the pad. Press lightly.

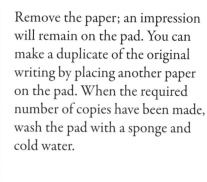

Remove the paper; an impression will remain on the pad. You can make a duplicate of the original writing by placing another paper on the pad. When the required number of copies have been made, wash the pad with a sponge and cold water.

Whitewash

To make whitewash, slake ½ bushel of lime in a barrel. Add 1 gallon of sweet milk, 1 pound of common salt, and ⅓ pound of sulfate of zinc.

White Paint

You can make a beautiful white paint by mixing the following: 9 ounces of slaked lime, 2 quarts of skimmed milk, 6 ounces of linseed oil, 2½ ounces of Burgundy pitch, and 3 pounds of Spanish white.

Machine Polish

To make an excellent polish for machinery, blend 3 parts of oil of turpentine, 3 parts of blood coal, and 1 part of stearine oil. Dilute this mixture with alcohol, and brush it onto the machine parts to be cleaned. When the alcohol has evaporated, rub the coaling with crocus (powdered iron oxide) or some other polishing agent.

Piano Polish

To make a good piano polish, mix ⅔ cup of vinegar, 1 cup of turpentine, and 1 cup of boiled linseed oil. Using a flannel cloth, rub the polish well into the wood. Finish by polishing the piano with a chamois skin.

Boot and Shoe Polish

For a good shoe polish, combine the following in a saucepan: 1 pint of soft water, 1 quart of cider vinegar, ¼ pound of clear glue, ½ pound of logwood chips, and 2 teaspoons each of powdered indigo, isinglass, and soft soap. Boil for 10 minutes. Strain when cool. First clean boots or shoes, and then apply the polish with a swab.

Waterproof Blacking

Melt and stir 16 parts of beeswax and 1 part borax to form a jelly. In another pot, stir the following mixture: ⅓ part of oil of turpentine, 1 part asphalt varnish, 1 part of melted spermaceti. Add to this the contents of the first vessel. For coloring put in 5 parts of ground Berlin blue and 12 parts of vine black. This waterproof blacking may be perfumed with 1 part of nitrobenzole. Store it in boxes.

Apply it to boots and shoes with a rag; then brush them.

Harness Blacking

Reduce to powder 1½ ounces of blue nutgalls. Put the powder into a bottle, and add 1 pint of soft water, ½ pint of alcohol, and 2 ounces each of tincture of muriate of iron and extract of logwood. Allow to stand for several days; shake the bottle twice daily. When the extract of logwood is dissolved, the harness blacking is ready for use.

Axle Grease

To make a good axle grease, put 2 pounds each of rosin and tallow, 1 pound of beeswax, and 1 quart each of castor oil and linseed oil into a kettle. Heat well and stir to blend. Continue stirring until the mixture cools.

Ice Chest

Select 2 boxes, one sufficiently smaller than the other so that there is a space of 4 inches on all sides when the smaller box is placed in the larger. Pack the free space between the boxes with sawdust. Make a cover for the larger box that fits snugly inside the top. Insert a small pipe in the bottom of the chest for drainage of waste water. This will make an efficient ice chest.

Making Ice

Into a cylindrical container pour 1⅓ ounces of water, 3½ ounces of sulfuric acid, and 1 ounce of powdered sulfate of soda. Set a vessel of water in the middle of this. The water will freeze. To make more ice, insert another vessel of water.

Fire Extinguishers

Dissolve 5 pounds of salimoniac and 10 pounds of common salt in 3⅓ gallons of water. Pour the liquid into bottles of thin glass that will easily break. Keep one in each room. When a fire starts, hurl the bottle into the flames forcefully enough

to shatter the glass. The contents will extinguish the fire.

Oiled Cloth

Over a low flame mix 2 ounces of lime water with 4 ounces of linseed oil. Beat separately 1 ounce of egg white and 2 ounces of egg yolk. Blend them into the other ingredients. Stretch close-textured white cotton cloth on frames, tacking it well. Apply the mixture with a brush. As each coat dries, brush on another. The oiled cloth will be waterproof after three coats.

Bushel Boxes

Make bushel boxes 17½ inches long, using lath for the length and bottoms. Use common pine wood for the ends, the boards to be 12 inches wide and 14 inches long. Plane the boards on both sides. Cut holes in them for the hands. With an inch bit bore 3 holes, and trim them with a pocketknife. An average wagon bed will accommodate from 32 to 36 of these bushel boxes. Potatoes, apples, and other produce packed in them will be less bruised than those in a loose load.

Mats

Wash a fresh sheepskin in warm water and strong soapsuds to which has been added a tablespoon of kerosene. Scrub it thoroughly on a washboard. Repeat the washing in fresh soapy water. When the wool looks clean and white, submerge it in cold water. Dissolve ½ pound of alum and ½ pound of salt in 3 pints of boiling water. Pour this mixture over the skin, and allow it to soak for 12 hours. Then hang it over a fence to drain. Next nail it on the side of the barn to dry, with the wool side against the wood. When it is almost dry, rub 1 ounce each of saltpeter and powdered alum into the skin for an hour. Rub it daily for three days or until completely dry. Scrape all impurities from the skin with a stick, and rub it with pumice stone. Trim it to a satisfactory shape. It will make a serviceable mat and can be dyed if color is desired.

Scarecrows

A stuffed coat and pants propped upright is customarily used to frighten crows from crops. Another means of keeping off these marauders is to string kernels of corn on long horsehairs and scatter them over the cornfields. Upon swallowing them, the crow will make such a raucous noise as he tries to free his throat of the corn that other birds will be driven away—sometimes, it is said, for the season.

A well-recommended method involves reflected sunlight.

Fasten two small mirrors back to back; hang them on a cord from a pole. As the glass dangles, sunshine is flashed over the field. A crow will leave as quickly as one of the startling flashes strikes him.

The following plan is efficacious in ridding fields not only of crows but of smaller birds and even domestic fowl: Make an imitation hawk, using a large potato and long turkey feathers. Stick the feathers into the potato in such a manner that they resemble the spread tail and wings of a hawk. Suspend it from a tall, bent pole. The wind will lend it realism by agitating it.

Christmas Wreaths

The sight and scent of fresh Christmas wreaths add to holiday pleasures. Wreaths can be fashioned easily with little expense if you have access to fir trees of some type: balsam, Douglas, grand, red, silver, or white. Consult your local nursery or forester to learn what suitable trees grow in your area's woods.

When you know where trees are available, set out on a bough-collecting trip equipped with garden clippers and a carrier for the branches. Take a long strip of canvas several feet wide and deeply hem its lengths. Run one continuous piece of rope through the resulting tubes, letting it extend beyond both ends of the cloth to serve as handles. Knot the rope ends together, and cut off any excess. (This carrier is also handy for transporting firewood from chopping block to woodpile and from woodpile to hearth. Use nylon rope. Not only is it strong and rotproof, but its elasticity will cushion the jolt when you lift a load of wood.)

Once you have found a good stand of firs, snip off branch ends to a depth of about 18 inches. Stack them on your canvas carrier. Trimming only the tips of boughs in this way will stimulate thicker, fuller growth; it will not damage the tree.

Transforming the greenery into wreaths will require a spool of thin wire (22–24 gauge) and the heavy wire hoops to which the evergreens are fastened. (Wreath frames range from 8 to 24 inches. You'll find a

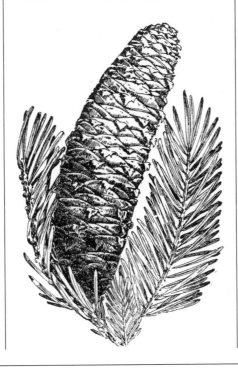

larger size easier to work with for your first attempt.) Both items can be bought at hardware stores.

Now follow these steps:

Place a hoop on a flat work surface, and attach an end of the wire to it.

Break a branch into three roughly equal pieces. Putting their thicker ends together, arrange them in a fan shape.

Lay the fan horizontally along the hoop, right side up.

Holding the twig ends together, bind the wire several times around them and the ring.

Fashion a second fan.

Turn the wire frame over. Lay the fan, right side uppermost, approximately 2 inches along the hoop from the first. Tightly attach it with a few turns of wire.

Continue in this manner, shaping fans and fastening them on alternate sides of the frame. Try to keep all twig bunches the same size. Always attach them right side up and wind the wire tightly.

Make the last two fans a little shorter than the others. Tuck them beneath the first fan to neatly complete the circle. Wrap them with wire, and tie it off. The knot will be invisible, covered by the twigs of the original fan.

If your finished wreath is somewhat shaggy, use the clippers to even up the central hole and to trim away any pieces elsewhere that protrude too far.

Your fragrant holiday wreath is ready to hang. You might want to brighten it with a fat red bow.

Christmas Tree Ornaments

Use decorative odds and ends and your imagination to create beautiful Christmas ornaments.

Begin with plain silver glass balls. Glue on leftover ribbon scraps of colored grosgrain or velvet and lace ruffles made crisp with spray starch. Apply designs from discarded gift wrapping paper, cutouts from last year's Christmas cards, or appropriate decals. Before gluing paper decorations on the balls, glue them to a backing of thin, flexible cardboard.

Whenever you prepare a recipe calling for eggs, save the shells. Keep them whole by puncturing both ends with an ice pick and forcefully blowing out the contents. After a good number has accumulated, transform the pale shells into bright Christmas tree ornaments.

Lacquer them in brilliant hues or pastel shades. When they are dry, glue on sparkling sequins, small pearls, and colored beads from broken necklaces. Gold or silver cord can be glued on in a spiral pattern or used to outline four ovals of vivid velvet spaced around the shells' circumferences. Decorating possibilities are almost limitless.

Finish each ornament by fastening a bead to one end of a thin wire and running the other end through the bottom hole in the shell and out at the top. Fashion a loop in the wire for hanging your shell ornaments on Christmas tree boughs.

Make a whole collection of original Christmas ornaments to enjoy season after season.

Christmas Tree Preserver and Fire Preventive

Dissolve the following ingredients in 1 gallon of hot water: 1 cup of ammonium sulfate (available at drugstores or chemical supply companies), ½ cup of boric acid (found in drugstores), 2 tablespoons of borax (found in hardware or grocery stores), and 8 tablespoons of 3 percent hydrogen peroxide (available in drugstores). If you like, add pine oil emulsion for an appropriate aroma. Store the mixture in a glass container.

For use, fill a spray bottle, and spray your Christmas tree with this fire-retarding solution. To prolong the life of your tree, keep the cup of its stand filled with the liquid. Help the tree absorb the solution by cutting the trunk anew at its base.

PART II

THE COUNTRY TABLE

10 | FARM FOODS AND KITCHEN WISDOM

Many of our commonest farm foods have histories stretching far back in time. In addition to their use in nutrition, they often served in other ways—to remedy bodily ills, to enhance beauty, and to fulfill superstitious beliefs. Here are some uncommon facts about some common foods.

Asparagus

Asparagus was cultivated as food before the Christian era in Persia and Arabia. It is a delicious vegetable rich in vitamins A and B.

The plant has no true leaves. Its so-called foliage consists of a great many slender branchlets, looking like green threads, which emerge from a tiny scale leaf at the tip.

Long ago, people believed that they could grow asparagus by planting the crushed horn of a wild ram. Its stalks were thought to have medicinal value. A broth made of them was said to relieve the pain of toothache and sprains. A drink of the plant's roots boiled in wine was administered to victims of snake bite.

In years past asparagus was known as "looking-glass weed."

Before the use of window screens, its feathery sprays were draped over bedroom mirrors for flies to alight on. Walking very cautiously, one might succeed in reaching an open door or window with a spray still black with flies!

Carrot

All carrots sprang from a common ancestor—that beautiful wildflower Queen Anne's lace.

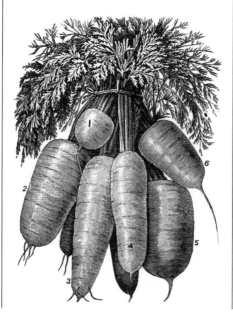

In the early 1500s the English were cultivating carrots in their gardens. Besides providing a delicious vegetable for tables, carrots furnished an adornment for women. In autumn their delicate, feathery foliage takes on a red or purple hue. Ladies used to pick the leaves and wear them on hats or in their hair instead of feathers.

Today a yellow pigment derived from the carrot is sometimes used to give butter a richer color. Furriers use the oil from this orange root on pelts to protect them from moths. Carrots also serve as nutritious food for livestock.

Cheese

A camel is supposed to have been responsible for the world's first cheese. Thousands of years ago, legend has it, a camel driver used a lamb's stomach as a container for fresh milk. The fermenting action of the enzymes remaining in the lamb's stomach, plus the constant swaying motion of the camel's gait, transformed the milk into cheese.

Cheese was said to have provided David with nourishment and strength when he challenged Goliath. It was brought to Europe by Crusaders returning from the Holy Land. Early Britons, in addition to getting subjugation from Caesar, got cheese. The eighteenth-century Italian lover Casanova advocated cheese and wine as a means of hastening love's blossoming.

Speaking of love, if you are a lover of cheese, you're known as a *turophile*.

Garlic

Garlic, that odoriferous member of the lily family, was native to southwest Siberia.

In olden times its odor was considered so intolerable that those guilty of heinous crimes were punished by being forced to eat garlic. Because animals as well as humans were believed to be offended by its strong smell and taste, domestic fowl were sprinkled with garlic juice to keep them safe from weasels and other predators.

The ancients valued garlic for its medicinal qualities. It was prescribed externally as a treatment for the bite of beast or insect and internally as an antidote for poison. Garlic was supposed to improve eyesight. When cattle lost their vision, farmers hung roots of it about their necks. A very ancient use of garlic was as a disinfectant in the cremation of corpses. During the First World War, when antiseptics were scarce, garlic oil was used as an acceptable substitute.

Magical protective powers were attributed to garlic. Throughout ancient times it was considered a sure defense against the influence of the evil eye. Hung on doors and around windows, it was supposed to provide protection against vampires. Midwives kept garlic cloves handy to place about a baby's neck immediately following birth or after baptism to guard him from harm. Country dwellers fastened garlic around their cows' necks to deter goblins from stealing milk in the night. To prevent a snake from crawling out of its hole, a clove of garlic was laid at the entrance.

A very practical use for garlic was to keep heavy drinkers from becoming intoxicated. Putting a few crushed cloves at the bottom of their sizable wine pitchers was supposed to do the trick. In Europe, garlic accompanied by chunks of coarse dark bread was a standard breakfast for peasants. In the United States, it is used chiefly for flavoring. High in iron content, it may eventually be regarded as a staple food in the American diet.

Meanwhile, rural folks claim that it's a dependable corn cure. Kermit Zog of North Carolina says to rub a pesky corn with a crushed clove of garlic every night before going to bed, or to bind a sliver of it on the corn with a plaster. This procedure should be repeated until the corn drops off, usually within eight to ten days. Kermit cautions that you may find yourself sleeping alone!

By the way, if you're fond of garlic, you're an *alliophiliac*.

Honey

In olden times honey affected people's lives virtually from cradle to grave. Regarded as pure, it was the first food given to newborn infants. Marriage contracts often

specified a quantity of honey that the groom was obliged to give his future wife every year of their married life. Marriage ceremonies were sticky affairs. In addition to honey's being served in food and drink, it was smeared on the bride's ear lobes, forehead, eyelids, and lips. Its purity served as a kind of talisman to protect the couple from evil and ensure their happy future.

Honey became known as an aphrodisiac and was the chief ingredient in love potions designed to increase virility. People believed it could influence fertility in women, cattle, and crops.

Esteemed for its nutritional value, it formed part of the daily diet. The ancients considered it an elixir of youth and predicted longevity for faithful users of honey as nourishment.

Since it was felt to be a magical substance, soothsayers used it in their ceremonies. It was regarded also as sacred and was generally included as a sacrificial offering during religious rites.

Over the centuries honey has been considered a cure-all for internal and external woes: gastric disorders, respiratory troubles, inflammation of the kidneys, epilepsy, labor pains, skin diseases, and inflammation of the eyes and eyelids. It has been used for dressing wounds, to spread on the skin of smallpox victims, and to treat obesity, typhoid fever, pneumonia, rheumatism, and insomnia. Because of its antiseptic quality, it was recommended as a gargle.

Peasants paid their taxes in honey. As a widely accepted medium of barter, it served as purchasing power.

Country folks valued it not only as a stimulant for the appetite and an aid to digestion, but as a supernatural agent to protect their cattle. Honey fed to cows and applied to their eyes were sure to guard them against pestilence. Rural folk added honey to their wells so that the water would not become contaminated. It was regarded as a cure for persons of disagreeable temperament and for those poisoned by mushrooms, bitten by snakes, or attacked by rabid animals. Used externally, it was said to kill lice and nits. Country people maintained that lightning never struck where there were honey and bees.

At life's end honey continued to play a role. Since honey represented eternal bliss, vessels of it were placed near the coffin and later in the tomb. Outstanding members of society were embalmed in

honey. The belief prevailed that the souls of those whose bodies were preserved in it would be reincarnated.

Nowadays honey might be associated with a country breakfast of hot biscuits spread with butter and honey or the aroma of split acorn squash baking in the oven, honey and spices steaming in the hollows. Yet among country dwellers today, honey is often mixed with hot lemon juice and used as a cold remedy or administered, combined with roasted onions, as a poultice for congested lungs.

To all the uses for honey down through the ages there has been added a modern one. Because of its low freezing point, honey mixed with an equal amount of water has been utilized as an emergency substitute for antifreeze.

Jerusalem Artichoke

Though the Jerusalem artichoke is a true native of North America, facts about it are not widely known. It is not an artichoke, but a member of the sunflower family, having a thick, fleshy root. The indigenous peoples of North America ate the root raw, boiled, or roasted. In the western part of the United States the plant grew wild, but Native Americans in the East cultivated it along with other crops of beans, maize, and squash.

French explorers carried it back to their homeland, where it was favorably received as table fare and used as feed for livestock. Upon reaching Italy, it was called girasole, the Italian word for sunflower. The English mispronunciation of this word brought about the first part of the name "Jerusalem artichoke;" a comparison of the tuber's flavor to that of the artichoke accounts for the latter part. After its introduction to the English, it was looked upon initially as an unusual delicacy. Since the Jerusalem artichoke grows prolifically, it was soon considered common and shunned.

The plant is similar to other small wild sunflowers but grows to a greater height. During the summer months the edible root grows very little, because the lengthening stalk and maturing flowers consume most

of the nourishment. Fortunately, the Jerusalem artichoke is resistant to frost, since its chief growing season extends through the cool months, from October to June. This vegetable is more widely cultivated in Europe than in America, its homeland.

Lettuce

In ancient times travelers from the Mediterranean area eastward were guided by the "compass plant." This plant was wild lettuce. Along its tall stalk climbed upturned leaves whose edges pointed due north and south. One's direction could be determined by it as surely as by the sun. Thirsty journeyers could rely upon its juicy leaves for refreshment, and so it became known as the "water plant."

Not long afterward the leaves, cooked as greens, were found to be a wholesome, palatable food. From then on and that was probably three thousand years ago lettuce was a cultivated plant.

Partaking of lettuce salad at the beginning of a meal, it was believed, would stimulate the appetite; eating it at meal's end would prevent inebriation from the wine imbibed while dining.

Because lettuce has a white juice similar to that of opium poppies, it was thought to have narcotic and sedative properties and was recommended as a treatment for pain, fevers, and insomnia.

Onion

The onion is one of the world's earliest-cultivated plants. The Bible relates that it was a food much craved by the Israelites in the wilderness.

Egyptians were said to have placed their right hand on the onion as they took an oath. They sometimes used it as a sacrificial offering to their deities. Divine honors were bestowed upon one variety, and it was depicted on Egyptian monuments. The nutritional value of the bulb was appreciated by Egyptians, who fed it to slaves erecting the pyramids as a defense against scurvy. In later centuries ships of other lands, destined to be long from home port, put to sea with holds laden with onions for the same purpose.

The onion reached the New World through the West Indies, where it was introduced by the Spanish. It spread throughout the Americas and was grown by early colonists and Native Americans, who had been eating wild onions for centuries.

According to folklore, the onion was an aphrodisiac. From this belief developed the custom of carrying onion soup to a newly married couple.

In the past it was believed that various ailments could be remedied by the onion. A few drops of onion juice in the ear would cure deafness or ringing. Onion juice applied to bald areas of the head would rejuvenate hair growth. For

the relief of gout, the juice mixed in a tea of pennyroyal should be spread with a feather on affected areas. Onion juice blended with capon grease was recommended as a cure for blisters on the feet. Today country people of America use raw onion to draw out the poison from a bee sting.

Parsley

Long ago parsley was used for both the living and the dead.

It was considered a healthful food for man and other creatures. The herb was used in meat dishes, poultry stuffing, omelets, soups, salads, and gravies. Eating parsley was said to benefit the brain and memory, beautify the skin, and counteract the effects of a mad dog's bite. One variety boiled in ale was a drink prescribed for the bite of a poisonous spider.

Ailing fish were cured, it was believed, if parsley leaves were tossed into their ponds.

Victors of athletic games were crowned with chaplets of parsley. As for the dead, their graves were customarily spread with it, for parsley was long regarded as the death herb.

To account for parsley's tendency to germinate slowly, legend said that it is the property of the Devil and must make seven trips to him before sprouting. During the Middle Ages it was believed that an enemy would meet sudden death if one uprooted parsley while repeating his name. To this day there are those who avoid transplanting the herb, fearing it might cause bad luck.

Potato

The potato grown in this country, often called the "Irish" potato, followed a rather circuitous route in reaching us. Though its history is spotted with unauthenticated information, there is general agreement that its original home was Chile.

From indigenous tribes in the Andes of South America, potato cultivation spread to other tribes, gradually finding its way to the West Indies and, to what is now Virginia, even before colonial days. Sir Francis Drake's ships, bearing supplies for settlers there, returned to England with potatoes obtained by barter from Native Americans. These curiosities were presented

to Sir Walter Raleigh, who planted them on his estate in Ireland. When the English imported them from that country, they became known as "Irish" potatoes.

Grain was the chief crop of Ireland at that period, and it was a long time before the potato was established as a staple food. By many it was regarded as unfit for human consumption. Its denouncers organized the "Society for the Prevention of Unsatisfactory Diets." From the initials of this group came the word "spud," used for the potato.

The potato was rejected in Scotland as a product of the Devil, since no mention of it could be found in the Bible.

Spaniards became acquainted with the vegetable when they invaded South America early in the sixteenth century. They carried it to Spain, from which country it spread to other parts of Europe.

For a considerable time the French would not accept the potato, believing it was poisonous because of its membership in the nightshade family. It was also believed to cause leprosy. Later, however, it was found to be a cure for scurvy on long sea voyages. In Germany it became a chief crop food as a result of a grain failure. Eventually the potato won its way into the hearts and stomachs of most of the civilized world.

The potato is actually the enlarged tip, or tuber, of an underground stem. In addition to their nutritional value for both humans and farm animals, potatoes are utilized in manufacturing potato flour, starch, alcohol, glucose, and syrup. Country dwellers use the potato as a remedy for lumbago by carrying a small one in the pocket, replacing it when it becomes dried out.

The most reliable written record shows that potatoes were first cultivated on a large scale in New Hampshire from a stock of "Irish" potatoes brought from Ireland. To do its ancient lineage justice, the potato should actually be called the "Chilean" potato.

Radish

The radish was cultivated so long ago that it's unclear where it originated. In ancient times it was food for the people of China, Japan, India, and southern Europe.

The plant is believed to have been cultivated at first for its leaves along Mediterranean shores.

Constant tending caused its root to enlarge, providing a second vegetable. Possibly its ancestor was the wild radish of Europe, credited with the power of detecting the presence of witches.

Medicinal properties were ascribed to the radish. Taken internally, it was believed to quicken mental capacities; used externally, to cure bruises. Mixed with honey vinegar, it served as a soothing gargle for tonsillitis. The radish was also considered efficacious in the event of snake bite. Cosmetically, it was recommended for renewal of hair growth and the removal of freckles.

In addition to the pleasantness as food of the crisp, pungent root of the radish plant, its pods are enjoyed when pickled.

Raspberry

Old-timers attached much importance to raspberries when hunting season arrived. Bears are particularly fond of them. When the fruit ripened, bears were easily located.

In olden times people believed that vinegar made from raspberries was a good protection against plague. The juice of the berries was used to dissolve tartar on the teeth and to treat scrofula.

Rhubarb

Rhubarb, usually served as a dessert, is a vegetable of the buckwheat family. Its origin was the Mediterranean area.

In ancient China a variety of rhubarb was cultivated for the use of its roots in medicine.

Benjamin Franklin, in the late 1700s, was responsible for introducing rhubarb to America. While in England, he sent a gift of it to a friend in Philadelphia. Its popularity soon spread. Only the stalks were used for pies and wine making; hence rhubarb is often called "pie plant" and "wine plant." The leaves are discarded because of their poisonously high content of oxalic acid, which can cause a skin rash.

Rice

Rice was probably a native crop of India some five thousand years ago. It soon spread and was cultivated throughout Asia.

The Greeks and Romans did not plant this cereal grass but imported it. Rice cultivation was introduced to the Mediterranean area by Arab armies in the seventh and eighth centuries, and by the fifteenth century it was raised in Italy and France.

On his second voyage to North America, Columbus brought rice from Spain, but its growth was not successful. Then late in the seventeenth century, a storm-tossed ship sought safe harbor along the coast of South Carolina. Some of its cargo was unhusked rice from Madagascar. The captain gave a quantity to a plantation owner, who cultivated it with good results. It was the start of a new money crop for the South. Today the states of Arkansas, California, Louisiana, and Texas produce most of America's rice.

Long ago rice was prescribed as a treatment for hemorrhages and lung disease. Powdered and mixed with milk, it was used as a poultice for skin inflammations. Today a standard country cure for diarrhea is rice water.

Soybean

One of the very earliest food crops grown by man was the soybean. It was a common food among the ancient Chinese well before the Christian era; yet not until the seventeenth century did it find its way to Europe.

In the United States, soybeans were first cultivated to a limited extent in the late nineteenth century, and by the early 1900s home-grown soybeans were processed for the first time.

In China, rural superstitions cling to the soybean. One wearing a concealed necklace of the beans is supposed to be capable of great feats. Diviners are able to predict future events by consulting soybeans that have been soaked in sesame oil for three days.

Besides being a nutritious food containing ten times the protein of milk, soybeans provide oil that is important in the finishing of automobiles.

Spinach

Spinach was first cultivated in ancient Persia and surrounding areas. Not until the Christian era did the plant become widespread. It was introduced to China in the seventh century. Moors were responsible for carrying it to Europe in the twelfth century. For generations a variety of spinach was grown in secluded monastery gardens of Europe.

Finally, in the early part of the sixteenth century, colonists transported the plant to North America. Today Arkansas and Texas produce our major spinach crops.

Nature included an acceptable amount of oxalic acid in spinach. However, with man's constant hybridization of the plant, the acid content has been substantially increased and can cause formation of small stones of calcium oxalate in the body. Eaten occasionally and in moderate amounts, spinach is a good source of vitamin B2.

Recently the plant has been processed to form a film of chlorophyll which produces electricity when under the sun's rays. The resulting energy is stored in batteries. So spinach has twofold potential energy: food power and electrical power.

Tomato

Spanish padres are credited with the initial dissemination of the tomato plant. After the Spanish conquest of the Aztec Empire, the Spaniards examined plants in Mexico used by the native

people for food and medicine. The indigenous people cultivated tomato plants on their floating gardens and ate the red fruit. Tomato seeds were among the first sent by the monks to Spain for planting in monastery gardens.

Some years later a Moorish visitor to Mexico, intrigued by the plant's beauty, carried seeds to Morocco. It was here that the bright fruit caught the eye of an Italian sailor. He took the *pomo dei Mori*, the apple of the Moors, to his homeland, where it spread quickly. The French received it from Italy and cleverly changed the name to *pomme d'amour,* the apple of love. The tomato reached England from France and continued being called the "love apple" for centuries.

The tomato plant of those times differed considerably from that of today. The fruit was very much smaller and deeply furrowed. Considered poisonous because it belongs to the nightshade family, it was cultivated not in the vegetable garden but amid flowers, solely as an ornamental plant. Stalks of the shiny red fruit were kept in vases as colorful centerpieces for dining tables or as decorative touches for fireplace mantles. Because of the supposed poisonous quality of tomatoes, they were thrown to marauding wolves, along with poisoned meat chunks.

During the days when tomato plants were relegated to flower beds, ketchup was made from

English walnuts. By the mid-1800s, however, walnut ketchup had lost favor to ketchup made from tomatoes. The Italians extracted an oil from the seeds, which they used in making soap. Today tomato-seed oil, along with other oils, is still incorporated in soaps.

After centuries of cultivation the tomato has developed into the large, smooth-skinned sphere of red we know today, delicious to eat and nutritious as a source of vitamin C. We think of the tomato as a vegetable; actually it is a berry.

The tomato really came into its own as a food in America just about the time that hoop skirts went out of style. Resourceful country housewives used discarded hoop-skirt frames as improvised trellises for training tomato vines.

A Hash of Kitchen Wisdom

Baking
A cup of water placed in the oven when you bake will keep the crust of bread and cake from getting hard.

Baking Powder
To make a good baking powder, thoroughly mix the following: 4 ounces of flour, 5 ounces of bicarbonate of soda, 10 ounces of cream of tartar, and 1 ounce of tartaric acid.

Butter
Butter can be made firm during hot weather in this way: Mix 1 teaspoon of powdered alum with 1 teaspoon of carbonate of soda. At churning time put this mixture into the amount of cream that will produce 20 pounds of butter.

Cabbage
Odorless cabbage cooking is accomplished by adding half a green bell pepper without seeds to the cabbage pot. It flavors the cabbage and kills the odor in the kitchen.

Cake
When cake sticks to the pan, wrap a damp warm cloth around the baking pan. The steam will cause the cake to loosen.

Citrus
Roll an orange, grapefruit, or lemon vigorously on a hard surface before squeezing it and you will get a lot more juice.

Currants
To clean dried currants, shake them about in a sieve with a little flour until only the currants remain. Wash them thoroughly, and remove any twigs. Spread them on a flat surface in some warm spot to dry. Don't use the currants until you are sure that they are completely dry, or else they will sink to the bottom of your puddings and cakes.

Eggs
When boiling eggs, add a little salt to the water and the shells will slip off easily. To boil an egg that is cracked, add a teaspoonful of salt to the water and the egg will stay in the shell.

To keep eggs fresh, follow this procedure: Gather new-laid eggs, and coat each with salt butter so that the shell is completely sealed.

Dry some bran in the oven. Place a layer of the bran in a box, and pack the eggs in it with their small ends down. Continue to fill the box with alternating layers of bran and eggs. Keep the box in a cold, dry place, and the eggs will remain fresh for 10 months.

Fish

Dip fresh fish in hot salt water until the scales curl and they will be a lot easier to clean.

Flavoring Extracts

Homemade flavoring extracts are found to be more delicious than those that are bought. To make lemon extract, put 1 pint of good alcohol in a jar and add 1 ounce of lemon oil and the peel of 2 lemons. Allow it to stand for a week; shake it 3 times each day. Now take out the peel, and bottle the liquid for use. All essences can be made according to the same proportions as the lemon-flavored extract.

Fruits

Fruits of an acid nature should be cooked in tin, brass, or porcelain vessels.

Herbs

Gather herbs on a sunny day of low humidity. To dry them, you may spread them in the shade on such a day, or hang them near a stove, or place them in an open moderate oven. When the herbs are very dry, powder and sift them. Store them in bottles with snug corks or in air-tight tins to preserve their flavor.

Milk

Raw milk curdles quickly when boiled. This can be corrected by adding a pinch of soda.

A pinch of salt in raw milk will keep it from souring quickly.

Sprinkle table salt on scorched milk and it will help eliminate the bad smell.

When cooking with milk, put a little water in the pan first and heat it to boiling, then add the milk. It will keep the milk from burning or sticking to the bottom of the pan.

Molasses

Molasses and syrup will pour completely out of a cup or any container if you will first grease it with butter or cooking oil.

Nuts

Soak hard-shell nuts in salt water overnight. They will break open easily and the kernels will shell-out whole.

Onions

When cooking onions set a cup of vinegar on the stove to kill the odor.

Preserving Apples

First pile them in a heap to sweat. Then pack them in barrels or boxes in hemlock sawdust. In this manner they can be kept fresh until Nature provides new fruit in the spring.

Preserving Root Vegetables

Put root vegetables into a large box. Pack them in such a way as to leave a space of an inch or more around the sides of the box. When it is filled to within 6 inches of the top, shake in sand or dry road dust and cover with a layer of fresh earth. This will nicely keep vegetables— especially beets and turnips—for winter use.

Restoring Tainted Meats

To remove the odor from tainted (not rotten) meat, prepare this solution: Boil 1 quart of water, and allow it to cool. Then add 1 ounce of permanganate of potash. Put

the liquid in a tightly closed bottle and shake well. Into a container of water sufficient to cover the ill-smelling meat, put 1 tablespoon of the solution. Stir it with a long stick to avoid staining hands or clothing. Submerge the meat and allow to stand for 10 minutes. Then rinse well, and all trace of unpleasant odor will be gone.

Soup Coloring

To impart an amber color to soup, add finely grated carrot. If a reddish color is desired, use red tomatoes, straining out their skins and seeds. Press the juice from spinach; dry and powder the leaves. To give soup a green color, add both the juice and the powdered leaves. For brown soup a clear stock should be used.

Soup Flavoring

Wash the large leaves of 5 celery stalks. Boil them in 1 quart of water until the liquid is reduced to ½ pint. Allow it to cool, strain out the celery leaves, bottle the liquid, and store it in a cool place. Use it as a flavoring for soups, gravies, and stews.

Substitute Jelly

If jelly is desired and fruits are not available for its making, the following method will produce a satisfactory substitute: Boil ½ ounce of powdered alum in 1 quart of water for 3 minutes. Put in 8 pounds of white sugar; boil for a few minutes, and strain. Add any preferred flavoring.

Tomatoes

To easily slip tomato peels off place the tomatoes in boiling water for one-half minute then place them in cold water until they are cool. The skin will slip off and leave a firm, full, unbroken tomato.

Vinegar Uses

• When cooking rice, add 1 teaspoon of vinegar to the water. This will keep the grains whole.

• You can make lettuce and other greens clean and crisp by soaking them for 5 minutes in water with a little vinegar added.

• Put vinegar in the water for boiling eggs. This will keep the whites from running out if the shells crack.

• Add a few drops of vinegar to uncooked icing during the mixing, and it will remain softer.

• To keep cheese fresh, wrap it in a cloth moistened with vinegar.

Vegetables

The taste of oversalted vegetables can be removed by covering the bowl with a wet cloth for a few minutes.

Whipping Cream

If whipping cream won't whip add the white of an egg.

Moon Signs in the Kitchen

Country women who heed the zodiac signs in their kitchen work agree with these tips:

Baking

Bread prepared when the moon is in the first and second or waxing quarters tends to "rise" more. Baking is best done when the moon is in Aries, Cancer, Libra, or Capricorn, the movable signs. Some believe this makes the bread lighter.

Brewing and Winemaking

The third and fourth waning moon quarters are usually best, especially when the moon is in the watery and fruitful signs of Pisces, Cancer, or Scorpio.

Canning

Can fruits and vegetables during a waning moon in the third and fourth quarters, preferably in the watery signs of Pisces, Cancer, or Scorpio. Put up jellies and preserves during a waning moon in the third and fourth quarters, but in the fixed signs of Aquarius, Taurus, Leo, or Scorpio (especially Scorpio since it is both a fixed and a water sign).

11 | FROM THE SPRINGHOUSE

Butter

Back in the old days when butter was homemade, the process began with the care of cows. Some farmers, believing that a diet of corn fodder did not result in good butter, advocated a blend of half bran and half cornmeal. Others swore by a twice-daily feeding of early-cut hay and a mixture of scalded cornmeal and wheat bran, moistened with sweet skimmed milk.

The milk produced was strained through a cloth and "set" for cream. It was poured into deep tin pails either standing in vessels of ice or maintained at low temperature by cold spring water running through the milk house, if the building was so favorably situated. Cream setting lasted for a period of twenty-four hours or more, some dairymen claiming that a preliminary heating to a temperature of 130°F would cause the cream to rise more quickly.

The temperature considered ideal for cream at churning time was 57°F. After being skimmed from the pails, the cream was put in a churn and worked for twelve to twenty minutes. The cylindrical dash churn, with a stick handle protruding through the top, was generally made of pottery or stripped cedar banded in brass hoops and powered by hand. Another old-time means of butter making was the dog churn. The sheep or cattle dog was recruited to run the equipment, freeing farm folks for other duties. Harnessed

on a sort of treadmill, the animal set in motion an attached container for cream as it trotted in place. To each 20 pounds of butter, 3 ounces of white sugar and 6 ounces of salt were added.

In the absence of pasturage during the winter months, butter generally lacked sufficient yellow; so country housewives colored it with annatto, a dyeing material prepared from the seeds of a tropical tree. A lump about the size of a hickory nut was dissolved in 8 ounces of water. One tablespoon of the mixture was used to color 5 pounds of butter. Coloring the butter was also done with carrots. For each 3 gallons of cream, 6 large carrots were washed and coarsely grated. Boiling water was poured on them to extract their color. The carrot juice, allowed to cool, was then strained through coarse muslin into the cream prior to churning. Besides improving the appearance of the butter, the carrot juice gave it a sweet taste, similar to grass butter. Powdered turmeric,

too, served as a yellow dye and was said to impart a richer flavor to sweet butter.

Tin pails and other dairy utensils were often scoured with the aid of nettles and plenty of suds from homemade lye soap.

Today, a simpler way of making butter is with your electric mixer. Attach the mixers, set the machine at its lowest speed, and slowly pour in all the cream while the mixer is running.

When pale butter grains appear, drain them in a muslin bag. Then put the substance in a bowl, and wash it thoroughly by spooning cold water over it until the water becomes clear. Finally, press the grains into one mass. If you wish to add salt, use about 1 teaspoon to the pound.

Perhaps the easiest means of making butter is provided by your blender. Put 4 cups of fresh cream into the machine. Let the cream reach close to room temperature (about 68° F). Then run the blender at its slowest speed. After about three minutes, yellowish flecks should appear on the surface. Continue running the blender until the cream turns to butter, within eight minutes or so.

When butter has formed, drain off the buttermilk, reserving it for cooking purposes, and replace it with an equal amount of cold water. Cap the blender and churn the contents for ten seconds. Strain off the water. Repeat this cleaning method until the water is quite clear.

Drain the butter. Transfer it to a bowl, and press out excess moisture with a spoon. Add salt if desired.

Cheeses

Hard Cheese
Yield: 1½ to 2 pounds

If you have access to milk fresh from a farm, let 4 quarts of the evening's milk stand overnight in a cool place where the temperature ranges between 50 and 60°F. The next morning, mix in 4 quarts of fresh morning milk. Either cow's or goat's milk may be used. The best store-bought milk for cheese is fresh homogenized milk.

Be sure all utensils are completely clean. In a stainless steel pot or enameled or tin pail, heat the milk to 86°F. Use a dairy thermometer. You may add cheese coloring (optional) at this time by dissolving about one eighth of a cheese color tablet in 1 tablespoon of water and stirring it into the milk. In a glass of cold water, thoroughly dissolve one quarter of a cheese rennet tablet by stirring and crushing it with a spoon. Set the pail of milk in a larger container of warm (88–90°F) water, and place it in a warm spot protected from drafts. Thoroughly stir in the rennet solution for about one minute.

Leave the milk undisturbed for approximately forty minutes while a curd forms. Test the curd's firmness by inserting your finger at an angle and lifting. When it breaks clean over your finger, it is ready for cutting. With a knife long enough for the blade to reach the pail's bottom, cut the curd into small pieces. Cut in all directions so that the pieces will be quite small. Using your well-washed hand or a wooden spoon, gently stir the curd from around the sides and from the bottom upward. Carefully cut any large chunks that rise to the surface into smaller pieces; do not mash them. Try to make the curds of uniform size. To prevent their sticking together, continue the stirring for fifteen minutes.

Gradually raise the temperature of the pail's contents to 102°F at the rate of 1½ degrees every five minutes. Stir frequently with a spoon to prevent the curds from sticking to each other. By this time, the curds should hold their shape and fall apart easily when they are held without being squeezed.

The next step in the process lasts one hour. Take the pail from the heat, and stir the contents often enough (about every five minutes) to prevent the curds from coagulating. Let the curds stay in the warm whey until sufficiently firm so as to shake apart after being pressed together in your hand. Turn the curds into a piece of cheesecloth 4 feet square, spread in a container. Gather up two corners of the cloth in each hand, and rock it gently for about three minutes so that the curds move about while the whey drains through.

(When making cheese with cow's milk, don't discard the whey. It can be used to prepare butter that will taste like the salted variety, but with a delicate cheese flavor.)

Lay the cloth holding the curds in a clean pail. Sprinkle 1 tablespoon of salt over the contents and mix thoroughly. Add another tablespoon of salt and blend well.

Now tie the corners of the cloth together, forming a ball of the curd. Hang it so that it drips for a half hour or more.

Have your cheese press ready. Cheese-making kits are available in stores, complete with a cheese press, dairy thermometer, cheese coloring, and rennet tablets with directions for use. However, you can make your own cheese press by taking two pieces of wood, 8 by 12 inches, and putting a 1-inch dowel through both at either end. The dowels will keep the boards in place.

Take the cloth away from the sides of the curd ball. Fold a long cloth, such as a dish towel, into a 3-inch-wide strip, and wrap it tightly around the ball. Form the ball into a round, flat wheel. Smooth the surface of the cheese with your hands. Put several thicknesses of cheesecloth under and on top of the wrapped cheese. Set the cheese on the bottom board of your cheese press, and lower the top board to rest on the cheese. Place two bricks on top. That evening turn the cheese over, placing four bricks on top. Allow to stand until morning.

The next day remove the cloth from the cheese. Leave it on a board for half the day, turning it now and then to let the rind dry completely. Or put it on a wire rack; air will circulate around it, making turning unnecessary. Then paint on liquid paraffin with a brush. If you prefer, you can wrap the cheese tightly in plastic wrap. Store it in a clean and cool but frost-free place. Turn it over daily for the first few days and then several times weekly for four weeks. At the end of that time, your homemade cheese should be good to eat. However, you may leave it longer to develop a higher flavor if you like.

Cottage Cheese
Yield: 1 cup
2 quarts skim milk
6 tablespoons homogenized milk
1½ teaspoons vinegar
½ rennet tablet
1 tablespoon cold water
½ to 2 teaspoons salt

Combine milk and vinegar in the top half of a double boiler with water beneath. Gradually warm the milk to a temperature of about 70°F (not more than 75°). Take the top of the double boiler from the heat. Blend into the milk one half of a rennet tablet that has been dissolved in 1 tablespoon of cold water. Cover the mixture, and set it in a warm spot (between 75 and 80°F) for about fourteen hours. Leave it undisturbed.

After twelve hours, examine it. There should be whey on the milk's surface. Tilt the pan a little; the curd should separate. If these signs are not evident, allow it to stand several hours more.

Then place a colander, lined with a towel, in the sink. Pour the mixture into the colander, letting the whey drain off. Occasionally stir it lightly with a fork, and lift the towel, moving the curd about to further the drainage. Add salt to taste when the curd has thoroughly drained.

Creamed cottage cheese can be made by stirring in 1 or 2 tablespoons of cream or milk. Caraway seeds, chopped parsley, chopped olives, and pimentos may be used for flavoring, if desired.

Homemade Rennet
Here are ways to make rennet from four different sources:

Rennet from Calf Stomach (dated 1887): Ask the butcher for a calf's stomach. Scour it well with salt, both inside and out. Tack it to a

wooden frame, and dry it in the sunshine for one or two days.

Cut the stomach into ½-inch squares. Put the pieces in a large jar; pack them in salt. Before using the rennet, soak it in water for thirty minutes and then wash it well. As an alternative to packing the pieces in salt, pour enough alcohol into the jar to cover them. With this method the rennet does not require soaking.

To easily remove the rennet from the curd when making cheese, tie the rennet sections together with a string before immersing them.

Rennet from Lamb or Kid Stomach: Remove the stomach from a nursing lamb or kid that has eaten no solid food. Tie the opening securely; roll the organ in ashes until well coated. Hang it to dry out of direct sunlight in a warm, dry, well-ventilated spot. (Old-timers used to hang the stomachs in their grape arbors or from house rafters.) Once it is

completely dry, the milk inside will have become brown powder.

When making cheese, pulverize a bit less than ¼ teaspoon of the powder in a mortar. (If you lack mortar and pestle, use a bowl and an old china doorknob instead.) Add enough water to form a paste. Then thin it, using a little more water. With the added water, the total liquid will equal about ¾ cup, enough rennet to help make twelve 2-pound cheeses, each made from 8 quarts of goat's milk plus 1 tablespoon of the solution.

Whey Rennet: Reserve 1 quart of whey for use as rennet. About ¼ cup cuts 5 gallons of milk. Replace the whey used each day; the quart of rennet will last two weeks before it is too weak to work as it should.

Nettle Rennet: It is said that a vegetable rennet for cheese making can be prepared from nettles. We haven't been able to learn the particulars concerning this method. You might like to experiment, however, with the idea on your own.

Goat's-Milk Cheese
Yield: 1½ pounds
Pour 1½ gallons of raw goat's milk into an earthenware bowl. Leave it for seven days or until it becomes clabbered, when thick curds will rise to the surface. Heat the clabbered milk in a vessel until very hot but not boiling. Stir often to separate the curds and whey (the liquid). Continue to cook and stir for thirty minutes. When the curds

are tough, drain them in a piece of cheesecloth. Remove as much of the whey as you can by squeezing and wringing. Put the cheese, still wrapped in the cloth, beneath a heavy weight in a pot. Leave it overnight to allow more whey to drain out.

The following morning, add 4 tablespoons of fresh sweet butter and ¾ teaspoon of soda. Mix the ingredients thoroughly, and chop the curd until very fine. Press the mixture flat on a board. Leave it in a warm spot for two hours.

Transfer the cheese to a double boiler over low heat. Put in ⅔ cup of very sour heavy cream and 1¼ teaspoons of salt. Stir until it starts to become a runny mass. Then empty the double boiler into a well-buttered bowl, and allow the cheese to cool. When solid, it is ready for serving.

To cure and store your goat's-milk cheese, take it from the bowl when cool and solid and coat the surface with melted paraffin, using a brush. Keep it in a cool place.

Clabbered Cheese

These are the necessary ingredients for clabbered cheese:

- 3 gallons clabbered, skimmed milk
- 1½ teaspoons soda
- ½ cup butter
- 1½ cups sour cream
- ¼ teaspoon dandelion-butter coloring
- 2 teaspoons salt

Heat the clabbered milk in a vessel until just bearable to the touch. Set the pot on the back of the stove; keep it hot for ½ hour.

Drain the curd through cheesecloth, thoroughly squeezing out the whey. Blend the soda and butter into the curd. Allow to stand for two hours.

Put the mixture in a double boiler, stir in 1 cup of sour cream, and melt it until smooth. In the meantime, blend the salt and dandelion-butter coloring into the remaining ½ cup of sour cream until the color is uniform. Add this to the contents of the double boiler.

Pour the mixture into a buttered pan, preferably one of stainless steel (do not use aluminum). Allow to stand uncovered for five days. Then coat the cheese with paraffin.

Cream Cheese

The best cream for making cream cheese is that skimmed from fresh whole milk. If you buy cream in a store, avoid the kind that has been treated for long shelf life. Allow the cream to sour at room temperature.

After two days put the sour cream into a cheesecloth bag. Suspend it over a bowl to let the whey drip through. Hang it from a cupboard door handle or the kitchen faucet.

A lump of cheese will remain in the bag. If desired, mix in a little salt. Form the cream cheese into a cake; chill it. Should it be too soft to make into a cake, shape it after chilling.

Save the whey; it contains valuable nutrients. Use it as a substitute for water in baking. You'll find potato or spinach soup taking on a new, delicious flavor from its addition.

Ricotta-Style Cheese

Slowly bring 2 quarts of milk to the boiling point, stirring it now and then. Turn off the heat, add 3 tablespoons of lemon juice, and stir twice. Set the vessel in a warm place for twenty-four hours.

Bring the mixture to a boil once more. Allow it to cool, and then strain it through cheesecloth.

If desired, the cheese may be seasoned with salt. To heighten its flavor, you may let it age in an uncovered dish for a few days.

Yogurt

Yogurt, a semisolid, cheeselike food that can be used in a variety of ways, is prepared from milk fermented by a particular bacterium.

All utensils used in making yogurt must be extremely clean. Wash them in hot soapsuds, followed by rinses first in hot and then in boiling water.

Assemble these ingredients:

1 quart skim milk

1 cup nonfat powdered milk

¼ cup plain, unflavored yogurt

Blend the skim milk and powdered milk in a saucepan. Put in a dairy thermometer and heat the liquid to about 180°F over low heat. Be careful not to boil it. Take the pan from the stove, and cool its contents to somewhere between 100° and 115°F. Thoroughly blend in the yogurt.

Warm some containers by rinsing them in hot water. Fill them with the milk mixture and cover tightly.

Put the containers in an incubator. You can purchase an electric yogurt maker or improvise one by placing the containers on a heating pad set on low and inverting a cardboard box over all. Maintain the incubator at 90°F for three hours, undisturbed. For a stronger flavor, you may incubate the yogurt longer, checking its taste every thirty minutes.

Put it in the refrigerator. As the yogurt cools, it will thicken. Save ¼ cup of your homemade yogurt to start the next supply. Use yogurt that is no more than five days old for the starter.

Yogurt Dressing
Yield: 1 serving

3 tablespoons yogurt

1 tablespoon homemade mayonnaise

1 teaspoon Dijon mustard

dash garlic powder

salt and pepper to taste

Combine yogurt and mayonnaise. Blend in well the mustard and garlic powder. Chill.

On a bed of chopped lettuce moistened with basic dressing (oil and vinegar), arrange a double row of alternating slices of beets and hard-cooked eggs, slightly overlapping. Spoon yogurt dressing over the beets and eggs; sprinkle lightly with paprika.

This dressing is also excellent on crisp, shredded cabbage.

Or fold diced beets into the yogurt dressing, and fill the hollow of half an avocado with the mixture.

Strawberry Yogurt Mold

1 cup homemade yogurt

4 tablespoons homemade strawberry jam (more or less to taste)

1 cup orange juice

1 envelope unflavored gelatin

¼ cup sugar

Thoroughly blend the strawberry jam with the yogurt. Pour ½ cup of orange juice into a small saucepan, and sprinkle it with the gelatin. Put the pan over low heat, stirring its contents until the gelatin dissolves. Remove the pan from the heat; stir in sugar. Add the remainder of the orange juice.

Pour the mixture into four dessert dishes. Chill until firm.

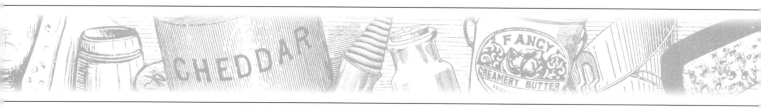

Yogurt Topping
Yield: 1 cup

¼ cup light corn syrup
¼ cup mayonnaise
½ cup plain yogurt

Stir together the corn syrup and mayonnaise. Fold in the yogurt. Serve over unfrosted cake.

Miscellaneous

Honey Mayonnaise
Yield: about 1 cup

Put the following ingredients into a blender: 1 egg, 1 teaspoon of honey, 2 tablespoons of vinegar, 2 tablespoons of lemon juice, ½ teaspoon of dry mustard, ½ teaspoon of salt, and ½ cup of safflower or peanut oil. Churn them until smooth. Now blend in an additional cup of salad oil, pouring it into the center of the mayonnaise. Transfer it to a jar and refrigerate.

Wine Mayonnaise
Yield: about 1¼ cups

2 egg yolks
1 tablespoon red wine
1 tablespoon white-wine vinegar

1 tablespoon herb-flavored vinegar
½ teaspoon lemon juice
¾ teaspoon dry mustard
½ teaspoon salt
½ cup salad oil
½ cup olive oil

Put the egg yolks in an electric blender; run it on high speed until they are frothy (about ten seconds). Blend in vinegar, wine, lemon juice, mustard, and salt at medium speed for slightly longer than one minute, very gradually adding oil in a thin constant stream while the blender is running.

Transfer the mayonnaise to a container, and remove every last bit from the blender with a rubber spatula. Store it in the refrigerator, where it will keep for two weeks. Before blending, you may add various fresh or dried herbs to the egg yolks.

Potato Mayonnaise

3 egg yolks
¾ cup olive oil
1 lemon
salt to taste
1 small potato, boiled and mashed

Beat the egg yolks until they are thick. While continuing to beat them, add oil in drops. Slowly pour in the juice of one lemon. Put in the mashed potato and salt, beating until the blend is very smooth.

Store in a tightly closed jar in the refrigerator. When cooked vegetables and fish are garnished with this mayonnaise, their flavor is enhanced.

Country housewives of bygone days maintained that mayonnaise prepared when a thunderstorm was in the offing wouldn't thicken and emulsify. Whether or not the claim is valid, if your mayonnaise fails to thicken, be the weather foul or fair, remedy the matter by constantly beating one egg yolk while very, very gradually (drop by drop at the start) adding the unsuccessful, thin mayonnaise.

Vanilla Ice Cream
Yield: 1 gallon

2 quarts light cream (half-and-half)
1 quart milk
3 cups sugar
2 tablespoons pure vanilla extract
1 teaspoon salt

Mix all ingredients until the sugar dissolves. Thoroughly chill, overnight if possible.

Wash the dasher, can, and cover of the ice cream freezer in hot, sudsy water. Rinse well in hot, clear water. Dry. Chill them in your freezer or refrigerator. Crush from 20 to 25 pounds of ice in an ice crusher. Return the can and dasher to the freezer bucket. Fill the can from one half to two thirds full with the ice cream mixture. Cover the can. Follow manufacturer's directions for fitting the crank assembly or motor into the cover and securing it to the bucket. Place the freezer on several layers of newspapers. Allow the motor to warm up for about sixty seconds. During this time, add ice and salt.

Be guided by the instructions accompanying your ice cream freezer. Freezers vary in their required proportions of salt and ice. Put in about 2 inches (6 cups) of crushed ice. Spread ¼ cup of rock salt over the ice. Continue these layers until they surround and cover the can. Keep the hole in the upper side of the bucket free to permit drainage of the brine. Place a plastic container beneath the hole to receive any drips.

A hand freezer should be cranked rapidly and steadily, with an increase in speed as the mixture thickens so as to whip air into it. Beating air into the ice cream gives it a smooth texture. Stop when the mixture becomes so thick that cranking is nearly impossible. When using an electric mixer, disconnect the freezer at once when the motor stops or runs sluggishly. Carefully tip the freezer to drain off the brine. Take out the ice and salt to a depth of two inches below the cover. Remove the cranking assembly or motor. Wipe away ice and salt from the cover, and take out the dasher. Scrape ice cream from the dasher into the can and from the upper sides of the can, using a rubber spatula. Blend it for a few minutes.

Next comes the ripening stage. Place several layers of waxed paper, plastic wrap, or foil over the mouth of the can, and then put on the cover. Fill the hole in the cover with some sort of plug; use wadded foil or paper towels. Add more ice and salt layers, using ½ cup of salt to each 6 cups of crushed ice. Cover the can completely with the layers. Wrap thicknesses of newspaper about the freezer, enclose it with a heavy cloth (an old blanket will do), and set it in a cool spot for three hours. (There are other ways of ripening ice cream. After the machine has been turned off, the can of ice cream can be transferred to your food freezer for ripening. Or you can immediately pack the ice cream in plastic containers and put them in the food freezer for the ripening process.)

Drain away the brine, and remove the ice and salt. Take the can from the freezer. If not eaten immediately, ice cream can be stored in plastic containers in the food freezer.

For a variation of flavor, you may add almost anything to the mixture just prior to freezing.

12 | GRAINS AND SPROUTS

Grains

Grinding Grain

Whole grains, high in vitamin E, iron, and the B vitamins, are a nearly perfect food. To be eaten at their most nutritious, flavorful stage, they should be ground immediately prior to cooking; vitamins and flavor start to diminish with each hour that grains are exposed to air after grinding. However, if you prefer preparing a larger amount at one time, avoid grinding more grain than will be used within a period of three to four weeks. Store it in clean, airtight containers. Unground grain will keep almost indefinitely in closed containers stored in a dry, cool place.

Unless you are raising your own grain, purchase it (clean or uncleaned) from feed and grain stores, health food stores, or farms. Buy fresh grain that is untreated by chemicals.

You will need to winnow uncleaned grain. Make a frame of convenient holding size, using 1- by 2-inch lumber, and cover it with window screening. Pour uncleaned grain on the winnowing screen. Remove chaff and dust by shaking it. Most of the chaff will be blown away if you winnow on a windy day. Pick out any foreign material, such as heavy grit. To clean grain indoors, pour it back and forth from container to container in the breeze from an electric fan.

Barley, millet, oats, rice, rye, soybeans, and wheat are grain that can be ground successfully at home in a hand (or electric) mill, coffee grinder, or some blenders. Depending on its intended use, grain may be roughly ground or converted to very fine flour. About four grindings will produce fine flour.

Whole or ground grains can be used for all baking purposes and cereals. Cracked wheat imparts a nutlike flavor to breads and waffles. A combination of grains provides a delicious and unusual breakfast cereal.

To prepare a hot cereal, put cleaned, unground wheat in an iron skillet, which will not heat up too quickly and will maintain steady temperature. Spread the grain in a thin layer and stir continuously. It will double in size and turn brown. The kernels will pop but won't burst open. Grind your toasted wheat, and then cook it as you would regular wheat breakfast cereal.

Granola

Mix the following ingredients:
   4 cups rolled oats (or rolled wheat)
   1½ cups unsweetened coconut, shredded
   1 cup wheat germ
   1 cup chopped nuts
   1 cup sunflower seeds, hulled
   1 cup sesame seeds
   ½ cup bran
   1 cup soybeans, ground and toasted
Heat these ingredients:
   ½ cup oil
   ½ cup honey
   1 to 2 teaspoons vanilla
Add the honey-oil-vanilla mixture to the dry ingredients; blend well. Spread on oiled cookie sheets. Bake for twenty to thirty minutes in a 375°F oven. Stir occasionally.

If you would like to prepare freshly shredded coconut but avoid doing so because of the difficulty in opening the coconut shell, here are two tips to make the task an easy one: Either heat the coconut in a 350°F oven or freeze it for about two hours. A blow from a hammer will then quickly crack it.

This recipe may be changed according to your taste. Substitute any suitable, wholesome ingredients that you prefer, but always maintain the same ratio of seven parts dry ingredients to one part wet ingredients for successful granola.

Hominy

To make hominy, first shuck ears of firm, dried corn. (*Hominy* comes from a Native American word

meaning "parched corn.") Take off the underdeveloped kernels from either end of the cob. Then shell the corn by hand.

Put the kernels into an iron vessel. Cover it with cold water. Add 1½ tablespoons of lye to every gallon of corn. Boil until the husks start to separate from the kernels.

Transfer the corn to another vessel, and wash it seven or eight times in clear, cold water. Rinse out the first pot to prevent sticking when the hominy is boiled again later.

To completely remove the husks, put the kernels in a coarse-meshed sieve. Wearing rubber gloves as protection against the lye, run a forceful stream of water on the corn, at the same time rubbing it over the mesh. The water will carry away the unwanted husks. After husking, return the corn to the iron vessel and boil in fresh water until tender.

Hominy may be canned for future consumption. But if its golden goodness sets you to craving some immediately, try frying it in bacon drippings for a real treat. It can also be eaten just salted, rather like boiled peanuts.

In the old days, hominy was chiefly made during the winter months when country folks had fewer farm chores.

Southern Fried Corn
    4 ears corn
    ¼ cup all-purpose flour
    ⅛ cup fine bread crumbs
    ½ teaspoon salt
    ½ teaspoon paprika
    ⅛ teaspoon black pepper
    1 egg
    cooking oil

Husk the corn and remove the silk. In a shallow dish, blend flour, bread crumbs, salt, paprika, and pepper. Lightly beat the egg in another shallow plate. Heat oil in a skillet. Dip the ears of corn in the egg. Drain slightly. Roll them in the flour mixture. Shake off any excess and fry in the hot oil for about four minutes. Turn occasionally. When golden brown, serve with meat, poultry, or seafood.

Sprouts

Essentials for Producing Sprouts

Produce inexpensive, unprocessed fresh food in all seasons by growing seed sprouts. Besides seeds you will need water, air, a few readily available containers, and—in certain cases—some sunlight. Just about any legume, grain, or seed can be sprouted for nutritious food (potato sprouts should never be eaten): garbanzos, kidney beans, lima beans, mung beans, pinto beans, soybeans, chickpeas, peas, corn, alfalfa, barley, oats, rye, wheat, unhulled sunflower and sesame seeds, the seeds of cress, parsley, radishes, and many more.

Choosing Seeds

Choose whole seeds that have not been treated chemically. They can be purchased from health food stores or through mail-order sources. Wash them thoroughly. Discard seeds that float; they are probably sterile.

Yield

A fairly small amount of seeds yields a considerable quantity of sprouts: 1 tablespoon of alfalfa seeds produces about 30 square inches of sprouts; 3 tablespoons of beans or peas produce a similar quantity. As a general rule, ½ cupful of seeds swells to 1½ cups when soaked, making a quart or more of sprouts.

Put the seeds in a vessel containing three times their volume in warm (70–80°F) water to soak overnight in some dark, warm spot, such as a kitchen cabinet. The following morning, drain off the water. Reserve this vitamin- and mineral-rich liquid for cooking rice, potatoes, and vegetables, or for adding to soups and fruit or vegetable juice drinks. Rinse the seeds, now double in size, to prevent mold. Put them in a moist (not wet) container. Keep it in a dark place where the temperature ranges between 80 and 90°F. If you prefer, instead of putting the container in a cupboard, you can invert a paper bag over it to keep out light. Rinse the seeds twice a day (three times daily in warm weather) to cleanse them and provide sufficient moisture for their growth. After each cleansing, drain them well to avoid rotting. Utilize the rinse water to feed your plants; they will thrive on it.

Begin a new batch of seeds each night to have a continuously fresh

supply on hand. For variety in your menu, have about three containers of different sprouts developing at one time: a grain, a bean, and a seed. Don't crowd larger beans like black-eyed peas, kidney beans, and soybeans. Some folks maintain that garbanzos, lentils, mung beans, and soybeans grow better in the same container than when sprouted separately.

Procedure for Germination

Sprouts can be grown successfully in common kitchen containers: colanders, the strainers of coffee percolators, flour sifters, sink strainers, vegetable steamers, and tea strainers. A wide-mouthed jar can be used by stretching cheesecloth over the opening and fastening it on with a rubber band. A circle of wire mesh secured with a screw-on canning ring can substitute for the cloth. Put the jar in a bowl, top down, at a 45-degree angle to facilitate drainage. An unglazed earthenware flowerpot can serve as a sprout garden. It will absorb moisture, maintaining the sprouts in a moist, not wet, condition. Plug the drain hole with cotton or cheesecloth. Place a saucer on top, and set the pot in a shallow container of water. Regularly rinse the sprouts, as with those in other types of sprouters, to prevent mold from developing. Yet another way to germinate legumes, grains, or seeds is to place a rustproof metal rack in a glass baking pan. Put warm water in the container, but not

enough to reach the rack. Spread a wet terry cloth towel (or several thicknesses of cheesecloth) on the rack, letting an end hang into the water beneath. This arrangement will provide the seeds with moisture without wetness.

Harvesting Sprouts

Within three to six days, depending on the type of seed, the sprouts will have greatly increased in volume and be ready for harvesting. If you like, during the last few hours of development, you can place them in indirect sunlight to generate healthful chlorophyll. Be sure to limit the exposure, however, since too much chlorophyll will toughen the shoots.

Seeds	Proper Size of Sprouts for Harvesting
Alfalfa	Two to three inches long
Peas	Two to three inches long
Soybeans	Two to three inches long
Grain	No longer than the length of the kernel
Sunflower	No longer than the seed length
Lentils	One inch
Mung Beans	Three to four inches

Most shoots are at their peak from sixty to eighty hours after germination, but you may wish to use personal preference in taste and texture as a guide for determining the harvest time.

The nutritional value of sprouts produced by the water method is high, but higher still when they are raised by the earth

method. Eliminating the necessity to periodically rinse them is an additional benefit.

Soak beans or seeds for twelve hours. Then scatter them evenly on a layer of good soil in a wooden box or large flowerpot. Sprinkle on enough earth to cover them, water lightly, and spread a cloth over the container to retain moisture and exclude light. Several days later, pull out the entire sprout, wash away the soil, and enjoy this extra nutritious harvest in your favorite recipes.

If the sprouts develop before you are ready to use them, put them into a colander and steam them for several minutes. Then immerse them in cold water. Drain and refrigerate the sprouts until they are needed. To preserve them for an extended time, freeze or dry them; their nutritional value will not be diminished.

Sprout Uses

It is unnecessary to remove the seed hulls from sprouts before serving them. Use sprouts as meatloaf filler, as steamed vegetables, in stews, sprinkled on soups, mixed into beverages (with a blender), and raw in salads.

13 | BREADS, SPREADS, PRETZELS, AND CRACKERS

Dough Starters

Some dough starters, kept active for more than 100 years, have been handed down from one generation to the next like family heirlooms.

Buttermilk Yeast Starter
1 quart buttermilk flour
½ cup sugar
1 cup yeast
3 pints water

At midday, heat the buttermilk until it commences to boil. Put in the yeast and sugar. Stir, adding sufficient flour to form a stiff batter. Allow to stand in a warm spot until nightfall. Then add 2½ cups of water and allow to stand until the following morning.

Add the rest of the water. Your buttermilk yeast is ready for bread baking.

Peach-Leaf Yeast Starter
Steep 1 quart of fresh, well-washed peach leaves in 3 cups of boiling water for fifteen minutes. Drain, adding enough water, if necessary, to make 3 cups. The water will have a greenish hue, but this will disappear during fermentation. Bake three medium-sized potatoes. Peel them, and put them through a sieve or food mill. Scald ½ cup of cornmeal in 1 cup of water until it boils and thickens. Stir to prevent lumps from forming.

Put all these ingredients in a bowl with 2 teaspoons of salt and 3 tablespoons of sugar. Cover and allow to ferment in a warm place for twenty-four hours, stirring well every two or three hours.

Pour it into a glass jar, and keep it in the refrigerator. Stir it down several times until foaming ceases. When approximately ½ inch of clear liquid rises to the surface, it will be ready for use. Stir thoroughly each time you use it.

When the starter is reduced to 1 cup, add 3 cups of water, three baked potatoes, the scalded cornmeal, salt, and sugar as you did the first time. Leave it in a warm spot. In about seven hours it should become active.

Peach-leaf starter improves with age. It is advisable to use it about twice each week. If not, stir it every couple of days, adding 1 teaspoon of sugar.

You can make this starter into a dry yeast. Begin by sterilizing 2 quarts of cornmeal for one hour in a low oven. Mix it into the starter. Spread it in flat pans to a thickness of ½ inch. When it is set, cut it into 1½-inch squares. Move them apart to dry and harden. Wrap the cakes. Store them in the refrigerator; they will keep a year or more.

A starter can be made from the dry yeast in this way. In a bowl, mix 1 cake of yeast, ½ cup of warm water, ½ teaspoon of ginger, and 1 teaspoon of sugar. Keep it covered until you see white foam on top. Then stir in ½ cup of water, ½ cup of flour, and 1 teaspoon of sugar. After it foams again, add 1 cup of water, 1 cup of flour, and 1 teaspoon of sugar. Allow to foam, stirring often. Pour it into a jar and refrigerate. Put the lid on loosely until the foaming stops. When ½ inch of clear liquid has risen to the surface, the starter is ready to use.

Potato Yeast Starter
Cook three potatoes, peeled and cubed, until tender. Mash them, blending in the pot liquor, and add sufficient cold water to equal 3 cups. Put in ¼ cup of honey. Cool the mixture to lukewarm. Soak one package of dried yeast in 1 cup of lukewarm water. Add it to the mixture. Allow to stand in a warm spot overnight.

The following day, store 1 cup of the starter in the refrigerator; use the rest to bake four loaves of any recipe.

Sourdough Starter
2 cups all-purpose flour
1 package dry yeast
2 cups warm water

Thoroughly blend all ingredients in a large bowl. Leave it uncovered in a warm spot for forty-eight hours. Stir occasionally.

Just before using the starter, stir it well.

Take out the amount needed; replenish the remainder by

blending in 1 cup of flour and 1 cup of warm water.

Leave the starter uncovered in a warm spot for several hours. When it bubbles once more, put it into a nonmetal container, cover loosely, and store in the refrigerator until needed.

The night before you plan to make sourdough bread, remove the starter from the refrigerator so that it can warm and commence working. The starter must be used at least once in a two-week period and be replenished each time. Using it daily is even better.

Sourdough Breads

The oldest of breads may well be sourdough bread. It dates back to 4000 B.C.

Sourdough Bread

3 cups all-purpose or whole
    wheat flour
1 cup sourdough starter
2 cups warm water
2 tablespoons sugar
1 teaspoon salt
1 teaspoon baking soda
3½ cups (about) unbleached
    all-purpose flour
cornmeal
melted butter

Put the first six ingredients into a large bowl; beat until smooth. Cover the dough with waxed paper. Allow to stand in a warm spot (80 to 85°F) for a minimum of eighteen hours.

Stir it down. Blend in the remainder of the flour, making moderately stiff dough. On a lightly floured board, knead the dough until satiny smooth for eight to ten minutes. Divide it in two. Form each equal portion into a ball. Roll them beneath your hands to make long thick ropes, more or less 12 inches in length.

Grease cookie sheets, and sprinkle them with cornmeal.

Place the loaves on the cookie sheets; slash the top of each with a sharp knife and brush with butter. Cover them with transparent wrap. Allow to rise where it is warm for approximately one and a half hours until doubled. Bake from forty to fifty minutes in a preheated 400°F oven.

Remove them from the oven, and brush the tops with melted butter. Place on a rack to cool.

Onion Sourdough Bread
yield: 2 large, long loaves or 4 small, round loaves

1½ cups sourdough starter
3¾ cups (approximately)
    unsifted all-purpose flour
3 tablespoons sugar
2 teaspoons salt
1 package active dry yeast
1 cup milk
2 tablespoons margarine
    cornmeal
egg white, beaten
1 tablespoon water
⅔ cup finely chopped onion
caraway seed

Measure out the sourdough starter, and set it aside. In a large bowl,

combine 1 cup of flour, the sugar, salt, and undissolved active dry yeast. Put the milk and margarine in a saucepan and heat over low heat. When the milk is very warm, somewhere around 125°F, slowly add it to the dry ingredients. Beat in a mixer at medium speed for two minutes, scraping the bowl now and then. Add ¼ cup of flour and 1½ cups of starter, beating for two minutes at high speed and scraping the bowl from time to time. Blend in additional flour to make a soft dough. Knead it until elastic and smooth on a lightly floured board for about nine minutes. Put it in a greased bowl. Then turn it over to grease the top. Cover it, and allow it to rise for one hour in a warm spot, away from drafts, until doubled.

Punch down the dough. Turn it out on a lightly floured board, and divide it in two. Cover and allow to stand for fifteen minutes. Shape as preferred. Form large, long loaves by rolling each section of dough into an oblong—8 by 12 inches. Roll the dough tightly from the 12-inch side, pinching the seam. Then pinch the ends and fold them underneath. To form small, round loaves, divide the dough in two again. Shape each into a round ball, and flatten slightly.

Sprinkle cornmeal on greased baking sheets. Place the loaves on them and cover. Allow to rise for one hour in a warm spot, away from drafts, until doubled.

Combine water and egg white. Brush this mixture on the loaves.

Sprinkle them with chopped onion and caraway seed.

Bake in a 400°F oven for twenty-five minutes or until done. Take from the baking sheets and let cool on wire racks.

Sourdough Rolls

1½ cups warm water
1 package active dry yeast
1½ cups sourdough starter
2 tablespoons salad oil
2 tablespoons sugar
2 teaspoons salt
½ teaspoon baking soda
1 cup flour

Into a large mixing bowl, measure 1½ cups of warm water. Blend in one package of active dry yeast. Add the sourdough starter, salad oil, sugar, and salt, stirring vigorously with a wooden spoon for approximately three minutes. Put in a large greased bowl, cover with a towel, and allow to rise for one and a half to two hours in some warm spot until doubled in bulk.

Blend ½ teaspoon of baking soda into 1 cup of flour and stir in, making the dough stiff. Knead it on a floured board, and add 1 cup of flour or an amount needed to control the stickiness. After eight minutes or more, it should be satiny smooth. Separate the dough into two sections. Shape into rolls by rolling the dough between your hands. Place them on a greased pan, cover, and leave in a warm spot. Leave for one to one and a half hours to rise and almost double in bulk.

For a crusty top, brush with water just before baking. If a softer crust is desired, brush with melted butter. Bake for seventeen to twenty minutes in a 400°F oven.

Corn Bread Variations

When preparing your favorite corn bread recipe, try using 8 ounces of cracklings in place of the shortening.

Basic Corn Bread

1 cup flour
1 cup cornmeal
4 tablespoons baking powder
2 eggs
1½ cups sweet milk
1 tablespoon cooking oil
1 teaspoon salt

Blend these ingredients thoroughly. Bake in a greased pan at 400°F for thirty minutes or until crusty and brown.

Buttermilk Corn Bread

1 cup cornmeal
1 cup unbleached white flour
⅓ cup sugar
¼ teaspoon baking powder
¾ teaspoon salt
1 cup buttermilk
2 eggs, well beaten
2 tablespoons oil
1½ teaspoons baking powder

Sift all the dry ingredients into a bowl. Mix in the milk, eggs, and oil. Stir only enough to blend. Empty the batter into a greased cake pan (8 inches square).

Bake it for approximately twenty minutes at 425°F. When the top is nicely browned, take the bread from the oven.

Clabber Corn Bread

1 cup cornmeal
1 cup sifted flour
¼ cup sugar
4 teaspoons baking powder
½ teaspoon salt
1 egg
1 cup curd
1 tablespoon oil

Sift the dry ingredients into a bowl. Put in the eggs, curd, and oil; beat the mixture until smooth. Empty the batter into a greased pan (9 inches square).

Bake for about twenty-five minutes in a 425°F. oven. When a knife inserted in the center of the bread comes out clean, remove your clabber corn bread from the oven.

Honey Corn Bread

Thoroughly mix these ingredients:
1¾ cups yellow cornmeal
½ cup wheat flour, plus
2 tablespoons
¾ teaspoon salt
3 teaspoons baking powder

Beat well the following ingredients:
2 eggs
2 tablespoons honey
2 tablespoons butter
(or margarine)

Stir in 1 cup of milk.

Combine the liquid mixture with the dry mixture. Gently blend until the whole mixture is moistened.

Spread the batter in a greased 9-inch pan. Bake for twenty-five to thirty minutes in a preheated 400°F oven.

Johnnycake

2 cups cornmeal
1½ teaspoons salt
1 teaspoon baking soda
2 tablespoons sugar
2 cups sour milk
2 eggs, beaten
2 tablespoons shortening, melted

Sift together the dry ingredients. Add milk, eggs, and shortening. Blend thoroughly.

Pour the batter into a greased 8 by 10 inch loaf pan and bake in a 400°F oven for thirty minutes.

Molasses Corn Bread

Mix together these dry ingredients:

3 cups yellow cornmeal
1 cup whole wheat flour
2 tablespoons baking powder
1 teaspoon salt

Mix together the following wet ingredients:

3 eggs
½ cup butter
½ cup sorghum molasses
2 cups buttermilk

Blend the two mixtures until the dry ingredients become moist.

Bake the batter in a greased 12-inch pan for approximately thirty-five minutes in a 350°F oven.

Southern-Style Corn Bread

1 cup yellow cornmeal
1 cup flour (whole wheat or white)
2 to 3 tablespoons powdered milk
4 teaspoons baking powder
1½ teaspoons salt
1 cup milk (or buttermilk)
1 egg
2 tablespoons vegetable oil
2 to 3 tablespoons wheat germ

Sift all the dry items, except the wheat germ, into a bowl. Mix in the remaining ingredients, making a uniformly moist batter. Put it in a well-greased 8-inch-square pan and bake for twenty to twenty-five minutes in a preheated 425°F oven until golden brown.

Spoon Bread

2 cups boiling water
1 cup white cornmeal
1 teaspoon salt
1 tablespoon shortening
1 cup milk
2 eggs, separated

Blend water, cornmeal, salt, and shortening. Cool. Thoroughly mix in the milk and beaten egg yolks. Then fold in stiffly beaten egg whites.

Pour the batter into a greased baking dish. Bake for thirty to forty minutes in a 400°F. oven. Serve the spoon bread directly from its baking dish.

Breads with Honey

To cut easily through freshly baked bread, use a heated knife.

Granola-Yogurt Bread
Yield: 2 loaves

2 envelopes dry yeast
1½ cups very warm water
1 teaspoon honey
8 ounces homemade yogurt
5 cups unbleached flour, sifted
3 teaspoons salt
2 cups homemade granola

Sprinkle the yeast into a 1-cup measuring cup holding ½ cup of the warm water. Add the honey and stir until the yeast dissolves. Let stand for ten minutes, more or less, until it is bubbly and the volume doubles.

Combine the rest of the water, yogurt, and salt in a big bowl. Stir in the yeast mixture. Beat in 4 cups of the flour for two minutes, setting your mixer at medium speed. Mix in the granola. Slowly blend in the remaining flour to form a stiff dough.

Put the dough on a lightly floured board, and knead it for about ten minutes until it is smooth and elastic. Use only enough flour to prevent the dough from adhering to the work surface.

Place it in a large buttered bowl; turn it to bring up the buttered side. Cover with a clean towel. Let rise in a warm, draft-free place for one hour or until double in bulk.

Punch down the dough. Put it on a lightly floured board and knead several times. Invert the bowl over the dough, and let it rest for ten minutes. Divide the dough in two equal portions; knead each half a few times. Shape them into two round loaves. Lay them on a greased baking sheet, about 5 inches apart. Allow them to rise in a warm spot, free from drafts, for forty minutes or until double in volume.

Using a sharp knife, cut a ½-inch-deep cross in the top of each loaf. Bake them in a 375°F oven for thirty-five minutes or until they are golden brown and have a hollow sound when tapped. Cool them completely on wire racks.

Honey-Oatmeal Bread
1½ cups milk
1 cup oatmeal (quick cooking)
2 tablespoons butter
1¼ cups light cream
½ teaspoon salt
½ cup honey
2 yeast cakes
2 cups flour, unbleached
3 cups whole wheat flour

Scald the milk, and put in the oatmeal, cooking it for three minutes. Add the butter. After it melts, put in cream, salt, and honey. Let cool. Add the yeast and the flour and beat well.

Mix in the whole wheat flour to make a soft dough. Knead it until smooth. Allow it to rise until double in volume. Shape the dough into three loaves. Let them rise until double in bulk.

Bake for fifty minutes at 375°F.

Peanut Butter Loaf
2 cups flour
4 teaspoons baking powder
1 teaspoon salt
¼ teaspoon baking soda
¼ cup honey
⅔ cup homemade peanut butter
1¼ cups milk

Sift together the first four ingredients. Thoroughly mix the milk into the peanut butter; blend in the honey. Add the peanut butter mixture to the dry ingredients and beat well.

Turn into a buttered loaf pan. Bake in a 350°F oven for forty-five minutes. Peanut butter bread is even tastier on the second day.

Whole Wheat Honey Bread
Mix the following dry ingredients:
12 cups whole wheat flour
1¾ cups instant dry milk
1 tablespoon salt
2 tablespoons yeast
Mix the following wet ingredients:
½ cup oil
2 beaten eggs
3 cups warm (110–115°F) water

½ cup honey (Dissolve it thoroughly.)

Add the wet mixture to the dry, stirring with a wooden spoon. When the dough is well blended, stir it a little about every ten minutes for an hour.

Now knead the dough slightly until it becomes elastic.

Form two large loaves and one small one. Put them in greased bread pans. Allow to rise for one hour.

Bake at 375°F for ten minutes. Reduce the heat to 350°F and bake thirty minutes longer.

Unusual Breads

Harvest Bread
1½ cups sugar
½ cup vegetable oil
2 eggs, beaten
1 cup canned pumpkin (or fresh)
1 cup oats
1 cup flour
1¼ teaspoons baking powder
1 teaspoon salt
½ teaspoon allspice
½ teaspoon cinnamon
½ teaspoon ground cloves
½ teaspoon nutmeg
½ cup chopped pecans

Combine sugar, oil, eggs, pumpkin, and oats. Beat well. Sift the dry ingredients, and add them to the pumpkin mixture.

Pour the batter into a greased 9- by 5-inch-loaf pan. Bake at 350°F. for an hour and fifteen minutes.

Tomato Bread
Yield: 1 good-sized loaf

    2 teaspoons dry yeast
    ¼ cup warm water
    1½ cups tomato juice
    1 tablespoon sugar
    ½ teaspoon salt
    1 tablespoon cooking oil
    ½ teaspoon powdered basil
    4½ to 5 cups whole wheat flour
    Grease a 9 by 5 inch bread pan.

Put the yeast in a big mixing bowl; pour the water on it.

Let the yeast dissolve (about five minutes). Then mix in the tomato juice, sugar, salt, oil, and basil. Gradually add the flour until a stiff dough is formed that no longer adheres to the bowl's sides.

Place the dough on a floured board; knead it until smooth and elastic, about six minutes. Shape the dough, and put it in the loaf pan. Cover it with a clean dish towel. Let it rise until about double in volume.

Preheat the oven to 350°F. Bake the tomato bread for about fifty-five minutes or until done.

Zucchini Bread
Yield: 2 loaves

    3 eggs
    2 cups sugar
    1 cup oil
    ¼ teaspoon baking powder
    2 teaspoons baking soda
    1 teaspoon salt
    3 teaspoons cinnamon
    3 teaspoons vanilla
    2 cups raw, unpeeled, shredded,
        and packed zucchini
    3 cups flour

Beat the eggs until light and fluffy. Add sugar, oil, and vanilla. Blend well. Stir in the zucchini. Add the dry ingredients to the creamed mixture.

Pour the batter into two well-greased 9- by 5-inch loaf pans. Bake at 350°F for one hour.

Unleavened Bread

Hardtack

Make a stiff mixture of the following ingredients:

    1½ cups graham flour
    3 cups unbleached white flour
    ½ cup cornmeal
    ½ cup shortening
    1½ cups milk
    1 teaspoon sugar
    1 tablespoon salt

Lightly grease several cookie sheets, and sprinkle them with flour. Dust a chunk of dough (about the size of an egg) with flour, place it in the middle of the cookie sheet, and slightly flatten it with your hand. Now roll the dough out to cover the surface of the baking sheet, making it as thin as possible. Dust with flour when necessary to prevent sticking. You may want to use a flour sock on your rolling pin. Trim off any excess dough, and return it to the mixing bowl.

Bake the unleavened bread in a 400°F oven. When the edges brown, turn it over; continue baking until the flat bread is almost as stiff as cardboard. Turn it once more, and when the hardtack actually is cardboard-stiff, remove it from the oven.

It may be eaten when freshly baked and hot but will last indefinitely if kept dry. Break it in pieces, and store them in an airtight container.

Bread Spreads

Apple Butter

Fill a kettle with cider, and boil it down to two-thirds of the quantity. Pare, core, and slice sweet apples. Add as many to the cider as the vessel will hold without boiling over. Allow to boil slowly; stir frequently to prevent burning. When the apple butter is smooth and thick, add cinnamon and sugar to taste.

Let cool. Keep it in the refrigerator in tightly closed jars.

Cherry Butter

Boil cherries until soft. Rub them through a sieve. Add 2 cups of sugar to each pint of pulp. Boil gently until a butterlike consistency is reached.

Store the spread in tightly covered jars.

Green Butter

Mash in a mortar two small green onions, one-half clove of garlic, some watercress, six sprigs of parsley, and salt and pepper. Blend these ingredients into softened butter.

Green butter is delicious when spread on toasted bread, fish, or bland vegetables.

Honey Butter

1 cup butter
½ cup honey

Cream the butter. Beat in the honey until uniformly blended. Honey butter is excellent on freshly baked breads.

Keep it in the refrigerator. Store any excess in an airtight container in the freezer.

Lemon Butter

Beat the yolk of one egg; mix it with the whites of three eggs. Stir in 1½ cups of sugar, ½ cup of butter, and the grated rind and juice of two medium-sized lemons. Set the vessel containing the mixture in a pan of water and cook for twenty minutes.

Let cool to serve or store.

Peach Butter

Pare ripe peaches. Boil them in a kettle of enough grape juice to cook them until soft. Rub the fruit through a colander to remove the stones.

Add 1½ pounds of sugar to each quart of peach pulp. Boil slowly for sixty minutes. Stir often to avoid burning.

When the peach butter is smooth and thick, season it with cinnamon or other ground spices to suit your taste.

Peanut Butter

Two tablespoons of peanut butter contain an amount of protein at least equal to that found in 6 ounces of milk or a medium-sized egg. This nourishing food may

be prepared in a variety of ways, depending on your preference, all with good results.

Peanuts can be ground raw or given a slightly roasted flavor by first putting them, unshelled, in a 300°F oven for thirty minutes. For a full-roasted taste, leave them in for sixty minutes. Allow them to cool; then remove the shells and skins, or leave the skins on for their nutritional value.

Put 1 cup of peanuts and 1 tablespoon of peanut oil (the amount of oil may be increased for a creamier spread) into a blender. Grind them, periodically turning off the machine to scrape the sides. Add salt to taste.

Refrigerate your homemade peanut butter in clean, tightly closed jars. After some while, the oil may begin to separate out from the peanut butter; stir a few times to blend it in again.

Make other delicious nut butters by the same method. Some

nuts—for example, cashews and almonds—require little or no additional oil, having sufficient natural oils of their own.

Pumpkin Butter

8 cups pureed pumpkin
4 cups sugar
1½ teaspoons cinnamon
1 teaspoon ground ginger
¼ teaspoon ground cloves
¼ teaspoon ground nutmeg
4 lemons

Pare and cube a pumpkin. Steam the pieces in a kettle until they are soft. Drain the pumpkin, and rub it through a sieve to produce 8 cups of pumpkin puree.

Squeeze the lemons. Add their juice and the spices to the puree. Cook the mixture in a 300°F oven until it becomes thick and smooth.

Put the pumpkin butter into jars, and allow it to cool. Seal the jars.

Rhubarb Bread Spread

2 cups rhubarb, cut in pieces
⅔ cup brown sugar
1 cup molasses
1 teaspoon cinnamon
1 tablespoon butter
(or margarine)

Combine the ingredients in a pan. Cook over moderate heat, stirring continuously until well blended. Boil for ten minutes.

Transfer the pan to the oven. Cook its contents at low temperature until the rhubarb spread reaches the consistency of apple butter.

Tomato Butter

2 pounds tart red apples
5 pounds ripe tomatoes
juice of 1 small lemon
1 cup cider vinegar
3 cups brown sugar
3 cups white sugar
2 blades mace
2 cinnamon sticks
2 slices ginger root
½ teaspoon cloves

Put chopped apples, vinegar, and sugar into a big kettle. Blanch, skin, and chop the tomatoes. Add them to the kettle. Tie the spices in a cheesecloth bag, and place it in the pot. Slowly simmer for three hours or until the mixture is thick and smooth, stirring continuously.

Then take out the spice bag. Cool the tomato butter, and fill wide-mouthed jars with it. Store them in a cool place.

Crackers and Pretzels

Graham Crackers

⅔ cup graham flour
⅓ cup white flour
½ teaspoon soda
¼ teaspoon salt
3 tablespoons shortening
2 tablespoons milk
¼ cup honey

Blend the dry ingredients; cut in the shortening. Thoroughly mix in the milk and honey.

Make a ball of the dough, and roll it out very thin. (Be sure to flour the board.) Cut the dough into squares. Put them on an ungreased cookie sheet and bake at 325°F.

Remove the crackers from the oven when they are crisp and golden brown.

Soda Crackers

4 cups flour
1 cup butter (or margarine)
¾ cup milk
1 teaspoon vinegar
½ teaspoon baking soda
½ teaspoon salt

Work the butter into the flour with a pastry cutter or forks.

Stir the vinegar, baking soda, and salt into the milk; add this to the butter-flour mixture.

Form the dough into a ball. Then roll it out to a thickness of about ⅛ inch. Lightly score the dough in the size of cracker desired, and perforate the lines with a fork. Bake at 375°F for twenty minutes or until crisp.

Pretzels

Make dough as for white bread with the following ingredients:

¼ cup shortening
¼ cup sugar
1 yeast cake
1½ cups milk
4½ cups flour
¾ tablespoons salt

Scald the milk, shortening, sugar, and salt. Cool the mixture to lukewarm (80°F). Crumble the yeast into a little milk, and dissolve it. Then blend it with the rest of the milk and 1½ cups of flour. Beat until smooth.

Cover the sponge, and set it in a warm, draft-free place.

Let it rise for one and a half to two hours until it is full of bubbles.

Slowly add the remaining flour and blend until the dough is elastic and smooth. Put it on a lightly floured bread board, and pound it with a rolling pin to develop a velvety texture. Turn the dough over frequently while beating it.

Lay it in a greased bowl, brush with melted butter, and cover with a clean dish towel. Allow the dough to rise for about one hour until it is double in bulk.

Roll the dough in strips about 3 inches long and the thickness of a pencil. Tie the strips in knots, lapping the ends over each other. Place them on a lightly floured board; cover them with a towel and allow to rise until light.

Fill a large kettle with boiling water. Cook each pretzel in the water, turning it over to cook the other side.

Take the pretzels from the water, and drain them. Lay them on a well-greased, lightly floured baking pan; sprinkle with salt. Bake in a 400°F oven until brown and crisp.

14 | RACCOONBERRY WINE AND OTHER POTABLES

Coffee

Around A.D. 1000, Arab merchants carried home the coffee berry from Abyssinia. Not long after, coffee became the national drink of Arabia.

When Muslims were forbidden to use wine, a brew of coffee soon became a substitute. The drug properties of the beverage were recognized when people found themselves remaining alert in the evenings after drinking it. Probably because of this drug effect, it was given the name *kahweh* (from which our word coffee stems), meaning "wine and other intoxicating beverages."

In the sixteenth century the Arabs brought coffee to Europe, whence it spread to the New World.

Years ago coffee came in what we always called a tow-sack—some folks call it a gunnysack. The coffee beans were green and had to be roasted. Roasting was generally done in a long-handled cast iron frying pan, called a spider in New England, and a skillet in the

Southwest. A lid was put on this roasting device and the coffee beans would jump like Mexican jumping beans or popcorn. The trick was to roast the beans without scorching them, so a lot of coffee was made from scorched beans instead of the roasted kind.

Then the famous Arbuckle brothers, Charles and John, came into the picture. They got the money-making idea of roasting the beans themselves on a professional basis and packing them in a handy one-pound sack. Their pack became so popular that for a long time coffee wasn't called coffee any more in some parts of the country—it was called Arbuckle. A lot of old-timers in the country still call it that.

Arbuckle Brothers coffee, even though roasted, was still in the whole bean form and had to be ground. Coffee grinders were listed in the catalogues and were in almost every general store. Every home had to have one, and it took many a turn of the crank to grind a pound of coffee. Even today the best coffee you can pass over your lips is that made from a freshly ground whole roasted coffee bean. Here are a few more pointers on making really good country coffee:

Use the very best water. Alkali water, high mineral content (hard) water, and deep well water *do not* make the best coffee. Rainwater, melted snow water, and sparkling pure mountain spring water make the best coffee by far.

CORRECT FOR DRIP OR PERCOLATOR — NEW CUT — ONE POUND NET — CORRECT FOR ALL METHODS

White House Coffee

PACKED BY DWINELL-WRIGHT COMPANY BOSTON, MASS.

fire keeps the coffee rolling around the side of the pot. If you keep the coffee plenty hot but just below boiling it will be fine for hours. You can add more water and more fresh ground coffee if needed and it will be good. You must keep the coffee hot, not boiling but very near. If it ever cools it will never be good again and you will need to make a fresh pot. Here is another way good country coffee is made:

To every cup of water add a teaspoon to a tablespoon of ground coffee; then add one for the pot. Put it in cold water and allow to boil just once. Remove from fire. Settle with ¼ cup of cold water and serve piping hot.

Some country folks like it this way: bring water to boil first. Add coffee, boil five minutes, settle, and serve. (You can put your coffee in a small muslin bag tied loose, then boil five minutes longer and your bag of grounds can be removed before serving.)

Economy Coffees

Sometimes it is necessary to find a substitute for coffee when rations are low. Here are three ways to do it:

• Parched barley, beans, rice, and breadcrumbs make a fair coffee substitute. Scorch them a bit and grind. An improvised coffee mill can be a bag and a stone, pounding the materials to a fine pulp.

• Wash carrots and slice into pieces about half-inch thick. Dry them in the sun or oven but do not cook. When they are dry, brown them well and use as coffee. If you have a

The best coffeepot is one made of cast iron and the gallon size is the best.

Be sure the pot is absolutely clean before making coffee. Modern scouring soaps are not recommended for this cleaning job as they leave a taste that is far worse than the taste of the old coffee.

Fresh mud, wet clay, or caliche mud is the best cleaning agent you can use to scour the inside of a coffeepot. Don't worry too much about the outside as it will get smoke black again anyway.

When the pot looks and smells clean, fill it about three-quarters full of good, cold water never warm water. Fresh grind about a third of a pound of roasted coffee beans. Dump these into the water and set the pot on the fire. Do not cover the pot but keep your eye on it and when the brew begins to bubble then stir it. It will foam at this point so stir until the foaming stops to keep it from boiling over. When the deep boiling sets in, move the pot away from the fire but still near enough that the heat of the

little real coffee left to mix with the carrots it makes a fine brew.

• Okra seeds should be roasted or browned the same as coffee beans. Alone, they make one of the finest coffee substitutes but if you can add just a little coffee with them it is even better.

Chicory Coffee

Coffee should have aroma, flavor, clarity, and strength.

When chicory is blended with it, these characteristics are developed. The first mention of chicory occurred in an ancient papyrus roll dating about 4000 B.C. In the ninth century, monks of Holland cultivated chicory and found that its ground, roasted root enhanced the flavor of their coffee.

The addition of chicory not only results in a more aromatic, richer-tasting coffee; it also cuts by one half the standard measure of coffee required. Besides its use as a coffee adulterant, chicory can serve as a substitute for that beverage.

The plant grows most anywhere—along country roadsides and in city vacant lots. You will know it by the leaves sprouting from its tall, jointed stalk, which resemble dandelion leaves but are somewhat wider and darker green. If ragged blue flowers bloom at the stem joints, you can be fairly certain that you have found chicory.

Dig up the plants; remove the leaves. Peel the roots, and cut them in narrow strips. Roast the root slices for four hours in a 250°F oven. Then grind them.

To prepare chicory coffee, use 1 teaspoon of the ground root for each cup of water. Boil for three minutes.

Barley Coffee

You can brew a delicious coffee drink, while using less of the product, by blending barley grains and coffee beans. First, roast the barley for forty-five minutes in a 400°F oven. Occasionally stir the grains to avoid scorching. Remove the barley when it is a deep brown.

Grind it in a blender or coffee mill. Then mix it with your usual coffee to taste, and brew the blend as you would regular coffee.

A decoction of barley alone makes a pleasing, caffeine-free beverage.

Chickpea Coffee

Chickpea (garbanzo) coffee can be prepared with an economical amount of coffee. Roast garbanzos in a 500°F oven for ½ hour or until they are very dark brown and very dry. Grind them coarsely (like coffee) in your grinder.

Use 1 tablespoon of the ground peas to 6 cups of boiling water. Continue boiling for three minutes, and then put in 2 tablespoons of coffee (regular grind). Let the mixture cool a few minutes before serving. Sweeten with honey or sugar.

A caffeine-free beverage can be made from chick-peas by roasting them in a 300°F oven until dark brown and then grinding them in a coffee mill.

Use 1 teaspoon of ground chickpeas per cup of water.

Prepare the drink in a percolator, or boil it in a saucepan for five to ten minutes and strain.

Sunflower Seed Coffee

Shell sunflower seeds easily by first crushing them with a rolling pin. Then drop them into a vessel of water. Kernels will sink; hulls will float.

Reserve the seeds for wholesome eating. Heat the empty sunflower seed hulls in a skillet until just brown. Put them through your grain mill.

Use 1 teaspoon (this amount may be adjusted to suit individual taste) of ground hulls to each cup of water. Steep for three minutes. If desired, sweeten with honey.

Dandelion Root Coffee

Wash dandelion roots thoroughly. Peel off the brown skin.

Roast them in a low oven (300°F) for about four hours or until they are brittle and stiff. Then reduce them to a powder in your food grinder.

Use 1 heaping teaspoon of the powder for each cup of water. Boil for three minutes.

Bran-Cornmeal Coffee

Thoroughly mix 1 pint of yellow cornmeal with 2 quarts of wheat bran. Stir in three well-beaten eggs and 1 cup of sorghum molasses. Beat the mixture well, and spread it on a flat pan. Dry it in a 300°F oven, stirring it often during browning.

Use the concoction as a coffee substitute, a handful being the right amount for two persons.

Bran-Molasses Coffee

Bran with molasses also makes a delicious caffeine-free drink. Combine 1 cup of bran with 4 tablespoons of unsulphured molasses. Mix the ingredients with your hands.

Spread the mixture in a shallow pan, and put it in a 300°F oven. Stir it now and then until browning takes place, usually in about ½ hour. Then remove it from the oven. Break up any lumps. The toasted granules will resemble freeze-dried coffee. Store bran coffee in an airtight container.

Pour boiling water on a heaping tablespoon of the granules to make each cup of beverage. Honey and cream or milk may be added.

Almond Coffee

Spread almonds on a flat pan, and roast them at 300°F until they are dark brown. Grind them in your coffee mill, and then reduce the ground nuts to a fine meal with mortar and pestle.

To serve, stir the resulting powder—in an amount to suit personal taste—into a cup of hot milk. Almond coffee is a delicious and nourishing drink.

Teas

Black Birch Tea

The black birch is a medium-sized tree, seldom exceeding 2 feet in diameter. Its bark is dark red to black, and the tree's twigs have a strong wintergreen flavor.

To brew a delicious, hearty tea, first gather 1 quart of twigs, and cut them into 1-inch pieces. Put them in a vessel; pour in hot (not boiling) water. Allow to steep until cool.

Remove twigs and impurities by straining the tea. Heat once more. Serve with milk and a little honey.

Hemlock Tea

The hemlock tree is often found in the company of black birches. Chop its needles into lengths of 1 inch. Pour boiling water on them. Allow to steep for a few minutes.

Strain your hemlock tea to remove the needles. Drink it warm.

Mint Tea

Mint is easily identified by its four-sided stalk and the minty aroma of its crushed leaves. Look for it in fields, along streams, or in sunny marshes. Bring home some of the plants, and spread them to dry on newspaper in some warm place away from the sun. The leaves, when thoroughly dry, can be quickly stripped from the stems.

Stored in a tightly closed glass or tin container, they provide fragrant tea throughout cold winter months.

Brew the tea by using 1 teaspoon of dried leaves to each cup of boiling water. Allow to steep for a few minutes. You can make mint tea from the plant's green leaves as well; use 2 teaspoons of fresh leaves to 1 cup of boiling water.

Strawberry Tea

If you know the location of a wild strawberry patch, you can prepare a good tea to combat winter's chill by digging beneath the snow and collecting tender green strawberry leaves. After they thaw, put two handfuls of them into a teapot; add boiling water. Sweeten with honey to serve.

Juices

Grape Juice

A glimpse of smoky blue amid vines twining through overhead tree branches probably means you've discovered wild grapes. Pick some of the fruit to make juice.

Crush the grapes, and simmer them for twenty minutes.

Keep the water well below the boiling point. Put the fruit in a jelly bag, letting the juice drip into a container overnight.

To store, freeze the juice or warm it to just short of boiling, and transfer it to sterilized jars, closing them tightly.

Because the grape juice tends to be concentrated, you may need to add water before drinking it. Sweeten to taste.

Tomato Juice

Select juicy, ripe tomatoes; wash them thoroughly. After removing the stem ends, chop them into pieces. Simmer the tomato chunks in a pot until soft, stirring frequently. Then strain the vessel's contents.

To each 1 quart of juice, add 1 teaspoon of salt. Serve chilled.

Preserve any excess by reheating the juice to the boiling point

immediately after preparation. Pour it into sterilized jars to within ¼ inch of the rim. Adjust the lids, and process for fifteen minutes.

Noncarbonated Drinks

Unique Eggnog
Yield: 4½ quarts

¼ teaspoon cinnamon
¼ teaspoon cloves
¼ teaspoon ginger
¼ cup sugar
6 eggs, well beaten
2 quarts orange juice, chilled
1 quart vanilla ice cream, soft
1 quart ginger ale, chilled
dash nutmeg

Beat the dry ingredients into the eggs. Blend in the orange juice and homemade ice cream. Just before serving, pour in the ginger ale and sprinkle with nutmeg. For extra zest, rum may be added.

Wassail Bowl

The word wassail was originally used as a salutation when offering a cup of wine to a guest or toasting the health of someone. It generally meant, "Be in good health." The word applied as well to the liquor in which healths were drunk. Long ago it was the custom to drink to cattle and fruit trees in wassail to insure that they would thrive.

Today, any festive occasion will thrive when the following drink is served:

2 pounds sugar
6 cardamom berries
6 whole cloves
½ teaspoon mace
1 stick cinnamon
1 nutmeg, cracked
1 teaspoon coriander
2 pieces candied ginger
1 cup water
4 bottles Madeira or sherry
12 eggs
½ bottle brandy
6 baked apples

Mix the dry ingredients in 1 cup of water. Add the wine and simmer. Separate the eggs, beating whites and yolks apart. Now combine the eggs, and slowly add them to the hot mixture. Just before serving, blend in ½ bottle of brandy and six baked apples. Put in a stone crock. Keep it hot in front of a glowing hearth.

Cordials

First make a sugar syrup. The recipe you choose may require a sweet or medium strength syrup. To make a sweet syrup, combine 2 cups of white sugar with 1 cup of water, and bring it to the boiling point. To make a medium syrup, combine 1 cup of sugar with ½ cup of water, and bring it to the boiling point. Let it cool for several minutes. Pour the specified amount of syrup into a clean bottle, and add the indicated amount of extract. Fill the bottle with the required spirits. Close it, and shake the contents until all are thoroughly blended. Allow the cordial to cool before serving.

Apricot Brandy

1 bottle apricot brandy extract
1 fifth (or 1 quart) brandy

This recipe needs no sugar. Follow the steps as already described, omitting the syrup.

Cherry Brandy

1 bottle cherry brandy extract
1 cup medium sugar syrup
1 fifth (or 1 quart) brandy

The amount of spirits you use depends upon the size of the bottle that will hold the cordial. Follow the steps as previously outlined.

Wines

Blackberry Bramble Wine

Gather 4 pounds of blackberry brambles, cut them into small pieces, and put them in a large crock. Using the bottom of a quart bottle or a mallet, mash them to a pulp. Add 2 quarts of boiling water, and cover the crock. Allow to stand for seven days; stir twice each day.

Strain the contents of the crock to remove the pulp. Pour in an additional quart of boiling water and 12 cups of sugar. Blend thoroughly. When the mixture is lukewarm, sprinkle one package of yeast on it. Cover the vessel, and place it in a warm spot for two weeks.

Strain the mixture into a 1-gallon jug so that the sediment is left behind. Seal the jug by slipping a large balloon over its mouth. This will prevent air from entering while allowing the escape of gases. Occasionally you will need to bleed off the gas that accumulates in the balloon. After ninety days in this container, the wine will be clear and ready to serve. However, it will be even better if strained, poured into bottles, and permitted to age for several months.

Carrot Wine

4 pounds carrots
4 lemons
4 oranges, sliced in ¼-inch pieces
2 cups raisins, chopped
8 cups sugar
12 peppercorns
1 ounce yeast, moistened
1 slice whole wheat toast

Thoroughly scrub the carrots; chop them fine. Boil for forty-five minutes in 4 quarts of water. When lukewarm, strain. Return the liquid to the vessel. Mix in the sugar, and add the fruit and peppercorns. Spread the toast with the moistened yeast. Let the toast float on the liquid. Place the container in a warm spot for fourteen days to ferment. Stir each day.

At the end of two weeks, strain the wine. Allow it to settle, then syphon your carrot wine into bottles.

Honey-Dandelion Wine

Put 4 quarts of water and 4 quarts of dandelion heads into a crock. Cover it. Allow to stand for eight to ten days.

Strain the dandelion heads, squeezing out the liquid. Add 3 pounds of honey, three sliced lemons, and one cake of wine yeast to the liquid. Let stand for nine days.

Strain the mixture into a jug. When the wine has ceased working, cork the jug.

Country Dandelion Wine

Pick 1 gallon of dandelion heads in the early morning while they are still fresh from dew. Put them in a 2-gallon crock; pour in boiling water. Spread a piece of cheesecloth over the mouth of the crock, and leave it for three days at room temperature.

Squeeze the juice from the flower blossoms, and discard them, reserving the liquid. Pour it into a large vessel. Add 3 pounds of sugar, three whole lemons, chopped, and four whole oranges, chopped. Cover the pot and boil for ½ hour. Let cool to lukewarm. Empty it into a crock; add 2 tablespoons of yeast. Cover with cheesecloth and allow to stand for two or three weeks.

When the bubbling stops, filter your dandelion wine through cheesecloth to remove the chunks.

Honey Wine: Mead

Into a 1-gallon glass jug, put 1½ to 2 pints of honey. The amount depends on individual preference;

the greater the quantity of honey, the stronger the wine. Fill the jug with warm water. Shake it vigorously.

Add one cake of yeast. Let the uncapped jug stand in the kitchen sink overnight, where it will foam. When the foaming largely subsides, slip a balloon over the jug's mouth to prevent air from entering and allow the escape of gases. Let sit for two weeks. After bubbles no longer rise to the top, transfer the honey wine to bottles, and seal them with corks so that small amounts of gas can escape.

May Wine

Essential for making May wine is the perennial herb sweet woodruff. It grows in areas of filtered shade and is hardy in every zone. Once planted, it will spread as a ground cover, seeding itself. Sweet woodruff gets along well in the company of other plants, making its appearance in spring. Its dried stems and leaves help to make May wine.

Pick six sprigs of sweet woodruff. Let them dry for several days in a light and airy spot, but away from direct sunlight.

Put them in a punch bowl. Pour two bottles of well-chilled dry white wine over them. Cover the bowl. Allow the herb to steep for two hours. Take out the woodruff. Pour in another bottle of chilled wine. Blend in 2 cups of crushed, sugared strawberries and 2 tablespoons of simple syrup (one part water to two parts sugar, boiled for five minutes).

Put your May wine in the refrigerator to chill.

At serving time you may garnish the wine with mint sprigs and float a few whole strawberries in it.

Rose Hip Wine

Collect 4 pounds of rose hips, those orange-colored fruits that grow behind wild or cultivated rose blossoms. They begin to form in July. Green at first, rose hips become orange by September, developing a red color with the approach of autumn.

When setting out to gather hips from thorny wild rosebushes, wear old clothes. It is advisable, also, to don an old pair of gloves for protection against briars. Snipping off their fingertips will allow you to work with freedom. To remove hips easily, use a twisting motion. Drop them into a bag suspended from your belt to free your hands for picking.

Put the fruits in a crock, pulverize them, and pour 2 quarts of boiling water over the pulp. Allow the mixture to sit for four days, stirring each day.

Strain the liquid to remove the pulp. Thoroughly mix in 2½ pounds of sugar, 6 ounces of orange juice (unsweetened), and 1½ quarts of warm water. Sprinkle in one package of yeast. Put the crock in a warm spot for two weeks.

Strain the wine into a 1-gallon jug. Plug the mouth with a wad of cloth. A seal of this kind allows extra air to enter, giving the wine

a flavor somewhat similar to sherry. In ninety days it will be suitable for bottling and ready for drinking.

Raccoonberry Wine

During late summer, mayapples—lemon-shaped fruits—hang half hidden beneath their plant's large, shieldlike leaves. You may know them as mandrake apples, raccoonberries, or hog apples. No matter the name, these yellow fruits can be converted into a delicious golden wine. Search for them in lush woodlands.

Crush the fruit in a good-sized crock. Cover the vessel and let stand for seven days. Strain the contents, squeezing all juice from the pulp. Measure the juice; add water in equal measure. Stir 2½ pounds of

sugar into each gallon of the liquid. Sprinkle it with yeast. Cover the crock, and set it in a warm place for ten days.

Strain the contents into 1-gallon jugs. Seal them with a piece of plastic wrap secured by a rubber band. Let stand for four months to clarify. Then strain and bottle your golden raccoonberry wine.

Clarifying Wine

When homemade wine is not clear, the best remedy is time. However, if your patience wanes before this cure is effective, try these methods for clarifying wine:

• Beechwood chips or shavings can be used to settle the haze in wine without affecting taste. Add several tablespoons per gallon; leave them until clearing takes place.

• Boil oak shavings for several minutes, drain them, and put 2 tablespoons of the wood bits into a gallon jug of wine. They will hasten clearing of the beverage and add a pleasant oak flavor; check the taste every few weeks to be sure the oak flavor doesn't become too strong.

• An old-time remedy for clarifying wine is egg white. Add one whipped egg white to each gallon of wine. Gently shake the container once a day for seven days or until the beverage has cleared.

• As a last resort, filter the wine through cloth.

• Remember that haze in no way affects the taste of wine, only its eye appeal.

Carbonated Drinks

Applejack

    5 pounds sugar
    1½ gallons cider (fresh from
        your local cider mill)
    5 pounds raisins, crushed

Put the sugar in a vessel; add sufficient water to dissolve it. Boil the solution for one minute. When the sugar water is lukewarm, mix it thoroughly with the cider in a jug. Add the crushed raisins.

Close the container tightly. Run a narrow hose from a hole in the cap to a pan of water below in order to free the gas during fermentation. Keep the jug where the temperature is maintained at 70°F.

When a few bubbles per minute agitate the water in the pan, the beverage is ready for drinking. Serve your applejack chilled on warm days and piping hot when the weather turns cold.

Birch Beer

Gather 4 quarts of black birch twigs, cut them into short lengths, and put them in a 5-gallon crock. In a large vessel containing 4 gallons of water, stir 8 pounds of brown sugar until dissolved. Heat to the boiling point and continue boiling for ten minutes. Immediately pour the bubbling liquid over the birch twig pieces in the crock.

Dissolve one yeast cake in 4 ounces of warm water. Stir this into the contents of the crock.

Cover and allow to work for ten days or until clear. Ladle into bottles

and cap tightly. Birch beer is best when served chilled.

Simple Root Beer
Yield: twelve 1-quart bottles

⅓ ounce root beer extract
4½ cups sugar
3 gallons lukewarm water
½ teaspoon wine yeast

Thoroughly wash and rinse all equipment, bottles, and caps. Dry them.

Shake the bottled extract well. Mix the sugar and extract in the water, blending until the sugar dissolves. Blend the yeast in well until it dissolves. Fill the bottles to within 1 inch of their rim. Close with plastic or crown lids.

When using plastic lids, stand the bottles up in a box. If using crown tops, lay the bottles in the box on their sides. Cover against drafts. Put the box in a warm spot. Where the temperature is approximately 70°F, the root beer will carbonate within one to five days; carbonation will usually take place in one day where the temperature is above 80°F. To check for carbonation, refrigerate a bottle after one day. When it is chilled, slowly open it over the sink. Inspecting and tasting it will tell you whether the root beer is sufficiently carbonated. If it seems a little flat, allow it to stand another day or longer.

Old-Fashioned Root Beer

If certain roots and barks are available to you, make root beer the old-fashioned way from natural ingredients. Here is a good basic recipe:

Mix 1½ gallons of molasses into 5 gallons of boiling water.

Let stand for three hours.

Put in ¼ pound each of wintergreen birch bark, sarsaparilla root, and bruised sassafras bark.

Add 1 cup of fresh yeast, and increase the water content of the vessel to a total of about 16 gallons.

Set the mixture in a spot where the temperature is kept at 65 to 75°F. Leave it for twelve hours to ferment.

Draw off the root beer, using flexible tubing, and bottle it. Secondary carbonation will now take place; maintain the same temperature as before throughout the process.

The percentage of alcohol in the drink depends upon the length of time it ferments before bottling and the depth to which the containers are filled. The lower the level to which the bottles are filled, the longer the period of fermentation and the greater the alcoholic content. By experimenting, you can develop the taste you prefer.

Other ingredients that can be used for flavoring are the bark or root of the following: anise, boxberry, cinnamon, clove, deerberry, spiceberry, teaberry, and vanilla. If they are not available to you, their oils are commercially produced.

Granddad's Home Brew

Home-brewed beer requires these ingredients:

3 pounds malt extract (light or dark)
3½ pounds corn sugar (you may substitute 1 or 2 pounds of honey for part of the sugar)
1 package brewer' yeast
½ teaspoon powdered gelatin (in case the beer is cloudy)
2 cups corn sugar

To brew beer, follow these steps:

Dissolve the malt extract in 2 gallons of boiling water.

Continue rapid boiling for 1½ hours. Stir frequently to prevent sticking and burning.

Put the corn sugar into a large crock. Pour the malt liquid on it. Add enough water to make 5 gallons of liquid. Allow to cool.

When the liquid is comfortable to the touch, thoroughly stir in one package of brewer's yeast (found at wine supply shops). Place cheesecloth over the mouth of the crock.

After the foam has begun to subside, usually within two or three days, syphon the beer into a 5-gallon glass jug with the aid of a rubber hose. Fill it to within 6 inches from the rim to leave space for gas.

Set the container on a table, and attach a gas lock. One can be purchased in a hardware store, or you can improvise your own. Run the rubber hose through a hole punched in the jug's cap. Do not let the end of the flexible tubing come in contact with the liquid. The other end should hang into a pan of water placed either on the floor or at least several

feet below the level of the table. Rising gas from fermentation will be conducted through the tubing and will bubble in the water. When the action has subsided to about three bubbles each minute, the fermentation process is all but complete. The length of time to reach this stage varies with temperature. In a warm area, fermentation takes place in four to six days; where it is cold, the process takes twice as long.

When bubbling has almost subsided, check for clarity. If the brew is not clear, dissolve ½ teaspoon of powdered gelatin in 8 ounces of water. Add it to the beer.

Return the flat beer to the crock. Ensure carbonation and a good head by stirring in 2 cups of corn sugar.

Siphon the beer into bottles. Let your home brew sit for seven to fourteen days before drinking it.

Beer

Put ¼ ounce (one packet) of dry yeast in a cup; add warm water and 1 teaspoon of sugar. Stir.

Heat 2 gallons of water to just short of boiling. Dissolve 3 pounds of malt extract and 5 pounds of sugar in it. Empty the mixture into a 5-gallon jug. Add 1 gallon of cold water. Gently shake the jug. Now put in the yeast mixture. Then fill the jug to within 6 inches of the rim with cold water, and set it on a table or counter top. The 6 inches of space will allow for bubbles and froth as the brew works.

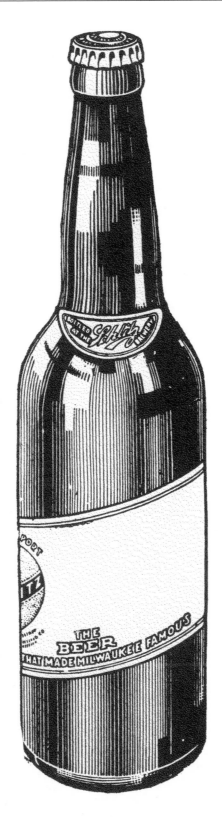

Attach a gas lock—a thin hose running from the air space in the container—through a hole in its cap, and into a vessel of water below. Let stand for four to six days or until only about three bubbles a minute disturb the water in the pan. The beer is then ready for bottling.

If the bottle caps you will use are cork lined, soak them in water on bottling day and they will seal much better.

Utilize your hose to siphon the brew into bottles. Add ¼ teaspoon of sugar to each bottle before capping it to insure a frothy head and proper carbonation.

Store the beverage in a dark, cool place for at least seven days before serving it.

Potato Beer

5 gallon container
6 good-sized potatoes
1 cup of sugar
3 packages active dry yeast
1 can malt syrup

Chop the potatoes. Put them in a 5-gallon container; a lard bucket will do nicely. Add the yeast, malt syrup, and sugar. Fill the bucket with water, and stir the contents thoroughly. Allow the mixture to ferment for five days. Do not cover the container.

At the end of five days, stir the brew until no sediment remains on the bottom. Then strain it through cloth. The beverage can be drunk now but will improve with time.

Different vegetables may be substituted for the potatoes to achieve a variety of flavors.

15 | GARDEN TO PANTRY SHELF

Canning Fruits and Vegetables

When I was a boy, canning season in the heat of a West Texas summer was a time to dread. It completely disrupted the rhythm of home life. Mother, weary from long hours in a steaming kitchen, set out only hastily prepared meals at irregular times.

Every member of the family participated in the chores. I was obliged to forego fishing along shady river banks. Endless bushel baskets, filled to brimming with garden and orchard produce, had to be lugged into the scorching kitchen, the twang and sharp slap of the screen door marking each delivered load. Here peaches were peeled, peas shelled, and other work doggedly pursued to keep pace with the maturing fruits and vegetables. No sooner was one crop safely sealed in its glass containers than another reached peak ripeness, necessitating immediate preserving.

With the waning day, and strength and spirits flagging, my only thought was to swim or shoot marbles with my friends. At this moment Mother always seemed to say, "Well, let's do just one more batch."

By summer's end, canning was over at last. Memories of hard work faded at the satisfying sight of pantry shelves gleaming with jar after jar of colorful, mouth-watering fruits and vegetables. As the incomparable taste of wholesome, homegrown foods continued to spark midwinter meals, we were convinced that our canning efforts had been more than worthwhile.

Assembled here are the basic methods for preserving fruits and vegetables as used by home canners for several generations.

Canning Methods

Open Kettle

In this method the food is completely cooked, put into sterilized jars, and sealed. Since the jars are not sterilized after sealing, spoilage is possible. However, the open-kettle method may be safely used for canning preserves in thick syrup and tomatoes.

Oven Steaming

To preserve food by oven steaming, seal jars completely. Then loosen the lids by turning them back ¼ inch. Self-sealing lids must be totally sealed. Space jars 2 inches apart in a shallow container of warm water placed on the middle rack of your oven. Preheat the oven to 275°F. Maintain steady temperature. Seal jars tightly right after their removal from the oven. Tighten the jar tops again during cooling, the exception being self-sealing tops; do not touch them. Set the jars on folded toweling or several thicknesses of cloth. Cool them rapidly and keep them out of drafts. When the jars are cold, test them for leakage.

Cold Pack

The cold-pack method is used for food that must be arranged in the jars and is put into them when cold. By heating the jars in steam or boiling water, the food is cooked and sterilized at the same time. Caution must be taken to seal containers only partially before processing. Expansion of the food during heating may crack the jars if they have been sealed too tightly.

Hot Pack

The hot-pack method involves filling the jars with boiling hot food and processing in steam or boiling water.

When processing is done in water, the jars can be tightly sealed. This method is generally preferred.

Equipment

Either tin cans or glass jars can be used as containers for preserving food.

Tin cans are available plain or lined with enamel. There are two kinds of lined cans: R enamel cans with shiny gold linings are suitable for very acidic foods and those of red color; the C type, having a dull gold lining, is used for vegetables of high protein content. Use plain cans for preserving meat. Lids for tin cans must be replaced each year. The cans themselves can be used three times by reflanging them.

Glass jars may be purchased with a variety of lids: zinc tops lined with porcelain or glass; metal ones with gaskets that melt during processing, automatically sealing the container; and glass lids. All tops, with the exception of those equipped with automatic seals, require rubber rings. Rubber rings and automatic seal lids must be replaced each year.

You can either buy a water-bath canner or substitute a large kettle for it. Use one deep enough for the boiling water to reach at least 1 inch above the jar tops. To keep jars from bumping and to allow water to circulate under them during processing, place a rack in the bottom.

Process nonacidic vegetables and meats in a pressure canner to kill bacteria that form spores. The pressure canner should be equipped with a safety valve, petcock, and pressure indicator. Use one of sturdy construction.

Preliminary Procedures

To insure safe, high-quality results, you must check and clean all equipment. Carefully inspect lids for bent, uneven edges and jars for nicks and cracks. If none are apparent, put a new ring on the jar, fill it partway with water, and seal. Turn the jar upside down, and check for leaks or for tiny bubbles rising as the water cools. An imperfect seal on jars with a wire bail can be remedied by taking off the top bail, bending it in at the ends and down in the center, and replacing it. Check rings by folding them in two. Those that develop cracks should be discarded.

Give cans and jars a thorough washing in hot, soapy water, followed by a rinse in hot water. Fill them with water, and set them upright or sideways, with space between each, in a deep vessel of cold water. Gradually bring the water to a boil, and continue boiling for fifteen minutes. Leave the jars in the hot water until needed; let tin cans drain on a clean cloth.

Wash all tops in soapy water. Leave glass and zinc lids in very hot, clear water for five minutes. Keep them hot until used. Turn them upside down to drain. Pour hot water over lids with a sealing composition. Let them stand until wanted for use. Scald rubber rings quickly; never boil them. Sterilize knives, spoons, funnels, and other utensils by putting them in boiling water after a preliminary washing.

When tin cans are used, a mechanical sealer is a necessity.

Test its adjustment each time you employ it by putting 2 tablespoons of water in the can, adjusting the lid, and sealing it. Put it in boiling water, keeping it beneath the surface until steam forms in the can and expands the ends. Air bubbles escaping from the can are evidence of improper adjustment of the sealer.

liquid and the rim. Since spinach and other kinds of greens tend to shrink, pack them down lightly, cutting through them with a knife several times.

Approximate Vegetable Yield

Vegetable	Weight	Yield
Asparagus	3 pounds	1 quart
Beans, Lima	2 pounds	1 quart
Beans, String	1¾ pounds	1 quart
Beets, Baby	2½ to 3 pounds	1 quart
Corn on the Cob	1 quart	7 small ears
Greens	2¾ to 3 pounds	1 quart
Peas, Green, Shelled	4 pounds	1 quart
Tomatoes	3 pounds	1 quart

Readjust it, and repeat the test. Clean the removable safety valves and petcocks on your pressure canner. Vinegar will remove any corrosion. Clean all openings in the canner lid. A toothpick or pipe cleaner is handy for the job. Be sure the gasket is free of dirt and grease, and examine it for a tight fit. If steam escapes or you have difficulty in removing it, grease with salt-free fat the closing surface of the canner cover that seals metal to metal. Tighten screws on the handle. Eliminate stains and odors with 2 tablespoons of vinegar in 2 quarts of water, processing for five minutes at 5 pounds pressure. With a master gauge tester or a maximum thermometer, check the dial gauge. A weight gauge should be cleaned according to the manufacturer's directions.

Preparation of Food

Select vegetables that are young and tender. Clean them thoroughly, and prepare them as for table use. Do not work with too great a quantity of vegetables at one time, particularly in hot weather. The various canning procedures must be accomplished rapidly to avoid flavor loss, called "flat sour." Large amounts of vegetables cannot be handled quickly enough. Can vegetables immediately after picking them. This applies especially to asparagus, beans, corn, and peas. To thoroughly heat nonacid vegetables, precook them, using the pot liquor to fill the jars. Pack vegetables evenly; do not crowd them. For a good pack, shake the jars. Because shell beans, corn, and peas are likely to swell, leave 1 inch of space between the

Choose firm, well-developed fruit that is not overly ripe. Try to can it soon after it has been picked. Prick unseeded plums and cherries a few times with a big pin. When canning fruit without sugar, use fruit juice or boiling water in place of syrup, filling the containers to within ½ inch of their rim. Before serving the fruit, drain it, add sweetening to the liquid, and bring to a brisk boil. Pour it on the fruit and allow to cool. Then chill it. You may wish to cook berries and fruits in syrup for several minutes to achieve a full pack. Prepare syrups according to the fruit's acidity and the taste preference of those for whom the food is canned. One cup of sugar to 3 cups of fruit juice or water will yield 3½ cups of thin syrup. One

cup of sugar to 2 cups of water or fruit juice will yield 2½ cups of medium syrup. One cup of sugar added to 1 cup of fruit juice or water will result in l½ cups of thick syrup. Blend the sugar and liquid, stirring over heat until the sugar dissolves. Bring the syrup to a boil. Use approximately 2 cupfuls of syrup to each quart of large fruit, such as peaches, pears, and plums. Use 1 cupful of syrup to each quart of small fruit, such as berries and cherries.

To avoid dark fruit, take these precautions:

• Process fruit for the correct amount of time; too-short processing results in dark fruit.

• Maintain sufficiently high temperature. Water should be boiling at the start of processing time and remain at a boil throughout.

• Accurately count the time of processing. Start counting time when a rolling boil commences. Check the timetable, making any adjustments that might be required for altitude.

• The level of boiling water should be between 1 and 2 inches above the lids of the jars during the complete processing time.

• Before packing large raw fruits, such as pears or peaches, treat them with an antioxidant. Put them in a solution of 2 teaspoons of salt to 1 quart of water.

To keep fruit from floating, follow these tips:

• Do not use overripe fruits; use those in their prime.

• Pack fruit closely.

• Don't allow the syrup to get too thick.

• Process for exactly the right length of time.

• Be sure the temperature is not too high.

Sort vegetables and fruits as to size so that each jar's contents will be approximately uniform. To peel foods like tomatoes and peaches, dip them in boiling water, until the skins loosen, and then in cold water for a moment. Once the vegetables and fruits have been heated, work quickly, filling only the number of jars that your canner accommodates. Don't allow the hot foods to stand prior to processing, for harmful bacteria develop between 105 and 150°F. Fill the containers to ½ inch from the top. For vegetables, use boiling water; for fruits, use boiling syrup. To help air bubbles rise to the surface and break, insert a spatula along the sides of the jar. If the contents of the jar are hot and processing is to take place in a water bath, seal the containers completely. Otherwise, seal them partially. If the food in tin cans is not hot at sealing time, rid the containers of air by boiling them for five minutes in 1 inch of water. After adjusting the lids, seal them immediately.

Approximate Fruit Yield

Fruit	Weight	Units	Yield	Bushels	Yield
Apples	2½ pounds	7–8	1 quart	1	28 quarts
Berries	1¼–1½ pounds	5 cups	1 quart	1	24 quarts
Cherries	1¼–1½ pounds	6 cups	1 quart	1	20 quarts
Peaches	2–2½ pounds	8–10	1 quart	1	21 quarts
Pears	2–2½ pounds	5–6	1 quart	1	30 quarts
Pineapples		15			15 quarts
Plums	1½–2½ pounds	24–32	1 quart	1	28 quarts
Tomatoes	2½–3½ pounds	8–10	1 quart		18 quarts

Processing

Hot Water Bath: Put hot, filled cans or jars on the rack in the canner. Cover them with boiling water to a depth of 1 inch above their tops. Heat rapidly to boiling. When bubbles commence breaking over the containers, begin the timing. Make sure that water covers the jars throughout the processing period. When necessary, add boiling water. Take the canner from the heat upon completion of processing.

Pressure Cooker: There should be sufficient boiling water in the cooker to reach the bottom of the rack. Put packed cans or jars on the rack, adjust the cooker lid, and clamp it down firmly. Have the petcock open. After permitting steam to escape for seven minutes, close the petcock, and watch for the pressure to reach the required point. From that moment count to nine. Regulate the heat to maintain steady pressure. Changes in pressure generally cause liquid loss in the containers, especially if the pressure builds to the extent of releasing the safety valve, causing an abrupt fall in pressure. Immediately upon termination of processing time, take the canner from the heat. When sufficient cooling has reduced the pressure to zero, slowly open the petcock. Wait until pressure is completely released before opening the canner. When using number 2 cans, open the petcock just as

EVEN STRAWBERRIES JELL PERFECTLY!

SURE-JELL NEW POWDERED PECTIN PRODUCT GIVES PERFECT RESULTS WITH ANY FRUIT!

quickly as processing is completed, permitting the pressure to drop rapidly. Open the canner and take out the cans. Submerge them immediately in cold water to avoid overcooking.

Cooling Containers

Take jars out of the canner. If they are partially sealed, complete the seal. Put them on folded towels. Invert those that do not have an automatic seal. From time to time, examine the jars. Rising bubbles or leakage indicates that the food should be used or immediately recanned. Never invert jars with self-sealing tops. Test them by tapping with a spoon. If the sound is dull instead of a clear-ringing note, the jar is not well sealed. After submerging tin cans in water, check for bubbles escaping from ends or seams. When containers are cold, wash and label them. Store them in a cool, dry spot.

Spoilage

If you detect any evidence of spoilage, dispose of the food.

An odor that is not characteristic of the product is an indication of spoilage. There should be no signs of leakage, bulging of the rubber, spurting of liquid, or expulsions of air with glass jars. Never taste-test a questionable food; destroy it immediately. Always boil all canned vegetables for ten minutes before serving or tasting.

Canning Recipes for Vegetables, Fruits, and Fruit Juices

Vegetables

When seasoning vegetables for canning, use 1 teaspoon of salt for 1 quart of vegetables; for 1 pint, use ½ teaspoonful.

Asparagus

Carefully wash asparagus. Cut it in 1-inch pieces or lengths to fit the containers. Put them into boiling water and boil for five minutes, keeping the tips above water. Pack immediately in hot jars, stem ends down. Pour in seasoned cooking liquid to within ½ inch of the rim. Partially seal jars. Process at once at ten pounds pressure for forty minutes (for pint jars, five minutes less).

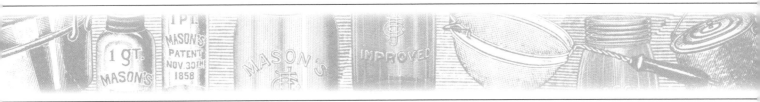

Beans, String

Wash beans and remove ends. Cut them into uniform lengths. Cover with boiling water. When the water commences boiling again, pack loosely in hot jars, adding salt and boiling cooking water to within ½ inch of their rim. Season, partially seal, and process immediately at ten pounds pressure for forty-five minutes (for pint jars, five minutes less).

Beans, Lima

Select small green beans. Wash well, shell, and precook for four minutes. Pack loosely in clean, hot jars to within 1 inch of the rim. Add boiling cooking liquid to the same level. Season, partially seal, and process at ten pounds pressure for sixty minutes (for pint jars, five minutes less).

Beets

Choose very small beets. Wash carefully. Cut off tops. Leave 1 inch of root and stem. Scald until skins slip. Remove skins, and pack the beets in jars at once. Fill with liquid to within ½ inch of the rim. Season. Partially seal jars. Process immediately at ten pounds pressure for forty minutes (for pint jars, five minutes less).

Broccoli, Brussels Sprouts, Cabbage, Cauliflower

Wash vegetables and remove stems. Discard coarse leaves. Precook for three minutes. Pack in hot jars. Fill them with fresh boiling water up to ½ inch from the rim. Season. Seal, and process immediately at ten pounds pressure for forty minutes.

Carrots

Wash young carrots. Precook for five minutes. Skin. Pack at once in hot jars. Fill jars with boiling liquid up to 1 inch from the rim. Season. Partially seal jars. Process immediately at ten pounds pressure for forty minutes (for pint jars, five minutes less).

Corn, Whole Kernel

Cut corn from the cob. Weigh. Add one-half the weight in boiling water. Season each quart with 2 teaspoons of sugar and 1 teaspoon of salt. Heat to a boil. Pack in hot jars, adding boiling liquid to 1 inch from the top. Partially seal jars. Process immediately at ten pounds pressure for seventy-five minutes (for pint jars, ten minutes less).

Corn, Cream Style

Remove uncooked corn from the cob with a shallow cut. Using 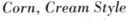 the back of a knife, scrape the cobs. Follow directions for whole kernel corn. Process immediately at ten pounds pressure for eighty minutes (for pint jars, the same time).

Greens

Discard imperfect leaves and stems. Wash well. Add water and simmer until thoroughly wilted. Drain, saving liquid. Pack the greens in jars. Cut through their centers several times with a knife. Add boiling cooking liquid up to ½ inch from rim. Season with salt. Partially seal jars. Process immediately at fifteen pounds pressure for sixty-five minutes (for pint jars, five minutes less).

Mushrooms

Wash well. Skin mature mushrooms. Put them in boiling water with 1 teaspoon of salt and 1 tablespoon of vinegar per quart.

Drain. Pack in hot jars. Pour in fresh boiling water to within ½ inch of the rim. Partially seal the jars. Process immediately at ten pounds pressure for thirty-five minutes (for pint jars, ten minutes less).

Okra

Thoroughly wash the okra. Discard the stem ends. Precook for five minutes. Pack hot into hot, clean jars. Pour in boiling cooking water to within ½ inch of the rim. Season. Partially seal and process immediately at ten pounds pressure for forty minutes (for pint jars, five minutes less).

Peas

Shell tender young peas. Precook for four minutes. Pack the hot peas loosely in hot, clean jars. Pour in boiling cooking water to within 1 inch of the rim. Season, and partially seal jars. Process immediately at ten pounds pressure for one hour (for pint jars, ten minutes less).

Potatoes, New White

Wash well. Cook for five minutes. Remove eyes and skin. Pack while hot, adding boiling cooking liquid to within ½ inch of the rim. Season. Partially seal the jars, and process immediately at fifteen pounds pressure for seventy minutes.

Fruits

Rules for processing in boiling water are for an altitude of 1,000 feet or less. Increase processing time by 20 percent for each additional 1,000 feet.

To use the cold-pack, hot-pack, and open-kettle methods, see the procedures under those headings.

These recipes are for quart and pint jars. Consult the directions already given for packing and sealing jars to be processed by the following methods.

Making Preserves

When fruits become plump from absorbing thick sugar syrup and appear bright and clear in color, you have successful preserves. Stew hard fruits before putting them in syrup.

Sweet apples, citrons, hard pears, pineapples, underripe peaches, quinces, and watermelon rinds must be cooked until soft enough to absorb the syrup. Foods that have had this preliminary stewing should be thoroughly drained before being added to the syrup. Use this cooking water to make the syrup. Berries, cherries, ripe peaches, and other tender fruits can be put directly into heavy syrup. Don't cook fruits too long in the syrup, just long enough for them to become filled with it; otherwise a dark, stiff product will result. Bring it quickly to a boil, and continue the rapid cooking until the fruits are shiny and sparkling, indicating that they are saturated with syrup.

For extra-fine preserves, place the fruit in the heavy syrup, and heat it until bubbling begins. Remove from the stove and let stand in a covered enamel preserving pot for a few hours or overnight. Then commence the cooking again. In

Fruit	Hot Water Bath	Oven	Pressure Canner
Apples: Peel, core, and quarter. Precook or steam for five minutes in thin boiling syrup. Process immediately for	20 minutes	75 minutes at 250°F	10 minutes at 5 pounds
Apricots: Wash. Leave apricots whole, pit them, or halve them. Pack in jars. Pour in thin boiling syrup to cover. Process immediately for	20 minutes	68 minutes at 250°F	10 minutes at 5 pounds
Berries: Pick over berries. Wash and hull them. Fill sterilized jars. Pour in boiling syrup to cover. Process immediately for	20 minutes	68 minutes at 250°F	10 minutes at 5 pounds
Cherries: Wash and stem. Prick with a large pin if unseeded. Fill jars. Cover with thick or medium boiling syrup. Process immediately for	25 minutes	68 minutes at 250°F	10 minutes at 5 pounds
Fruit Juices: Crush (Remove seeds from cherries.) Gradually bring to the simmering point. Strain. Add water and sugar to taste. Heat the juice, and pour it into hot jars. Seal and process at once for	30 minutes		
Peaches: Skin, halve, and pack in jars. Pour in boiling medium syrup to cover. Process immediately for	25 minutes	1 hour at 275°F	10 minutes at 5 pounds
Pears: Remove skins, halve, and core. Boil 1 quart of pears at a time in thin syrup for about six minutes. Pack in hot jars, adding syrup. Process immediately for	30 minutes	1 hour at 275°F	10 minutes at 5 pounds
Pineapple: Peel and remove eyes. Cube the pineapple and pack it in jars, pouring in boiling thin syrup to cover. Process at once for	30 minutes	1 hour at 275°F	10 minutes at 5 pounds
Plums: Wash plums. Prick them with a large pin. Pack jars and cover the contents with boiling medium syrup. Process immediately for	20 minutes	1 hour at 275°F	10 minutes at 5 pounds
Rhubarb: Wash. Cut into· pieces. Pack in jars, pouring in boiling thin syrup to cover. Process at once for	16 minutes	50 minutes at 275°F	10 minutes at 5 pounds
Strawberries: Wash and stem. Add 1 cup of sugar to each quart. Allow to stand for two hours. Simmer for five minutes. Fill the jars. Seal and process immediately for	0 minutes	68 minutes at 250°F	10 minutes at 5 pounds

this manner the fruit absorbs more syrup. For an extra fine quality product, repeat the plumping process of heating and cooling a few times. Particularly suited to plumping are citrons, crab apples, green tomatoes, whole tomatoes, peaches, pears, and melon rinds. Always plump fruits that are to be candied.

Seal your preserves in hot, clean jars. Sterilize in boiling water all utensils used in filling the jars with preserves. As a precaution against mold, place the packed jars in boiling water or steam for ten minutes.

Making Jam

Making jam requires mashing or cooking to a pulp small whole fruits with sugar. Ideally, its texture should be tender and soft, its color sparkling bright, and the mixture's consistency uniform.

A jellying substance, pectin, is a necessity for good jam. Broken fruit or pieces remaining from canning may be used for jam making, but part of the fruit must be underripe because pectin is absent in overripe fruit. To develop the pectin, cook the fruit several minutes before adding sugar. When fruit lacks enough juice, add a little water to prevent burning, and cook it in a covered vessel. Porcelain or enamel cooking utensils are best. Use ½ pound of sugar to 1 pound of fruit. After putting in sugar, cook rapidly until the jam takes

on a jellylike appearance. To check whether it's done, test it by dropping a bit on a cool dish. If it sets quickly or hangs from the spoon in sheets, it is ready. Keep in mind that upon cooling, jam thickens. Make allowance for this so that the product will not become tough and thick from overcooking. Cooking for too long also darkens the jam.

Because jam is a highly concentrated substance, it will burn easily. To avoid this, always stir from the bottom with a wooden spoon, lifting the jam from the bottom of the kettle. Cook jam rapidly, watching it closely for twenty to thirty minutes.

To protect jams from mold, seal them in hot, clean jars.

Fig Jam
Yield: 3 pints

> 4 pounds fresh figs
> 1 lemon

> 1 cup water
> 4 cups sugar

Wash figs; peel them. Slice the lemon. Cook water and sugar together for five minutes. Add lemon and figs. Cook briskly until clear.

Seal in hot clean jars.

Grape Jam
Yield: 2 pints

> 4 pounds Concord grapes
> 1½ cups water
> 3 cups sugar

Wash grapes. Remove the skins and seeds. Combine water and sugar; boil for five minutes. Add grape pulp and continue cooking until thick and clear.

Pour into hot, clean jars. Seal immediately.

Peach Jam
Yield: eight ½–pint jars

> 4¼ cups crushed peaches (about
> 3½ pounds of the fruit)
> ¼ cup lemon juice
> 7 cups sugar
> ½ bottle liquid pectin

Wash ripe peaches. Remove their stems, skins, and pits. Crush the fruit.

Put the peach pulp in a kettle, and mix in the lemon juice and sugar. Set over high heat, stirring continuously. Quickly bring to a rolling boil and boil hard for one minute, stirring all the while.

Take from the fire, and stir in the pectin. Skim. Fill and seal jars.

Making Marmalade

Generally, marmalades are made from fruits containing both acid and pectin. The fruits are thinly sliced and suspended in a clear jelly. If fruit is used in which the jellying properties of pectin and acid are absent, tart apple juice or slices of lemon or orange can be added to supply them.

The preparation of marmalade is the same as for jams, except that the fruit is in cut pieces or slices, not mashed. Successful marmalade should be of sparkling clarity.

Grapefruit Marmalade

Cut the sections from three grapefruit. Discard seeds and white fiber. Grind the well-washed yellow rind (without the white) of one grapefruit in a food grinder. To the grapefruit sections, add the ground grapefruit peel and the grated rind and strained juice of three lemons. Cover with 6 cups of water; allow to stand overnight.

The following morning, boil the mixture for forty minutes. Repeat for two days more.

Then put in 1 cup of crushed pineapple. Measure the mixture, and add 1½ cups of sugar for each cup of fruit and juice. Cook for thirty minutes or until jellylike.

Seal in sterilized jars.

Tomato-Apple-Ginger Marmalade

Skin enough ripe tomatoes to make 2 cupfuls. Drain. Peel and core enough apples to make 2 cupfuls. Chop. Mince one lemon.

Mix these ingredients, and cook them for fifteen minutes.

Add 3 cups of sugar, and cook until the mixture reaches the consistency of marmalade. For the last ten minutes of cooking, add 4 tablespoons of chopped preserved ginger.

Seal in sterilized jars.

Making Jellies

To make jelly, sugar and fruit juice are combined in proper proportions and cooked until the mixture jells when cool. Jelly of good quality has the natural flavor and color of the fresh fruit, its clarity unmarred by crystals or sediment. It retains its shape when emptied from the jar but is supple enough to quiver. When cut, the jelly does not stick to the knife.

Fruit for jelly must be high in acid and pectin. When fruit is not rich in both of these, it must be combined with a fruit containing whichever substance is absent. The following fruits have pectin and acid in sufficient quantity: crab apples, tart apples, blackberries, gooseberries, loganberries, raspberries, currants, grapes, plums, and quinces. Those with insufficient pectin are as follows: cherries, peaches, pineapples, rhubarb, and strawberries. Fruits lacking enough acid are sweet apples, blueberries, huckleberries, and pears.

Although the flavor isn't as good, fruit that is a bit underripe generally has more pectin and acid than completely ripe fruit. A correct proportion is one-quarter underripe fruit to three-quarters ripe fruit. If either acid or pectin is lacking in a fruit, it can be combined nicely with tart apples, because apple juice has the most minimal effect on the flavor and color of the jelly.

When using commercial pectin, follow exactly the directions accompanying it.

The juice from almost any kind of fruit can be used by adding a large quantity of sugar and the commercial pectin. Jelly is made in less time, but due to the shorter cooking period, the flavor is less rich and full than fruit juice boiled over a longer period. However, success is usually assured with the use of commercial pectin.

Extraction of Fruit Juice

Carefully inspect the fruit, and remove stems and areas of decay. Cut large fruits into pieces. Crush juicy fruits, adding little or no water. Fruits with less juice require adding just enough water until it is visible among the pieces, but not so much that they float. Cook the fruit in a covered vessel until tender and the juice flows liberally. Do not overcook. Apples need approximately fifteen minutes, berries from one to three minutes, and citrus fruits one hour.

Empty the contents into a jelly bag. Use a clean flour sack, or make one of heavy muslin, flannel, or four layers of cheesecloth. Suspend it on a strainer above a bowl to allow the juice to drip through. More juice is extracted by squeezing the bag, but the jelly will not be clear. The first time, let the juice simply drip through; the resulting jelly will be clear and appropriate for special occasions. Squeeze the bag with the second extraction; jelly from this juice will be cloudy, but acceptable for general use. Pulp for a second extraction can be prepared by putting it in a pot, adding water almost to cover, and simmering for about twenty-five minutes. If only one extraction is made, you can press the pulp that remains through a sieve and use it for preparing fruit butter or jam.

Pectin Test

The amount of pectin in a particular fruit juice can be ascertained by combining 1 tablespoon of the juice, 1½ teaspoons of Epsom salts, and 1 teaspoon of sugar. Blend the mixture. When the salts have dissolved, allow to stand for twenty minutes. The formation of large flaky particles or a solid mass means that sufficient pectin is present in the juice to make a good jelly.

Sugar Content

Too much sugar results in weak, syrupy jelly; too small an amount of sugar produces a too-solid jelly. As a general rule, the right proportion is a quantity of sugar equaling two-thirds of the amount of fruit juice. When in doubt, use less sugar instead of more. It is not necessary to heat the sugar.

Cooking Jelly

To produce jelly with the best texture, flavor, and color, cook no more than 2 quarts of juice at one time. Use a 10-quart vessel of large diameter to permit rapid evaporation. When the juice begins to boil, gradually add sugar, stirring slowly.

Boil briskly until the jelling point, which can be determined by letting a little juice drip from the spoon. The running together in a continuous strand of the last few drops indicates the jellying stage. Immediately remove the jelly from the heat. Skim and pour into hot, clean glasses. Fill them to within ½ inch of their rims. Seal with paraffin either by pouring melted paraffin on the jelly at once or by covering the jelly with hot paraffin after it has cooled. Put metal covers on the jelly jars after the paraffin cools. Store them in a cool, dry place.

Butter Bean Hull Jelly

5 cups butter bean hull juice
7 cups sugar
2 packages (1¾ ounces each) powdered fruit pectin

Boil butter bean hulls for one hour. Strain them through cheesecloth. Add the pectin to 5 cups of strained juice. Bring the mixture to a boil, and stir in the sugar.

Allow to jell. Pour into clean jars and seal.

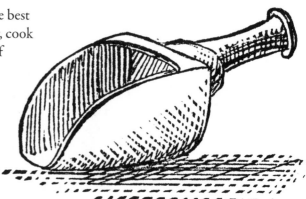

Amounts of Sugar and Fruit Juice for Jelly

Fruit	Juice	Sugar
Apple	1 cup	⅔ cup
Blueberry (with lemon juice)	1 cup	⅔ cup
Crab Apple	1 cup	⅔ cup
Currant	1 cup	¾ to 1 cup
Gooseberry (green)	1 cup	1 cup
Grape (underripe)	1 cup	¾ to 1 cup

Fruit Juice Combinations	Juice	Sugar
Apple/Black Raspberry	½ cup/½ cup	⅔ cup
Apple/ Blueberry	½ cup/½ cup	¾ cup
Apple/Cherry	½ cup/½ cup	⅔ cup
Apple/Peach	½ cup/½ cup	⅔ cup
Apple/ Pineapple	½ cup/½ cup	⅔ cup
Apple/Quince	½ cup/½ cup	⅔ cup
Blackberry/ Apple	¾ cup/¼ cup	⅔ cup
Cherry/ Currant	½ cup/½ cup	¾ cup
Currant/ Raspberry	½ cup/½ cup	⅔ cup
Damson Plum/ Apple	¼ cup/¾ cup	¾ cup
Elderberry/ Apple	½ cup/½ cup	¾ cup
Gooseberry (unripe)/ Cherry	½ cup/½ cup	¾ cup

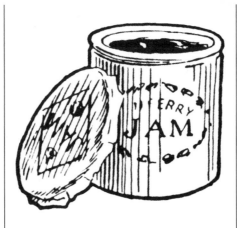

Corn Cob Jelly

12 medium-sized red corn cobs
¼ ounce package powdered pectin
2 quarts water
3 cups sugar

Wash cobs. Cut them into fourths. Put them in a vessel of water and bring to the boiling point. Lower the heat. Let boil slowly for about forty minutes.

Strain the juice. Measure 3 cups of it into a large saucepan.

Add pectin; bring to a boil. Add sugar; bring to a boil once more. Continue boiling for five minutes.

Skim the foam from the surface. Pour into sterile jars.

Corn cob jelly is said to taste like mild honey.

Mesquite Bean Jelly

3 quarts mesquite beans
1 box pectin (1¾ ounces)
5 cups sugar

Pick mesquite beans while they are still red. Cover 3 quarts of the beans with enough water to make 5 cups of juice. Add sugar as it simmers until the juice becomes yellow. Strain it.

Follow directions on pectin juice for making jelly, but boil a bit longer than specified. Use the spoon test to check when it has jelled.

Put into sterilized jars. Seal.

Parsley Jelly
Yield: six 8-ounce glasses

3 cups boiling water
4½ cups sugar
4 cups chopped parsley (2 big bunches)
several drops green food coloring (homemade)
2 tablespoons lemon juice
1¾ ounces powdered fruit pectin

Put the chopped parsley in a bowl; pour the boiling water over it. Cover. Allow to stand for twenty minutes.

Strain the liquid through cheesecloth. Put 3 cups of the parsley juice into a good-sized saucepan. Stir in the lemon juice and pectin. Cook over high heat, stirring until the mixture reaches a rolling boil. Put in all the sugar at once and stir. Mix in a few drops of green coloring. Bring to a rolling boil again and boil hard for one minute, stirring continuously.

Take the pan from the heat, and remove the foam with a metal spoon. Quickly pour the liquid into sterilized jelly glasses. Cover immediately with hot paraffin to a depth of ⅛ inch.

Homemade Pectin

Make apple jelly stock-sugar-free pectin-to preserve for future use

or to prepare jams and jellies immediately.

(Most commercial pectins contain sugar.)

For your homemade pectin select small, green, immature apples, available in early summer. Being rich in pectin and acid, they make excellent jelly stock and impart a snappy, tart flavor to the finished product. Apples cut or bruised by falling from orchard boughs, and even those damaged by birds and insects, can be utilized by cutting away the imperfect parts.

Wash the fruit thoroughly, retaining only the sound portions and cutting them into thin slices. Put them in a vessel, and add 2 cups of water for each pound of apples. Cover the vessel; boil its contents for fifteen minutes. Strain the juice with pulp through one thickness of cheesecloth; do not squeeze the pulp.

Put the pulp back in the vessel, once more adding the required measure of water. Cook the mixture again for fifteen minutes, but this time over lower heat. Let it stand for ten minutes. Now strain the juice with pulp through cheesecloth, without squeezing the pulp. When the pulp cools sufficiently for handling, press any remaining juice from it. You should have accumulated approximately 1 quart of apple juice for each pound of fruit.

If you don't have immediate plans for blending the pectin with the juice of other fruits to make jam or jellies, prepare it for storage in this way: Heat the jelly stock to the boiling point; then pour it into hot, sterilized canning jars. Seal them. Invert the jars, and allow them to cool. Instead of canning the pectin, you may freeze it by letting the liquid cool and pouring it into freezer containers. Leave 1 inch of headroom to allow for expansion.

To prepare honey jelly, use 2 cups of homemade pectin to each 2½ cups of honey plus ½ cup of water. These amounts will vary a little when fruit juice is used, depending on the kind involved. Remember that the greater the quantity of pectin, the thicker the finished product and the weaker the other fruit's flavor.

Grape Jelly with Homemade Pectin

Blend the following:

2½ cups grape juice (unsweetened and, if possible, homemade)

½ cup honey

2 cups homemade pectin

Rapidly boil the mixture for ten minutes. To prevent its foaming over, stir the jelly but don't lower the heat.

Pour it immediately into hot, sterilized jelly jars. Seal them. Do not disturb the jars until the contents have partially set. To complete the jelling, refrigerate them.

Making Vinegar

In the presence of a particular kind of yeast, the action of oxygen upon a solution of alcohol produces vinegar. The alcoholic liquors from which vinegar can be made result from the fermentation of almost any fruit or vegetable juices. The chief types of vinegar are wine vinegar from grapes; malt vinegar from barley; cider vinegar from apples; sugar and molasses vinegar from sugar cane; beet vinegar; corn vinegar; etc.

Cider Vinegar

Put cider into a jug. For each quart of cider, add ½ cup of molasses and ¼ cup of brewer's yeast. Leave the container partially open to admit air. Fermentation will begin at once. The cider will become vinegar in about a week's time.

Pour off the clear vinegar into bottles and close tightly. To repeat the process, leave the lees (which provide the necessary yeast) in the jug and fill with fresh cider.

White Wine Vinegar

Crush 1 pound of clean raisins. Add ½ gallon of pure soft or distilled water and put in a l-gallon jug, uncovered. Allow to stand in a warm place. It will turn into white wine vinegar in about a month.

Strain the clear vinegar through cheesecloth. Leave the raisins and sediment in the jug. Add another ½ gallon of water along with ¼ pound of raisins to repeat the process.

Fruit Vinegar

The juice of most fruits, such as currants, gooseberries, and raspberries, contains enough sugar to ferment and produce an alcoholic liquor for making vinegar, with or without adding molasses.

To make vinegar from fruits, extract the juice by boiling the fruit with its equal in water. Press out the juice through several layers of cheesecloth. You can do this by inserting sticks at either end of the cloth and twisting them. To each 2 quarts of fruit juice, add ¼ cup of yeast. Allow to stand in a jar or jug with the top slightly tilted to admit air. Keep it in a spot where the temperature ranges between 70 and 80°F. Or you may let the boiled fruit juice stand for two or three days to ferment before straining it. Add the yeast after the fermented liquor has been removed from the fruit pulp.

Preparing Pickles

Pickling is the process of preserving foods with vinegar or brine. A variation of seasonings and spices results in spiced pickles, sour pickles, and sweet pickles.

Vegetables and fruits can be pickled sliced, quartered, in halves, or whole. The most commonly pickled foods are cabbage, carrots, cauliflower, cucumbers, beets, onions, tomatoes, crab apples, grapes, peaches, and pears.

Preparation of Food for Pickling

Scrub vegetables thoroughly in clear water. Next, soak them in salted water (from ⅛ to ¼ cup of salt for each quart of water) for a few hours or overnight. The salt extracts moisture from the tissues, crisping the vegetables so that they more readily soak up the pickling solution.

Fruits do not require a preliminary soaking in water and salt. Prepare them as you would for canning, and put them in the pickling solution.

Pickling Pointers

- Lift or stir pickles with a wooden or granite spoon.
- Cool pickles in an aluminum vessel or porcelain-lined graniteware.
- Keep in mind that too much salt will shrivel vegetables and make them tough.
- Vinegar that is too strong can bleach vegetables and cause them to soften after pickling.
- Seal pickles in stone or glass jars.

Bread-and-Butter Pickles

    8 cups sliced cucumbers
    1 tablespoon mustard seed
    5 cups sliced onions
    ½ cup finely chopped green
        pepper
    ½ teaspoon celery seed
    ¼ teaspoon turmeric
    ¼ cup salt
    ¼ teaspoon ginger
    1 quart water
    1½ cups vinegar
    2½ cups sugar
    1 cup water

Put cucumbers, onions, and green peppers in a big bowl.

Dissolve the salt in a quart of water, and pour it on the cucumber mixture. Cover. Allow to stand for four hours at room temperature.

Drain the bowl's contents. Place them in a 6-quart kettle.

Heat the rest of the ingredients in a saucepan to the boiling point, stirring until the sugar dissolves. Pour over the cucumber mixture. Heat to a boil.

Pack in sterilized jars to within ½ inch of the rim. Seal.

Process in boiling water for ten minutes.

Pumpkin Pickles

Cut a pumpkin rind into strips. Peel and cut them in 1-inch pieces. Prepare 4 cupfuls.

Combine the following in a saucepan:

    1 cup sugar
    6 whole cloves
    ¾ cup white vinegar
    2 teaspoons ginger, freshly
        grated
    ¼ cup dark corn syrup
    ½ cinnamon stick, crushed

Bring these ingredients to a boil, and add the pumpkin pieces. Slowly cook the mixture for about forty-five minutes or until tender.

Put the pickles in a quart jar; close it tightly. Store in the refrigerator.

Sauerkraut

    5 pounds cabbage
    5 tablespoons salt

Take off the outer leaves wash and put them aside and any imperfect parts of the cabbage. Quarter it, removing the core. Slice the cabbage finely with a slaw cutter or sharp

knife. Toss cabbage and salt in a large bowl, mixing well.

Solidly pack it into a 1- to 2-gallon crock. Allow to stand for a few minutes. Forcefully press on the cabbage with a wooden pestle (a wooden spoon will serve) until juice makes its appearance. Cover the top with the well- washed outer leaves of the cabbage; place several thicknesses of cheesecloth over them. Lay a plate on the cloth that fits snugly within the crock. To insure that the cabbage remains beneath the liquid and that the cloth stays wet, weight the dish. A heavy stone will do nicely. Let the crock stand in a warm place (65–68°F) to ferment for about four weeks. When choosing the spot, take into consideration that the contents will give off a very disagreeable odor during the initial stage of fermentation. Check the crock each day. Skim off scum. Remove the cloth cover, rinse in cold water, wring dry, and replace.

After four to five weeks, the sauerkraut is ready for use and should be stored in a cool (below 60°F but above 32°F), dark place. Keep the top covered to prevent air from entering. For canning, simmer kraut and juice in a large vessel to heat; avoid boiling. Pack into clean hot jars. Fill them with juice to within ½ inch of the rim. Seal and process.

Watermelon Pickles
General Rules

Cut watermelon rind in long strips. (Leaving on a little pink flesh lends

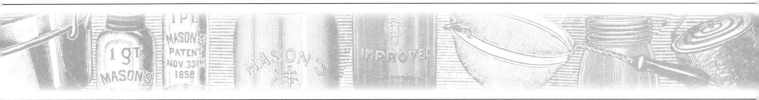

color to the finished product.) Peel them. Cut the rind into 1-inch chunks. Prepare 4 quarts.

In 2 quarts of cold water, dissolve 1 cup of salt. Drop in a few cherry or grape leaves to insure crisp pickles.

Pour this solution on the rind pieces, adding water, if necessary, to cover them. Allow to stand for six hours. (For a shorter soaking period, two to four hours, you may substitute 3 tablespoons of slaked lime for the salt and leaves. Check the bag's label to be sure the lime is intended for pickling.)

After the soaking period, rinse the rind thoroughly, and cover it with cold water. Cook the pieces until just tender. Drain.

Select your favorite watermelon pickle recipe, and tie the indicated spices in a bag of cheesecloth. Put it in a vessel with the rest of the ingredients mentioned in the recipe, except the rind, and simmer for ten minutes. Then add the rind pieces, and simmer them until they become transparent. Should the syrup get too thick, thin it with boiling water.

When the rinds are clear, take out the spice bag. Refrigerate smaller amounts to be used right away. Pack the remainder of the boiling-hot pickles with their syrup into sterilized jars to within ⅛ inch of the rims. Close tightly. Pumpkin, winter squash, and cantaloupe rind can be pickled in the same manner.

Ingredients for Spicy Watermelon Pickles
- 1 tablespoon salt
- 1 teaspoon whole cloves
- 1 teaspoon celery seed (Do not put this ingredient in the cheesecloth bag)
- 9 cups sugar
- 2 quarts vinegar

Ingredients for Lemony Watermelon Pickles
- 2 tablespoons whole cloves
- 1 thinly sliced lemon
- 8 cups sugar
- 3 sticks cinnamon
- 1 quart white vinegar
- 2 pieces ginger root
- 1 quart water

Zucchini Pickles
Yield: 6–7 pints
- 5 pounds squash
- 1 quart white vinegar
- 4 to 5 medium onions
- 2 cups sugar
- 8 cloves
- 1 cinnamon stick
- 1 dried red pepper
- ¼ cup salt
- 2 teaspoons ground turmeric
- 2 teaspoons celery seed
- 1 teaspoon dry mustard

Cut the unpeeled zucchini into ¼-inch slices. Thinly slice the onions, enough to make 1 quart. Mix the squash and onions in a big bowl.

Combine the remaining ingredients in a saucepan, mixing them well. Bring to a boil. Pour the bubbling liquid on the vegetables in the bowl. Leave it for one hour; stir now and then.

Now put the bowl's contents into a vessel. Bring to a boil; simmer for three minutes. Then let the simmering continue as you quickly fill hot sterilized jars to within ½ inch of the rim. Be sure that the zucchini and onion mixture is completely covered by the vinegar solution.

Spiced Crab Apples
Yield: 6 pints

    4 quarts crab apples
    2 sticks cinnamon
    5 cups brown sugar
    1 tablespoon whole allspice
    2 cups vinegar
    1 tablespoon whole cloves

Wash the crab apples, but do not pare them. Prick their skin a few times with the tines of a fork. Remove the blossom ends. Mix the remaining ingredients, and simmer them for twenty minutes. Add several apples at a time; simmer until tender.

Put the apples in hot sterilized jars and cover with syrup.

Seal.

For spicier apples, include a bit of ginger root and one blade of mace with the other spices when preparing the syrup.

Strain the leftover syrup to pour on vanilla ice cream.

Pickled Prunes

    1 pound prunes
    2 cups light brown sugar
    1 lemon
    1 cup tarragon vinegar

Soak the prunes overnight. The following morning, simmer them until plump and tender in just enough water to cover. Add the remaining ingredients, except the red pepper. Cook until glossy; then put in the dried pepper.

Seal the prunes in a 1-quart jar.

Chow Chow
Yield: 9–10 pints

    1 peck (12½ pounds) green
        tomatoes
    1 tablespoon cinnamon
    8 large onions
    1 tablespoon allspice
    10 green bell peppers
    ¼ teaspoon cloves
    3 tablespoons salt
    3 tablespoons mustard
    6 hot peppers, chopped
    several bay leaves
    1¾ cups sugar
    1 quart vinegar
    ½ cup horseradish

Chop tomatoes, onions, and green peppers. Mix them in a bowl and cover with the salt. Allow to stand overnight.

Drain the mixture, and add the hot peppers (chopped), vinegar, and spices tied in a bag of cheesecloth. Bring the ingredients to a boil.

Pack the chow chow in clean jars and process for fifteen minutes.

Making Mincemeat

Apricot Mincemeat
Yield: 3 quarts

Coarsely grind the following, even the sugar, if need be:

    1 pound dried apricots, soaked
        overnight
    1 pound apples, peeled, cored,
        and chopped
    1 pound pitted dates
    1 pound seedless raisins
    1 pound currants
    2 cups brown sugar
    2 cups suet
    ¼ cup almonds

Add to these ingredients the juice and rind of one lemon and 2 tablespoons of grated nutmeg. Use at once, or can at ten pounds pressure for ten minutes.

Green Tomato Mincemeat

    1 peck green tomatoes, finely
        chopped
    1 tablespoon salt
    ½ peck apples, finely chopped
    2 pounds raisins
    4 pounds brown sugar
    2 tablespoons cinnamon
    1 cup weak vinegar

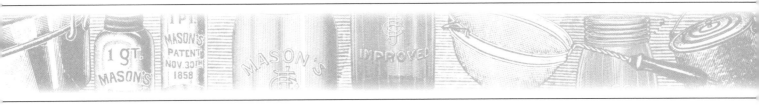

2 tablespoons cloves

1 cup suet, finely chopped

1 tablespoon nutmeg

Put the finely chopped tomatoes in a large vessel. Cover the contents with cold water; add salt. Heat to boiling. Drain. Cover with cold water; heat to boiling. Repeat the procedure a third time, cooking the tomatoes until tender. Drain.

Add the remaining ingredients. Cook them gently. Once the apples are tender, fill sterilized jars with the mincemeat. Seal at once.

Traditional Mincemeat

4 pounds lean beef, chopped

2 pounds beef suet; chopped

1 peck sour apples, peeled, cored, and sliced

3 pounds sugar

2 quarts cider

4 pounds seeded raisins

5 pounds currants

1½ pounds citron, chopped

½ pound dried orange peel, chopped

½ pound dried lemon peel, chopped

1 lemon, juice and rind

1 tablespoon cinnamon

1 tablespoon mace

1 tablespoon cloves

1 teaspoon pepper

1 teaspoon salt

2 whole nutmegs, grated

1 gallon sour cherries and their juice

2 pounds broken nut meats (if desired)

Slowly cook these ingredients for two hours. Stir them often.

Fill sterilized jars. Seal.

Making Catsup

Apple Catsup

½ bushel sour apples

1 cup sugar

1 teaspoon pepper

1 teaspoon cloves

1 teaspoon mustard

2 teaspoons cinnamon

1 tablespoon salt

2 onions, finely chopped

2 cups cider vinegar

Wash, quarter, pare, and core the apples. Put the apple pieces in a vessel, and cover them with boiling water. Bring to the boiling point, and then simmer the fruit until soft; by this time almost all the water should have evaporated.

Rub the vessel's contents through a sieve, making 4 cups of pulp. Combine the remaining ingredients and add them to the pulp. Bring the mixture to the boiling point and simmer for sixty minutes.

Bottle and seal the apple catsup while it is hot.

Grape Catsup

20 pounds grapes

5 pounds sugar

2 quarts vinegar

1 tablespoon cinnamon

1 tablespoon allspice

2 tablespoons cloves

1 grated nutmeg

Wash grapes and remove their stems. Barely cover the fruit with cold water, bring to the boiling point, and simmer until softened. Press it through a sieve; discard seeds and skins.

Put 10 pounds of grape pulp and the other ingredients into a kettle. Bring to the boiling point; simmer until the consistency of catsup is reached.

Fill and seal bottles.

Raspberry Catsup

4 quarts ripe raspberries

4 cups cider vinegar

½ teaspoon white mustard seeds

1 slice ginger root

1 cinnamon stick, in pieces

6 cloves

2 cups sugar

Put the fruit and vinegar in an enameled pot. Simmer gently for sixty minutes. Strain through a fine sieve, pressing the pulp through with the back of a wooden spoon.

Rinse out the pot, and return the puree to it, adding mustard seeds and spices. Cook slowly for twenty-five minutes. Again strain and then measure.

To each quart of berry puree, add 2 cups of sugar. Simmer over a low fire, stirring continuously until the mixture is thick and smooth.

When the raspberry catsup is cool, bottle it.

Tomato Catsup
Yield: about 1 quart

¼ cup cider vinegar
6 large ripe tomatoes (red)
1 3-inch cinnamon stick (broken in small pieces)
½ cup water
¼ cup minced onion
½ teaspoon whole cloves
3 tablespoons sugar
1 teaspoon salt
½ teaspoon celery seed
dash cayenne pepper

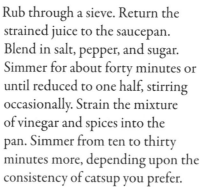

Put the first four ingredients into a saucepan. Boil for one minute. Take from the heat and pour into a container.

Cut tomatoes into quarters, after removing their stems, and place them in the saucepan. Add the onion and water. Heat to the boiling point, using a wooden spoon to stir and mash the tomatoes. Reduce the heat. Simmer about twenty minutes, stirring now and then to avoid sticking.

Rub through a sieve. Return the strained juice to the saucepan. Blend in salt, pepper, and sugar. Simmer for about forty minutes or until reduced to one half, stirring occasionally. Strain the mixture of vinegar and spices into the pan. Simmer from ten to thirty minutes more, depending upon the consistency of catsup you prefer.

Take from the stove and cool. Fill a clean container with the catsup, closing it tightly. Store in the refrigerator.

Making Soy Sauce

Prepare soy sauce in autumn after the soybeans have been harvested. Boil them, using any preferred amount, until thoroughly cooked. Put the hot, wet beans through a meat grinder having very fine cutters. Keep the liquid along with the mash. Form the wet pulp into a cone shaped like an inverted flowerpot.

Spread a clean, white towel over a window screen (or fruit-drying rack), and place the mass on it to dry. During this time, any excess juice will leach out.

Lay down two strips of unbleached muslin, about 6 inches wide and 2 feet long, so that they bisect each other. When the cone has dried to a rather hard consistency, set it where the cloth strips meet. Bring up their ends, tie them together, and suspend the bean mass in a warm place while fermentation begins. After several weeks, take it down and put it in a cotton or muslin bag. Store the package in a warm spot through the winter. To avoid damage by insects or mice, it may be hung from a hook.

In spring, break the bean mass into a few chunks; put them in an earthenware crock. Fill it with water, and add salt to taste plus several lumps of charcoal, which will absorb gas and any impurities. (Activated charcoal can be purchased from chemical supply houses or wherever water treatment products are sold.) Set the crock in the sun for a few days to encourage further ripening of the contents. The water will turn black, and moldy pieces of the soybean mass will rise to the surface.

When the few days are up, ladle the liquid into a pot, adding a little garlic. Boil it, skimming off the scum during cooking. Once the liquid becomes sufficiently concentrated, cool, bottle, and store your patiently awaited soy sauce.

16 | FROM THE DRY HOUSE

Drying Foods

Drying vegetables, fruits, and herbs is the cheapest way of preserving food. It also requires little space and fills some needs more readily than frozen or canned foods.

A few generations ago, drying herbs, fruits, and vegetables was a standard way of keeping edibles. Metal racks 3 feet square and equipped with tiers of trays were used for drying sweet corn. The trays could be rotated from top to bottom, hastening the drying process. Corn cut from the cob was spread evenly and thinly on a cloth to prevent the kernels from slipping through the slatted trays. The bottom tray was about 10 inches above a fire or stove, which was used to enhance drying during rainy periods. The procedure was usually carried out in the kitchen or smokehouse. In dry weather, foods were spread or hung outdoors. Pumpkins were cut in circles and the rings hung on stretched lines. Sometimes they were cut in strips and strung on heavy twine. Green beans, snapped into pieces and strung on twine, were called "leather breeches." Folks often constructed small buildings designed for drying fruits. Known as "dry houses," they contained slatted trays attached to the walls, with a small stove for heating the interior.

Sun-Drying Method

Sun drying requires time and care. Spread foods on trays, cookie sheets, cake pans, wire racks, or butcher paper; space the pieces for air circulation. Shield them from insects with cheesecloth or wire screening. Most vegetables require about two days to dry properly. Foods should be stirred and inspected frequently during the process. They must be brought in from rain and night dew.

Here are ways to successfully dehydrate certain foods by sun drying them:

Cabbage

Select well-developed heads. Remove the outer leaves. Cut the cabbage in ¼-inch-thick strips. Spread them on trays. For 1 pound of dried cabbage, you will need 18 pounds of fresh.

Corn

Choose corn at its sweet, best-eating stage. Discard the husks. Blanch the vegetable for three to five minutes in boiling water. Cool rapidly in cold water. Remove the kernels from the cob. Spread them on trays to dry in the sun.

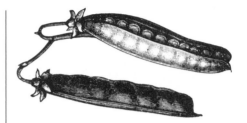

Peas

Pick peas in their ripe stage, not too old or too immature. Shell them. Spread the peas on trays placed in the sun for thorough drying. Approximately 3½ pounds of fresh peas make 1 pound of dried.

Pumpkin and Squash

Cut pumpkin and squash into slices ½ inch thick. Since they keep well without processing, you may not want to bother with drying them. However, it's a long time between autumn harvests.

Tomatoes

Bright sunlight is essential for drying tomatoes. Slice them thickly, and spread them on drying trays. To prevent mold from developing, turn them now and then. When leathery dry they can be packed in containers. Sprinkle a bit of salt between each layer.

Storing Sun-Dried Foods

Store dried foods only after they are completely cool.

Package them in plastic or paper bags, and close them securely. Put the bags in insect- and rodent-proof containers. Store them where it is cool and dry. If you live in a humid climate, store them in glass jars. You may keep dried foods in your freezer, particularly if insects are a problem.

Reconstituting Dried Vegetables for Cooking

Prepare dried vegetables for cooking by first soaking them; onions, cabbage, and finely chopped peppers are the exceptions.

To each cupful of cabbage, add about 7 cups of water.

Slowly bring to a boil in an uncovered vessel and boil for thirty minutes. Add salt and preferred seasonings. Dried cabbage in chicken or beef stock with a dollop of margarine makes a hearty, delicious soup.

Corn requires a preliminary soaking of two to four hours.

For 1 cup of corn, use 2 cups of water.

Peas should be soaked for about twenty-four hours. Pumpkins and squash need soaking overnight. Add 10 pints of water to 1 pound. They are then ready for use in breads, cookies, pies, or in any recipe calling for the canned or fresh kinds.

Tomatoes need a period of twenty-four hours or more for softening. Before soaking them, rinse them a few times under cold water to remove any excess salt.

All of these dried vegetables make excellent casserole dishes, either in combination or separately.

Oven-Drying Method

If your area lacks fairly long periods of steady, hot sun, prepare foods by the oven-drying method.

Meticulously pick over all foods to remove blemishes.

Blanch vegetables before drying them. To avoid vitamin loss, blanch by steaming rather than boiling. Use disease-free herbs, and select fruits at their ripest stage when sugar content is highest. Prevent discoloration by treating fruits with ascorbic acid solution.

Spread the food evenly on cookie sheets. Dry them in the oven for twelve to twenty-four hours. (Corn may require more than twenty-four hours.) Use an oven thermometer to maintain the temperature between 90° and 115°F. Do not allow the temperature to exceed 120°F. Stir the food from time to time with a spatula. Turn the pieces over, and transfer those in the center to the outside edges. When done, vegetables should be brittle; the fruit, leathery.

Here are ways to successfully dehydrate certain foods by oven drying them:

Carrots

Wash carrots well. Leave them whole and steam for twenty minutes. Lay them on paper towels to dry. Peel and cut them in slices ⅛ inch thick. Spread the carrots on a cookie sheet. Dry them in the oven until brittle and a deep orange. Don't let the temperature exceed 120°F.

Corn

To avoid the necessity of soaking dried corn prior to cooking it,

use this old-time recipe for oven drying the vegetable: Cut enough sweet corn from the cob to equal 16 cupfuls. (Speed the operation by utilizing this handy implement: Take a metal shoehorn and keenly sharpen its wide end. The curve of the shoehorn conforms to the shape of the cob so that its sharpened edge can speedily slice off kernels to just the right depth and over a wider area than a knife.)

Put 4 ounces of cream, 6 tablespoons of sugar, and 4 teaspoons of coarse canning salt into a kettle; add the unblanched corn. Boil these ingredients for twenty minutes. Stir continuously to prevent sticking.

Remove the mixture from the stove, and spread it on shallow pans. Put the corn in an oven set at its lowest temperature. Stir frequently.

Once the corn is dry and somewhat crisp, transfer it to clean paper bags. Close the bags securely, and hang them in a dry place to finish the dehydration process. When the kernels rattle in the bags, they are ready to be stored in tightly closed jars.

At serving time, no presoaking is necessary. Heat the vegetable, using a small amount of milk rather than water to enhance its flavor.

Onions

Onions do not require steam blanching. Peel them and slice thinly. Separate the rings, and spread them on a cookie sheet.

Dry in the oven until very crisp at no more than 120°F. Crumble the onions, and put them in airtight containers.

Grapes (Raisins)

Wash grapes; stem them. Lower them in a colander into briskly boiling water just long enough to split their skins. Spread on paper towels to dry. Place on a cookie sheet in an oven set no higher than 120°F. Remove when pliable.

Apples

Pare and core tart cooking apples. Slice them ¼ inch thick. For each 5 quarts of sliced fruit, mix 2½ teaspoons of ascorbic acid in 1 cup of water. Sprinkle this over the fruit slices, completely coating each piece. Spread on a cookie sheet and dry at a temperature not exceeding 120°F. Remove from the oven when springy and pliable.

Herbs

Collect herb leaves for drying just before the plant blooms. Wash the leaves quickly in cold water. Using paper towels, blot them dry. Remove the leaves from the upper two-thirds of the plant. Spread on a cookie sheet. Dry them at an oven temperature not exceeding 120°F. To check to see if they're done, pinch the leaves. If they are brittle and crumble, take them from the oven.

To dry the seeds of herbs, pick the whole plant. Put it upside down in a paper bag. Make holes at the top of the bag to allow air circulation, and hang it up. As the flower heads dry, the seeds will fall into the bag.

Put the seeds in airtight containers. Store them in a dry, dark, cool place.

Storing Oven-Dried Foods

Allow the foods to stand for complete cooling. Then store them in airtight containers. Keep them in a cool, dark, dry place.

17 | MEAT, FOWL, AND FISH

Smoking Meat, Fowl, and Fish

Smoking meat, fowl, and fish converts them into food with a special taste and texture, appealing to the most discriminating gourmet.

The process is a slow one and requires a smoker. Small-scale smokers can be purchased in hardware stores or made at home. Use a semi-enclosed box with some sort of heating element in the bottom, such as a hot plate, to support a pan of wood chips. The chips should be slowly heated and a temperature maintained somewhere between 150° and 200°F, 190°F being considered most favorable. Do not use chips from the wood of evergreen trees. Hardwood chips, such as hickory, keep the flames down and generate more smoke. Soak the chips in water for thirty minutes before use. Dried corncobs can substitute for the chips. As the wood chips smolder, the food gradually absorbs the smoke, which imparts a delectable flavor. Heat and smoke can be controlled by some kind of adjustable vents. To maintain steady temperature, use an oven thermometer. A meat thermometer will help you determine when the meat is done.

Smoked Roasts (Beef, Lamb, or Pork)

The smoker should be preheated to 225°F. Rub the roast with a mixture of salt and your favorite spices, or with seasoned salt alone. Insert a meat thermometer in the middle, away from bone and fat. Smoking time will depend on the size of the roast. Be sure that pork attains an internal temperature of at least 170°F.

Smoked Ribs or Chops

Trim fat from the ribs or chops, and rub them with seasoned salt. Hang the meat or lay it on racks in the smoker. Smoke for about two hours at 80 to 85°F. Slowly raise the temperature to 250°F and smoke for an additional thirty to forty-five minutes. The meat is done when it begins to fall from the bone. During the last fifteen minutes of cooking, baste the ribs or chops with barbecue sauce, if desired.

Smoked Sausage

Any sausage can be smoked; smoking will flavor the meat, not cook it.

Suspend uncooked sausages from hooks in the smoker.

Smoke from one to two hours at 70°F. Then cook according to the recipe.

Put bulk sausage in loaf pans in the middle of the smoker rack. Smoke from one to two hours at 70°F. Then cook according to the recipe.

Jerky
Yield: 1 pound
    4 pounds lean beef
    2 tablespoons lemon juice
    ⅓ cup soy sauce
    3 tablespoons vinegar
    1 teaspoon onion powder
    2 tablespoons sugar
    1 teaspoon seasoned salt

Select very lean meat for making jerky, and carefully trim away any fat. Partially freeze the meat. Cut it (across the grain for flank steak) in very thin slices.

For mild-flavored jerky, sprinkle one teaspoon of pepper and one teaspoon of seasoned salt for each pound of meat.

Smoke it immediately. For a stronger flavor, blend all the other ingredients, and marinate the meat in this mixture either for a few hours or overnight, keeping it in the refrigerator. Turn the meat a few times.

Thoroughly drain the meat, and arrange it on greased racks that are slightly separated to permit circulation of air. Smoke it until brittle and dry for approximately twenty-four hours at 85 to 90°F.

Smoking Pork in a Smokehouse

Preliminary Preparation
Each cut of pork may be wrapped in cheesecloth to protect it from soot, but this measure is not essential. Run wire or string through the meat, and loop it around cross poles in the smokehouse. Hang hams with the hock downward in order to retain juices. Allow free circulation of smoke to all areas of the meat by spacing the pieces.

Fuel
The ideal smoking temperature ranges between 110° and 120° F. Sawdust, chips, or small pieces of wood from alder, apple, beech,

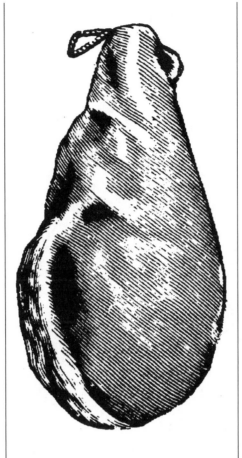

hickory, maple, or oak make good fuel. The wood of all nut and fruit trees is suitable, as are corncobs. Never use resinous wood. Since smoke, not heat, is desired, keep the lit fuel smoldering by lightly sprinkling it with water whenever it flares up.

Smoking Time
The longer the smoking period the better. During prolonged smoking the meat dries slowly, and the acid of the smoke permeates each piece. Quick smoking affects only the ham's exterior; the smoke's acid coats it but does not penetrate its fiber.

Hams may be smoked either for eight to ten hours or for a few weeks, depending on the quality desired. Generally, hams are satisfactory in about five days, bacon in three.

Smoking time can be determined by color. Meat that is mahogany-colored all over, either light or dark in hue, may be removed from the smokehouse. The darker the meat, the longer it will keep.

Storing
Wrap the meat pieces in cheesecloth and then newspaper. Place them in paper bags, tied closed. Store the smoked meat in a cool (43°F), dry place.

Smoked Fowl
Small game birds ducks, pheasants, and quail can be successfully smoked. Smoking will render them tender and succulent. The average pheasant requires about ten hours of cooking time, perhaps a bit longer. You will need to add wood chips three or four times during this period. Smoke should trickle constantly through the vents. If you prefer a heavy smoked flavor, continuously add wood chips to the pan; for moderate flavor, a handful now and then is sufficient.

Some game birds can be put directly into the smoker.

However, for the best results, brine them first. This applies as well to domestic chickens. Place the bird to be smoked in a glass or crockery vessel.

over low heat. Let the mixture cool. Leave the bird whole, or cut it in pieces. Marinate it in the refrigerator for at least eight hours, turning it several times.

When readying a bird for smoking, don't discard the giblets. They can be put to good use as tasty snacks. Prepare livers for smoking by putting them into boiling water and cooking them until all redness disappears. Drain and smoke. Hearts and gizzards do not require this preliminary boiling. Coat the gizzards, hearts, and cooked livers by shaking them in a plastic bag containing a mixture of the following seasonings: pepper, table salt, sugar, and garlic salt. Put the giblets on the racks inside the smoker for forty-five minutes to one hour at 80°F. Then raise the temperature to 225 or 250°F for thirty to sixty minutes more.

Take out the giblets; put them in a jar, adding a little vegetable oil. Roll them about in the jar until well coated. Keep the jar refrigerated for twenty-four hours to insure the best flavor.

Smoked Fish

For mildly salty, spiced fish, marinate for several hours; for more spiciness, let it stand in the marinade for at least six hours or overnight.

    lemon slices or grated lemon peel
    10 fish fillets of firm flesh
    ½ cup sugar
    1 quart water
    ½ cup salt

Cover it with water. For every 4 quarts of water, put in 4 cups of cider, several dashes of lemon juice, ¼ teaspoon of maple flavoring, 1½ cups of curing salt, ½ teaspoon of ginger, ½ cup of brown sugar, and 3 tablespoons of pepper. You can either cold soak the bird overnight in this brine or simmer it in the solution for approximately five minutes. When it is ready for smoking, dry it in the air for an hour, or wipe it with a towel. Combine brown sugar, garlic powder, and black pepper. Rub the bird generously with this mixture.

Thread a long, heavy string through the body, and truss up the legs, using the excess string to hang the bird in the smoker. Maintain the temperature as close to 190°F as possible. For each pound of bird, allow one and a half hours of cooking time. To determine how well it's done, twist a leg. If it moves easily, the bird is ready for eating.

You might like to give the brine an Asian flavor. Mix ⅓ cup of soy sauce, ⅓ cup of sherry, ⅓ cup of water, ¼ cup of honey, and ½ teaspoon of powdered ginger, all

one or two of these seasonings:
    garlic or onion salt
    black or white pepper
    leaves of bay, dill, or
      tarragon
    ground mace or ginger
    hot pepper sauce or
    dried red pepper flakes
    lemon slices or grated
      lemon peel

Mix the water, sugar, salt, and seasonings in a bowl until the salt and sugar dissolve. Put in the fish. Cover. Then weight the cover down to keep them beneath the brine. Refrigerate the fish either for a few hours or overnight.

Drain the fillets, and thoroughly rinse them in cold water.

Pat dry with paper towels and place on a wire rack to dry in the air for thirty minutes to one hour. Grease the smoker racks, and lay the fish on them, skin down, spaced for air circulation. Smoking should begin at 90°F. After fifteen minutes, slowly raise the heat to 135 to 140°F and smoke for one to two hours.

When the fillets are golden brown and flake at the touch of a fork, they are ready to be eaten;

or they can be tightly wrapped and stored in the freezer.

Smoked Oysters

Shuck and wash oysters. Mix 1¼ pounds of salt in 1 gallon of water. Soak the oysters in this brine for five minutes.

Drain them well. Lightly coat the oysters with salad oil.

Lay them on a well-greased rack wide enough apart to permit air circulation. A wire cake rack may be used if the spaces of the smoker rack are too wide. Smoke the oysters for fifteen minutes at 180°F.

If they are not eaten immediately, they can be refrigerated for a few days. They will last for two months when stored in containers in the freezer.

Sausage Making

Sausage comes from the Latin word *salsus*, meaning "salted;" that is, preserved meat. Here is the general procedure for making sausage.

Divide in half the amount of meat required for the recipe you have chosen. Put 3 rounded tablespoons of it in a blender, adding 1 tablespoon of crushed ice. Cover and liquefy at high speed for five seconds. Shut off the blender, uncover it, and move the meat to the blades, using a rubber spatula. Blend five seconds more. Turn off the blender, again moving the meat to the blades if need be, and add a little more ice. Blend five seconds more or until the contents have a peanut butter-like consistency. With the spatula, scoop the meat into a large bowl. Repeat this procedure until you have smoothly blended half of the meat. While allowing the blender to cool, measure all other ingredients into the bowl with the already processed meat. Now process the rest of the meat in your blender, and mix it thoroughly with all the ingredients in the bowl. Use your hands or a spoon (you may also find a potato masher handy for this) to insure that the seasonings are evenly blended.

Tie the end of a sausage casing with a string, and firmly pack in the meat. (Buy synthetic casings. They are easily stored and cannot spoil. The size generally preferred is 24 inches in length and 6 inches in diameter.)

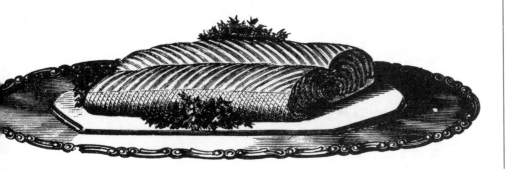

Try to squeeze out as much air as possible as you work. Tie the tip close to the meat, and snip off the casing. Cook according to the recipe you have selected. Or, if the recipe indicates, put the mixture into a loaf pan instead of casings and cook as directed.

Pork Sausage

12½ pounds fresh pork (approximately 11 pounds lean meat and 1½ pounds fat)
¼ cup salt
¼ cup brown sugar, firmly packed
1½ tablespoons sage
1 tablespoon black pepper
1 tablespoon red pepper

Trim away excess fat from the pork. Cut the meat into 2-inch cubes. Spread them on a piece of waxed paper. Blend the remaining ingredients, and sprinkle the mixture over the meat. Grind the seasoned meat twice in a meat grinder, and thoroughly mix it with your hands to help distribute the seasonings and fat. Stuff into casings.

Canned Pork Sausage

Shape the pork sausage into small patties. Bake them for twenty-five to thirty minutes at 350°F.

Then place them in quart jars. Pour in their juice to cover.

Seal the jars and process for fifteen minutes at ten pounds pressure.

Grandma's Cracklings Sausage

The crisp bits of skin and meat remaining after hog fat has been rendered are called cracklings. Grandmother used them as an ingredient in homemade sausage, that is, if she could keep the family from pilfering too many of those crunchy snacks right from the kettle.

Here is her recipe: With each cup of cracklings, mix 1 cup of grated potato. Season the mixture with salt, pepper, and grated onion to taste, adding any preferred herbs. Grandma favored marjoram and thyme.

When well mixed, the blend should be put in bread pans and baked for one hour at 350°F. Then cool and chill it.

To serve, cut the sausage in slices, and fry them for an old-time country breakfast.

Bologna (Fine-Cut Sausage)

3 pounds ground beef (75% lean)
2 pounds ground pork
1 tray ice cubes, crushed
1 cup instant powdered milk
3 tablespoons salt
1 tablespoon white pepper
1½ teaspoons ground coriander
1½ teaspoons ground cardamom
1 teaspoon dried sage
¾ teaspoon ground allspice
¾ teaspoon ground mace
1½ teaspoons sugar

Heat the oven to 275°F. Follow the general rules for preparing the meat mixture as already described. Pack the mixture into the casings, tying and cutting them.

Firmly press each stuffed casing into a loaf pan. If the casings fail to fit snugly against the ends of the pan, fill any empty spaces with wadded aluminum foil to keep the sausages tightly in place. Insert a thermometer in the middle of one. Place the pan in the center of the oven. Bake for two hours or until 160°F registers on the thermometer.

Take the meat from the oven. Remove the thermometer.

Allow cold water to run over the sausages for several minutes to cool them. Refrigerate them until serving time.

Braunschweiger
Yield: 1½ pounds

½ pound ground pork liver
½ pound ground pork
½ pound ground beef
1 medium-sized onion, minced
2 tablespoons powdered milk
½ teaspoon sugar
½ teaspoon pepper
¼ teaspoon ground cardamom
¼ teaspoon ground mace
¼ teaspoon margarine or butter
1 teaspoon salt

When grinding your own meat, use the grinder's fine cutter. If you have your butcher do the job, ask to have all the meats ground together twice.

Heat the oven to 275°F. Follow the general rules for preparing the meat mixture as described previously. Use less seasoning rather than a generous amount. Check the flavor of your sausage meat just before filling the casings by frying well 1 tablespoon of it. Add more seasonings if you find it too bland. Pack the meat into a loaf pan. Place a piece of waxed paper over it, and press down firmly and evenly. Remove the paper, and insert a thermometer in the middle of the mixture.

Set the loaf pan in a larger baking pan in the center of the oven. Fill the larger container with water

to a one-inch depth. Now and then check to see that the water does not boil. If it does, lower the temperature. Bake for one to one and a half hours or until the thermometer reaches 160°F.

Take the loaf out of the oven, and remove the thermometer. Place the pan in a container or sink of ice. Cool it rapidly, and put it in the refrigerator until serving time.

To store the Braunschweiger, remove it from the pan, wrap it in foil or transparent wrap, and keep it in the refrigerator, where it will remain edible for one week. It will keep in the freezer for six months.

Venison Sausage

When making venison sausage, first weigh the venison to determine the amount of pork required. Use two parts venison to one part pork.

The pork will compensate for lost venison fat (which many people dislike), keeping the sausage moist and imparting a pleasant flavor. Your butcher can supply you with pork trimmings, a combination of fat and pork meat, and with casings, if you intend to make link sausage.

After mixing the venison and pork, grind the meat twice to insure a good blend. A hand grinder is adequate unless you are processing more than 100 pounds, in which case a power grinder is practical.

Spread the ground meat on a table or countertop, and flatten it into an immense meat patty, some 4 inches thick. Sprinkle it with 1 tablespoon of black pepper and 2 tablespoons of salt (or garlic salt) for each 5 pounds of meat. If you prefer hot sausage, add 1 tablespoon of chili pequins (very small red peppers), dried and crushed.

Roll the meat into logs, 3 inches thick and 1 foot long.

Wrap them well; freeze for future use.

Bulk sausage may be cooked by cutting it into ½-inch-thick patties and frying them, seven minutes to a side, in an ungreased skillet.

To make link sausage, prepare the casings. Soak them for five minutes in warm water and rinse; turn them inside out and repeat the soaking and rinsing.

Attach the stuffer spout. Gather up a casing (as you would when putting on a sock), and slip it on the spout.

Approximately 3 inches of casing should extend from the spout

opening. Tie the lower end of the casing with a string. When 3 to 4 feet have been stuffed, tie the filled casing in individual sausages, using strong cotton cord. Cut the casing in lengths of 24 inches. Tie the ends of each 2-foot length together so that it resembles a loop.

You can broil or barbecue the venison sausage, fifteen minutes to a side. It can also be boiled for twenty to thirty minutes or fried. Before serving the sausage, prick the casings to release pressurized juices.

If smoked meat is desired, keep it in the smokehouse for twenty-four to forty-eight hours. Smoking should be done only in cold weather. Cook the sausage thoroughly before serving it.

Curing Pork

Methods

Meat can be cured by two methods: the wet cure involves immersing the meat in brine; the dry cure entails rubbing the meat with a salt mixture. The wet method is often preferred for smaller cuts, the dry cure for larger pieces.

Whichever method is followed, each piece of meat must first be weighed, rubbed with fine salt, and allowed to drain, flesh side lowermost, for six to twelve hours.

Procedure for Wet-Curing Pork

Pack the meat in earthen or glass crocks (never use metal with brine); fill them up with water. Take out the meat, and empty the water into a vessel. For each 100 pounds of pork, assemble the following: 9 pounds of medium-grain salt (10 pounds in warm weather); 4 pounds of unsulphured molasses (you may substitute 4 pounds of maple syrup or 2½ pounds of brown sugar for the molasses); and 2 ounces of saltpeter. Add these preserving ingredients to the vessel of water, and stir with a wooden spoon.

Fill the crocks with pork, placing the largest pieces on the bottom. Cover them with the curing brine. Put lids on the crocks, and weigh each down with a stone or some heavy object to insure complete submersion of the meat. Store the crocks in a cool place.

Once a week, pour off the brine, remove the meat, and replace it, changing the position of the pieces. Return the brine to the crock. If scum develops on the brine's surface, empty the crocks and wash them and the pork thoroughly. Repack the meat in fresh brine, if possible. Otherwise, use the original solution by boiling it and skimming off impurities.

Curing Time

Large pieces of meat need four days in the curing solution per pound of pork. Smaller pieces require three days in the brine to each pound. Record on a chart the weight of each cut and its calculated date of removal.

When the meat is taken out, soak it in clean water for thirty minutes.

Procedure for Dry-Curing Pork

Thoroughly mix the following ingredients for each 100 pounds of meat:

6 pounds salt (In warm weather use 8 pounds)

2 pounds molasses, maple syrup, or brown sugar (if the salt content is increased, use 2½ pounds)

2 ounces saltpeter (found in drugstores or meat-packing plants)

5 ounces black pepper

To this blend you may add any preferred seasoning, such as pickling spices, sage, or savory.

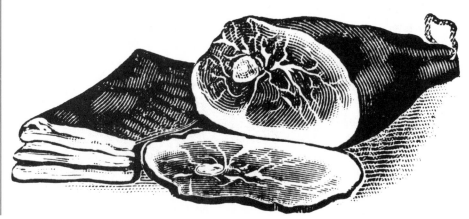

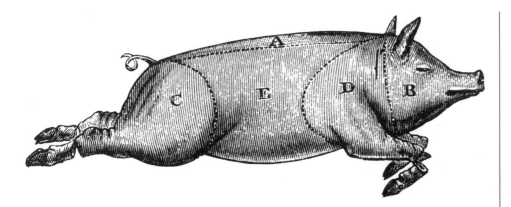

Using a kneading motion, rub the curing mixture on all meat surfaces. Work it in well around the bones.

Pack the pork in a crock (or barrel) with the larger pieces on the bottom, smaller ones on top. Remove the meat after several days, and repack it. This step insures that the cure completely coats all pieces.

Curing Time

The curing process will require two days per pound of each cut. Keep a chart of weights and the duration of curing periods for individual pieces.

Country Ham

1 ham (10–15 pounds)
4 quarts ginger ale

Place the ham in a very large pot of water heated to just below the boiling point. (If you lack a vessel of adequate size, use a clean lard can.) Allow to boil for ten to fifteen minutes. This will remove excess salt from the exterior of the ham. Take out the ham; discard the water.

Return the ham to the pot, and fill it to the halfway mark with hot water. Pour in 4 quarts of ginger ale and cover loosely. Bring to a rolling boil and continue boiling for thirty minutes. Ginger ale will develop the ham's flavor.

Lay down several thicknesses of newspaper; place the pot containing the ham on them. Cover the pot (or lard can) closely with its lid. Now bring the newspapers up and around the pot's sides and top, and bind them in place with twine. Cover with blankets and quilts. Allow to stand for ten to fourteen hours, depending on the size of ham. A 13-pound ham will need about ten hours.

Remove the skin and cut away fat. Serve your country ham baked or fried.

Country Ham and Grits with Red-Eye Gravy

Cut country ham in slices ¼ to ½ inch thick. To prevent curling, slit the fat around the edges. Cook the ham slices slowly in a heavy skillet, turning them a few times. When the ham is brown, add a little water and simmer for several minutes.

Take the ham from the skillet, and keep it warm.

Cook the gravy until it turns red. You may add a small amount of strong coffee to darken the color. Accompany your country ham with grits, serving red-eye gravy over both.

Corned Beef

Put 1 quart of water into an enamel pot with sufficient salt to enable an egg (still in its shell) to float. Remove the egg, and add a bay leaf, 8 peppercorns, and 2 tablespoons of pickling spice mix. Bring the contents of the vessel to a boil; then simmer for ten minutes. Let the liquid cool to room temperature.

Place a 4- to 6-pound beef brisket in a good-sized crock.

Pour the cooled brine into it. Cover the crock with foil topped by a weighted plate. Allow to stand for forty-eight hours. After that, wash the meat, and simmer it again for approximately three hours.

Bake the corned beef in a 300°F oven for one hour. Coat the cooked meat with a glaze of mustard and brown sugar. Serve warm or cold.

Hog Jowl and Black-Eyed Peas

Black-eyed peas are good any old time. But in Texas they are especially good on New Year's Day for luck. Including them in your dinner on the first of January is supposed to ensure a favorable year.

So, for good luck and good eating, prepare your black-eyed peas in this way:

½ pound hog jowl
¾ pound black-eyed peas
salt to taste
1 onion
1 or 2 jalapeno peppers

Cook the hog jowl until partially tender. Add the remaining ingredients. Slowly cook until the peas are just done, being careful not to overcook them.

Headcheese (Pork)

Scrape and clean a hog's head, washing it thoroughly.

Shove a hot poker into the nostrils and ears. Cover the head with lightly salted water in a large vessel. Put in onion and bay leaf. Simmer until the meat comes away from the bones, usually within several hours' time. Then drain the vessel's contents, saving a small amount of the liquid.

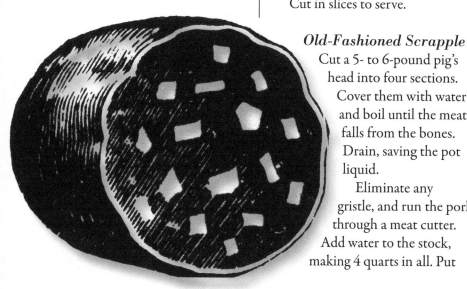

Remove all meat from the bones, discarding any gristle, and shred or chop it coarsely. Season it to taste with sage, thyme, salt, and pepper. Press the meat into a crock, and add a little of the pot liquid in which it was simmered. Cover the crock; place a weight on the lid. Allow to stand in a cold spot for three days.

When the headcheese has solidified, slice it for serving cold.

Headcheese (Veal)

Quarter a calf's head. Remove eyes, ears, brains, snout, and the greater part of the fat. Soak the four pieces in cold water to withdraw blood. Then put them in a kettle with enough cold water to cover and simmer until the meat separates from the bones.

Drain setting aside the liquid and dice the meat. Cover it with the stock, adding herbs, salt, and pepper. Cook for thirty minutes. Transfer to a mold. Cover with a cloth, putting a weight on top. Chill.

Cut in slices to serve.

Old-Fashioned Scrapple

Cut a 5- to 6-pound pig's head into four sections. Cover them with water and boil until the meat falls from the bones. Drain, saving the pot liquid.

Eliminate any gristle, and run the pork through a meat cutter. Add water to the stock, making 4 quarts in all. Put in the meat and sausage seasonings. Stir in enough cornmeal or buckwheat to give the consistency of mush. Let the mixture boil for several minutes.

Empty it into greased loaf pans to cool. Cut the scrapple in slices, and fry it without lard until crisp and brown.

Easy Scrapple

Make a thick porridge by cooking 1 cup of rolled oats in 2 cups of water. In another saucepan, cook 1 cup of cornmeal to like consistency in the same way. Then combine the two cereals. Mix in 1 pound of sausage meat plus some additional sausage seasoning.

Pack the blend into a crock and chill. When the scrapple is firm, slice and fry it thoroughly. Serve it plain, or trickle homemade maple syrup over the slices.

Aging Game

Aging tenderizes meat and improves its flavor. Hang game meat in a cool place, such as a garage or a basement, where the temperature remains in the low forties. Air must be kept circulating around the meat. To create this, hang a small electric fan close by.

Inspect the game two or three times each day. Check for souring, particularly in cracks and folds of the meat. If you detect a sour odor, trim off the area involved, and clean the place with a half-and-half solution of water and vinegar.

The length of aging time ranges from two to fourteen days, depending on personal preference; however, about five days generally suits the taste of most folks.

Venison Mincemeat

Make mincemeat of irregular venison cuts that are not suitable for any particular game recipe.

    3 cups venison, chopped fine or ground
    1 cup butter
    1 cup strong coffee
    9 cups apples, chopped fine or ground
    3 teaspoons salt
    2 teaspoons cinnamon
    3 cups each of raisins, sugar, cider, molasses
    1 teaspoon cloves
    1 teaspoon nutmeg

Blend all ingredients in a large pot. Bring to a boil. Then lower the heat, and simmer the mincemeat for four to five hours.

Put it into hot, sterilized jars. Seal and cool. Venison mincemeat may also be frozen.

Two Small-Game Recipes
Yield: 6 to 8 servings

    2 good-sized squirrels or 2 rabbits (even better, 1 of each)
    2 tablespoons butter
    1 large onion, chopped
    ½ pound smoked ham, diced
    2 quarts water
    1 teaspoon salt
    1 teaspoon pepper

Tie the following four ingredients in a cheesecloth bag:

    1 bay leaf
    1 celery top
    1 hot red pepper pod
    1 parsley sprig
    1 cup corn
    1 cup lima beans
    4 medium-sized potatoes, cubed
    1 cup sliced okra
    1 teaspoon soy sauce
    dash Tabasco sauce
    2 teaspoons Worcestershire sauce

Wash the game, and pat it dry with paper towels. Cut it into serving sizes. Melt the butter in a large stew pot, and cook the chopped onion. When they are soft, put in the meat. Fry it until brown, about three minutes on each side. Mix in the ham. Add the water, salt, and pepper, and the cheesecloth bag containing herbs and vegetables. Cover the pot. Simmer until the meat is tender, for approximately forty-five minutes to an hour, stirring occasionally.

Now put in the vegetables. They may be fresh, canned, or frozen. Fresh vegetables should be added in this order: corn, lima beans, potatoes. After twenty minutes add okra, soy, Tabasco, and Worcestershire sauces. Stir and cook until the potatoes are tender. Take out the cheesecloth bag. Do not add water; the stew should be very thick. It may be served over white rice.

    3–5 pounds small game meat
    ½ cup butter (or margarine)
    1 large garlic clove, minced
    1 large onion, chopped
    2 cups water
    1 teaspoon sweet basil
    1 cup white wine
    1 28-ounce can whole tomatoes
    2 cups chicken stock or broth
    salt and pepper to taste

Cut the meat into serving pieces; sprinkle it with salt and pepper to taste. Melt the butter in a pot, and brown the meat with garlic and onion. After the meat is nicely browned and the chopped onion is tender, add the white wine, basil, tomatoes and their liquid, chicken stock, and water. Cover. Simmer until the meat is tender, from forty-five to ninety minutes.

During the last twenty to forty-five minutes, put in any desired vegetables, and cook them for the required amount of time, adding liquid if necessary.

How to Pluck a Duck

For a fast, clean duck-plucking job, follow these steps:

In a bucket of boiling water, melt 1 pound of paraffin wax. Fill a second bucket with ice-cold water.

Cut off the feet and wings of the duck. Use the head as a handle.

Remove the roughest feathers from back and breast. This job should take no more than one minute.

Grasping the head, plunge the body to the bottom of the bucket of hot water and pull it out through the film of wax on the water's surface. Repeat this procedure a total of three times to thoroughly coat the duck.

Immerse the bird in the bucket of cold water to set the wax. Take it from the water to let the wax harden completely in some cool place. When properly hardened, the wax coating should feel cold to the fingers and crack down to the skin when the bird is flexed.

With the duck's back in your palms, split the coating along the breast with your thumbs. It should come away in about six large sections, taking all down, and feathers with it. Around the legs, work your thumb beneath the wax, and separate the skin from the wax. Removing the entire wax coating plus down and feathers should require less than sixty seconds. An essential for success is making certain that the wax coating is thoroughly hard and cold before removal.

Fresh Fish

Try the following recipe with bluefish or your favorite catch.

Grilled Bluefish
  4 pounds bluefish, dressed
  salt and pepper to taste
  lemon juice
  melted butter (or margarine)

Stuffing:
  2 tablespoons chopped onion
  ½ cup chopped celery
  ½ cup butter
  2 cups herb-seasoned bread
    crumbs
  ¼ cup chopped parsley
  4 ounces crumbled blue cheese
  1 tablespoon lemon juice

Rinse the fish; pat it dry. Lightly season the inside with lemon juice, salt, and pepper. Spread butter in the middle of a good-sized sheet of aluminum foil, and place the fish on it.

To prepare the stuffing, saute onion and celery in butter until tender. Put in the crumbs; toss to absorb the butter. Mix in the parsley and blue cheese. Moisten the stuffing with lemon juice and approximately ⅔ cup of water.

Fill the cavity of the fish with the stuffing. Close the opening by drawing the skin together and binding with soft string. Butter the top of the fish. Sprinkle with lemon juice, salt, and pepper.

Bring the sides of the foil over the fish and close them with a double fold. Seal the ends in double folds. Place on a grill over a medium fire for ten minutes on each side; turn a third time and grill for an additional ten minutes.

Serve stuffed bluefish garnished with parsley and lemon slices.

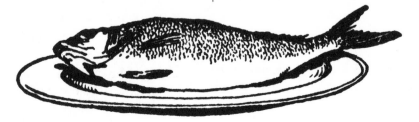

18 | SWEET THINGS

Sugar

Making Sugar from Beets

So highly valued was sugar several centuries ago that it was listed as a wedding present, along with precious gems and jewels, for a future queen of Bohemia and Hungary.

You can produce this once-greatly prized commodity at home from sugar beets. Scrub the vegetable well, and chop it into small pieces. Cook them in water to extract the juice; then strain the juice. Cook down the resulting syrup. Let it cool to crystallize.

Your homemade sugar will not be pure white, and a slight beety flavor will linger. It will be nutritionally superior, however, to treated commercial sugar.

Sugar Substitutes

Each of the following is a sweetening equivalent to 1 cup of white sugar and may be substituted for it when preparing food or drink:

• ½ cup of firmly packed brown sugar
• ¾ of strained honey, minus 3⅓ tablespoons of liquid per cup of added honey
• 1½ cups of molasses or sorghum, minus ¼ cup of liquid for each cup added
• 2 cups of corn syrup, minus ¼ cup of liquid per cup added
• 1½ cups of maple syrup, minus ¼ cup of liquid per cup added

Granny Barlow's Bran Brittle

1 cup granulated sugar
3 tablespoons corn syrup
½ cup brown sugar
½ cup water
1 cup bran
½ teaspoon lemon extract
2 tablespoons butter

Cook the sugars, syrup, and water to 290°F on your candy thermometer. Take the pan from the fire, and stir in the butter, bran, and flavoring.

Pour the mixture on a greased slab. Roll it very thin, using a greased rolling pin. When it cools, mark it into bite-sized squares.

Butterscotch Apples

2 cups sugar
1 cup corn syrup
½ cup water
¼ cup butter
1 teaspoon lemon extract
¼ teaspoon salt
red apples

Combine the sugar, corn syrup, water, and salt in a sauce pan.

Cook the mixture until the sugar dissolves, stirring constantly. Then, without stirring, continue to cook the syrup to the hard-crack stage (295°F). Add butter and cook until your candy thermometer reaches 300°F. Stir in the lemon extract.

In the stem end of each well-washed, unpeeled apple, insert a wooden skewer. Dip the fruit in the hot syrup. Stand the apples on a wire cake rack for drainage of excess syrup as they harden.

Cracker Jacks
Yield: 2½ quarts

2 quarts popped corn
1 cup molasses
2 cups shelled peanuts
½ cup sugar

Blend the popped corn and peanuts in a pan. Mix the molasses and sugar in a deep saucepan, and cook the syrup until it becomes threadlike when dropped in cold water or until the candy thermometer registers 234°F.

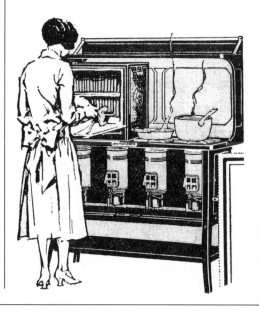

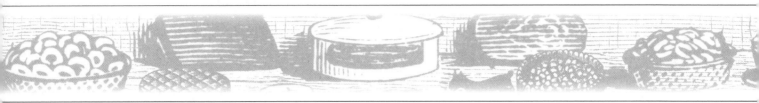

Pour the hot syrup over the popped corn and peanuts blend, mixing well. When the candy is cold and firm, break it into chunks.

Fruit Leather

Fruit leather, a nutritious, lightweight food, is an excellent addition to the outdoor menus of hikers and campers. Making this old-time confection is a good way to utilize overripe fruit.

Put 5 cups of any ripe fruit (apples, apricots, prunes, persimmons, etc.) in a saucepan. Add 1 tablespoon of lemon or lime juice and sweetening (preferably honey) to taste. Simmer until the mixture has the consistency of thick oatmeal. Stir and mash constantly to prevent burning and promote thickening.

Spread the thick fruit sauce on cookie sheets to a depth of ¼ inch. Dry in the oven at 120 to 150°F. for about 4½ hours, leaving the door slightly open. If the day is sunny and warm (over 80°F), dry the fruit paste in the sun for about 9 hours, covering it with cheesecloth to screen out insects.

Keep fruit leather in a dry, cool place until ready for use.

It lasts for thirty weeks at a room temperature of no more than 70°F; it can be stored in a refrigerator for months and in a freezer for years.

The idea for preparing food in this manner stems from certain Native American tribes who made plant leather. They cooked the bee plant to a soup, removed the stems, and boiled the mixture until it became a thick paste. It was then sun-dried in sheets and stored for future camp use or on-the-trail consumption.

Fruit leather is not only a staple food for outdoorsmen. By adding five parts water to one part leather and churning the mixture in a blender, you can turn it into a delicious beverage. It can also be used in cooking, and as pie fillings and dessert toppings.

Lemon Gumdrops
Yield: 60 pieces

    1 6-ounce bottle liquid pectin
    1 teaspoon grated lemon rind
    ¼ teaspoon baking soda
    3 drops homemade yellow
        food coloring
    ¾ cup sugar
    ¾ cup light corn syrup
    1½ teaspoons lemon extract

In a one-quart saucepan, mix the pectin and baking soda. Mix the ¾ cup of sugar and the corn syrup

in a 2-quart pan. Cook both mixtures simultaneously over high heat until foam leaves the first mix and the second comes to a fast boil within three to five minutes. Stir both vessels often. Continue stirring as you slowly empty the pectin mixture into the sugar mixture in a steady stream. Boil for one minute, stirring constantly.

Take from the stove and add lemon extract, lemon rind, and coloring. Put it in an 8-inch-square pan at once. Allow to stand at room temperature for about two hours. When the candy is cool and set, cut it in 1-inch cubes. Roll them in sugar. Keep gumdrops in the refrigerator.

Lollipops
Yield: about 80

    4 cups sugar
    2 cups light corn syrup
    1 cup hot water
    preferred extracts (lemon,
        orange, etc.)
    homemade food coloring
    7 dozen wooden lollipop sticks

An old slab of marble is handy for making lollipops. (A baking sheet can substitute.) Coat it with oil. Line up the sticks on it, about

4 inches apart, with their points all in the same direction.

Combine the sugar, corn syrup, and water in a four-quart pot. Cook them until your candy thermometer registers 270°F (the soft-crack stage). Then reduce the heat and continue cooking until the thermometer reaches 310°F (the hard-crack stage). Take from the heat; let cool for several minutes. Divide the mixture in half. Add any preferred flavorings and, if desired, the homemade food coloring. Stir to blend thoroughly.

When the candy thermometer falls to 280°F, drop tablespoons of the syrupy mixture on the points of

the lollipop sticks. Let stand until completely cold and hard.

Maple Sugar Candy
Yield: about 2 pounds

2 pounds homemade maple sugar
¼ teaspoon cream of tartar
1 cup water

Butter the rim of a good-sized, heavy saucepan. (This will keep the contents from boiling over.) Put in all three ingredients, and bring them to a boil, stirring continuously. Cook until your candy thermometer registers 234°F (the soft-ball stage). Let cool.

Now work the mixture with a wooden paddle until it becomes creamy and thick. Turn it into maple sugar molds. (If they are not available, twelve 2-inch cupcake tins will do nicely.)

When the candy is completely cold, invert the molds to remove their contents.

Marshmallows

2 tablespoons gelatin
¼ cup cold water
¾ cup boiling water
2 cups sugar
⅛ teaspoon salt
1 teaspoon vanilla
powdered sugar

Soak the gelatin in the cold water. When it has absorbed all the moisture, add the salt and vanilla.

Boil the water and sugar to the soft-ball stage (280°F).

Slowly pour this syrup over the gelatin, continually beating the mixture with a wire whisk until it is thick and cool.

Lightly butter a shallow pan; dust it with powdered sugar.

Turn the confection into the pan. Smooth the surface evenly; dust it with powdered sugar. Allow to stand overnight.

The next morning, cut the candy in small squares, and roll them in powdered sugar.

Honey Marshmallows

1 tablespoon gelatin
1 cup honey
¼ cup cold water

Thoroughly soak the gelatin in cold water. Dissolve it over hot water. Warm the honey, and add it to the gelatin. Beat the mixture for ten minutes in a blender until very fluffy and light. Spread it on a buttered pan. Allow to stand for twenty-four hours or longer.

Cut the confection into squares with a knife that has first been dipped in cold water. Store in airtight jars or tins.

Old-Fashioned Pulled Confection

2 cups water
chunk of butter (as big as an egg)
4 cups sugar
¾ cup vinegar
2 teaspoons vanilla
1 cup cream

Put all ingredients in a vessel. Boil them until a test sample "cracks" in water. Then pour the mixture out on a buttered platter.

When the candy is cool enough to handle, pull it (as you would for taffy) until white.

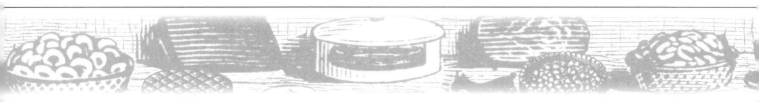

Old-Time Sugar Candy

Combine the following ingredients in a pot: 1 cup of water, 6 cups of sugar, and 1 cup of vinegar. Put 1 teaspoon of soda in just enough hot water to dissolve it. Add this solution plus 1 teaspoon of butter to the vessel.

Boil the contents for thirty minutes without stirring. Sugar candy may be flavored to taste.

Popcorn Balls
Yield: 12 to 15

1½ cups popcorn
1 cup sugar
4 tablespoons butter (or margarine)
⅓ cup corn syrup
1 teaspoon salt
⅓ cup water
1 teaspoon vanilla

Pop the corn, and remove imperfect kernels. Set the popcorn aside in a large bowl.

Mix the butter, water, sugar, and corn syrup in a saucepan.

Cook the blend to the medium-crack stage (280°F on your candy thermometer). Remove from the stove. Add the salt and flavoring.

Slowly pour the syrup over the popped corn, stirring constantly to evenly coat all kernels. As soon as the popcorn is cool enough to handle, shape it lightly into balls with oiled or slightly floured hands. Place them on waxed paper, wrapping them individually.

Potato Candy

Boil and mash a medium-sized potato. Mix in sufficient sugar to make it stiff. On a dough board sprinkled with powdered sugar, roll out the potato mixture. Spread on homemade peanut butter. Roll it up jelly-roll style. Slice in ½-inch pieces to serve.

Spun Carnival Candy

2 cups sugar
⅛ teaspoon cream of tartar
1 cup water

Combine the three ingredients in a saucepan, and boil them without stirring until the candy thermometer reaches 310°F. Immediately put the pan in a larger pan of cold water to halt the boiling; then set it in hot water. Add homemade food coloring if desired.

Lay broom handles across chairs set three feet apart.

Spread newspaper beneath. Dip a sugar spinner into the syrup, and quickly wave it back and forth over the broomsticks. From time to time gather up the spun sugar, and pile it on a cold platter or shape it into

nests. Should the syrup become sugary, melt it over heat for a moment.

Spun sugar candy can be eaten alone or used as a garnish for ice cream.

Taffy
Yield: ½ pound

1 cup light corn syrup
½ cup sugar
1 tablespoon vinegar
1 teaspoon butter flavoring

Lightly butter a platter. Combine the first four ingredients in a saucepan. Boil them until your candy thermometer registers 252°F. The mixture should now be firm.

Pour it on the platter. When it is cool enough to touch, add several drops of any preferred flavoring and pull the taffy with thumbs and forefingers until it is light. Pull away bite-sized pieces; wrap them in squares of waxed paper.

Vinegar Candy

2 cups sugar
2 tablespoons butter
½ cup vinegar

Melt butter in a saucepan. Add the sugar and vinegar. Stir until the sugar is smooth and the mixture starts to boil. When it is bubbly, put a drop in cold water. If it congeals, becoming brittle, empty the mixture onto a buttered pan.

When it is cool enough to pick up, pull it into strands, as you would taffy. Then cut it into bite-sized pieces with scissors or a knife. Place them on buttered plates to cool further.

Cakes, Cookies, and Frosting

Carrot Cake

1½ cups cooking oil
1¾ cups sugar
4 eggs, separated
¼ cup hot water
1 teaspoon nutmeg
1 teaspoon cinnamon
½ teaspoon ground cloves
2 teaspoons baking powder
2½ cups whole wheat flour
1½ cups grated raw carrots
½ cup raisins

Bake carrot cake in a preheated 350°F oven. Grease and flour a 10-inch tube pan.

Beat the oil, sugar, and egg yolks together. Stir in the hot water until the sugar dissolves. Mix in the spices, baking powder, flour, carrots, and raisins. Blend well.

In another bowl beat the egg whites until they are stiff but not dry. Gently fold them into the batter. Empty the batter into the prepared cake pan, and bake it for seventy minutes or until done.

Grandma's Gingerbread

½ cup shortening
½ cup sugar
1 cup molasses
2 eggs
2½ cups flour
2 teaspoons ground cinnamon
1 teaspoon salt
1½ teaspoons soda
½ teaspoon ground cloves
1 teaspoon ground ginger
1 cup buttermilk

Cream the shortening and sugar; blend in the molasses.

Add the eggs, one at a time, beating after each addition.

Combine the flour, salt, soda, and spices. Alternately add the dry blend and the buttermilk to the creamed mixture.

Grease a 9-inch-square cake pan. Spoon in the batter.

Bake in a 350°F oven for forty minutes or until done. Cool.

Oatmeal Cake

1 cup oats (quick cooking)
1 cup brown sugar
2 eggs
1¼ cups hot water
1⅓ cups flour
1 stick butter (or margarine)
1 teaspoon soda
1 teaspoon cinnamon
1 cup white sugar
1½ teaspoons salt

Pour the hot water over the oats; allow to stand for twenty minutes. Cream the butter and sugar together, and stir in an egg at a time. Add the oatmeal mixture. Sift the dry ingredients. Stir them in, blending thoroughly.

Grease and flour an 8-inch-square pan. Pour in the batter.

Bake in a 350°F oven for thirty to thirty-five minutes until done. Cool and frost.

Sugarless Frosting

Mix 4 tablespoons of cornstarch and 8 tablespoons of cocoa powder. Stir in 8 tablespoons of honey. While stirring continuously, slowly add small amounts of evaporated milk until the frosting reaches the desired consistency.

Country-Boy Ginger Snaps

1 cup molasses
½ teaspoon soda
½ cup butter
1 teaspoon ginger
3 cups flour, sifted
2 scant teaspoons salt

Put the butter and molasses in a saucepan; boil them for two minutes.

Mix and sift the remaining ingredients. Add them to the contents of the saucepan. Beat well.

Chill the mixture overnight. Roll the dough out thin, and cut it with a cookie cutter or knife.

Bake on buttered cookie sheets in a 375°F oven for about ten minutes.

Yogurt Cookies
Yield: about 60

½ cup cooking oil
1 teaspoon baking powder
1 cup sugar
2 eggs
3 cups rye flour
½ teaspoon salt
1 tablespoon grated orange rind
1 cup homemade yogurt

Grease two baking sheets.

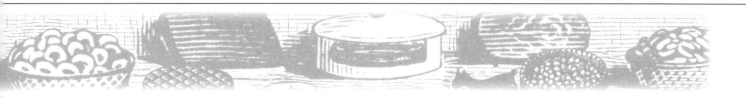

Beat oil, sugar, and eggs in a big bowl. Add the rest of the ingredients, stirring and blending well.

Drop dough by the tablespoon on the cookie sheets, spaced roughly 1½ inches apart. Bake in a preheated 350°F oven, until lightly browned, about 10 to 12 minutes.

Puddings

Molasses-Cranberry Pudding

2 cups cranberries
1½ cups flour
½ cup boiling water
1 cup sugar
2 teaspoons soda
½ cup butter
¼ cup molasses
½ cup cream
¼ cup corn syrup
½ teaspoon nutmeg
1 egg, well beaten
½ teaspoon vanilla

Chop the cranberries. Mix the soda into the boiling water; pour it over the berries.

Beat the egg well. Blend it with the molasses and corn syrup. Add the mixture to the cranberries, and stir in the flour. Blend well.

Pour into a well-greased pudding mold. Steam for three hours.

Cream the butter and sugar. When they are of a creamy consistency, add the cream. Cook until fluffy in a double boiler, beating continuously.

Mix in the nutmeg and vanilla. Serve as sauce over the hot pudding.

Persimmon Pudding

1 cup persimmon pulp
½ teaspoon vanilla
1 tablespoon butter, melted
1 lemon
1 orange
1¼ cups flour
1 cup sugar
1 teaspoon soda
1 egg
½ cup milk
2 tablespoons hot water

Sift together the flour and soda. Blend this dry mixture with the milk, persimmon pulp, melted butter, and vanilla.

Pour into a well-greased pudding mold; cover. Steam for 2 hours.

Lightly beat the egg. Cook it in the top of a double boiler along with the grated rind and strained juice of the citrus fruits, the hot water, and sugar until the mixture develops a creamy consistency. Serve the sauce hot over the steaming persimmon pudding.

Chocolate Pudding
Yield: 4 servings

Sift together the following ingredients:

¼ cup flour
dash of salt
6 tablespoons sugar
4 tablespoons cocoa
⅔ cup powdered milk

Store the blend in a tightly closed jar until ready for use. To prepare pudding, empty the mixture into a saucepan.

Gradually add 2 cups of water and 2 tablespoons of margarine, blending thoroughly all the while.

Put over a low flame and stir until the pudding thickens and starts to bubble when stirring is arrested for a moment.

Turn off the heat; blend in 1 teaspoon of vanilla. Cool.

APPENDIX | WEIGHTS AND MEASURES

Most everything you do in the country has a weight or measure associated with it in one way or another; buying and selling, building, planting and harvesting, even counting out the eggs the old hen lays. For this section we have accumulated weights and measures of every kind and description. This is by no means all the measures that exist, but it's a handy reference as almost all of them have a use at one time or another.

Weights

In our modern civilization we find many odd weights and measures, some which indicate a notable need for scales or measuring implements. For many of these, rather fantastic origins have been given. We know that Charlemagne found different, arbitrary measures of distance in every country, and struck his foot to earth, ordering that its length should be the sole standard for the world. It is said that the English standard, the "grain," was originally derived from the average weight of a grain of barley. The inch was determined from the length of three barley corns, round and dry. The

weight of the English penny, by act of Henry III, in 1266, was to be equal to that of thirty-two grains of wheat, taken from the middle of the wheat kernel and well dried. Among the nations of the East, we have the "finger's length," from that of the digit, or second joint of the forefinger, the finger's breadth, the palm, the hand, the span, the cubit or length of the forearm, the stretch of the arms, length of the foot, the step or pace, the stone, pack, etc.

Below we give a table showing some of these measures, now only used for special purposes:

A sack of wool is 22 stone, 14 pounds to the stone, or 308 pounds.

A pack of wool is 17 stone, 2 pounds, or 240 pounds, which is considered a pack load for a horse.

A truss of new hay is 60 pounds; old hay, 50 pounds; straw, 40 pounds.

A load of hay is 36 trusses; a bale of hay is 300 pounds; a bale of cotton, 400 pounds; a sack of Sea Island cotton, 300 pounds.

In England, a firkin of butter is 56 pounds. In the United States, a firkin of butter is 50 pounds. Double firkins, 100 pounds.

196 pounds = a barrel of flour

200 pounds = a barrel of beef, pork, or fish

280 pounds = a barrel of salt

3 pounds = 1 stone butcher's meat

7 pounds = 1 clove

2 cloves = 1 stone common articles

2 stone = 1 tod of wool

6½ tods = 1 wey of wool

2 weys = 1 sack of wool

12 sacks = 1 last of wool

240 pounds = 1 pack of wool

Distance

3 inches = 1 palm

4 inches = 1 hand

6 inches = 1 span

18 inches = 1 cubit

21.8 inches = 1 Bible cubit

2½ feet = 1 military pace

3 feet = 1 common pace

3.28 feet = 1 meter

Mariners' Measures

6 feet = 1 fathom

120 fathoms = 1 cable length

7½ cable lengths = 1 mile

5,280 feet = 1 statute mile

6,076.1 feet = 1 nautical mile

880 fathoms = 1 mile

A ship's cable = a chain 120 fathoms, or 720 feet long

A hair's breadth = one forty-eighth part of an inch

A knot, or nautical mile = one-sixtieth of a degree; 3 knots = a marine league; 60 knots, or 69½ statute miles = 1 degree

Dry Measure

2 quarts = 1 pottle
2 bushels = 1 strike
2 strikes = 1 coom
2 cooms = 1 quarter
5 quarters = 1 load
3 bushels = 1 sack
36 bushels = 1 chaldron
1 cup = ½ pint
2 pints = 1 quart
8 quarts = 1 peck
4 pecks = 1 bushel
32 quarts = 1 bushel
1 barrel (cranberries) = 5,826 cubic inches
1 barrel (other fruits, vegetables, and dry produce) = 7,056 cubic inches = 105 dry quarts
1 bushel = a cube measuring 12.90747 inches on each side.

The Standard Bushel

The standard is the Winchester bushel, which contains 2,150.42 cubic inches, or 77.627 pounds avoirdupois of distilled water at its maximum density. Its dimensions are 18½ inches diameter inside, 19½ inches outside, and 8 inches deep.

The heaped bushel requires six inches in the height of the cone above the top of the struck bushel, and contains 2,748 cubic inches in all.

Dry Measure: A Comparative Scale

Chaldron	Bushels	Peck	Quarts	Pints
1 =	36 =	144 =	1,152 =	2,304
	1 =	4 =	32 =	64
		1 =	8 =	16
			1 =	2

Liquid Measure

1 teaspoon = ⅙ ounce (oz.)
1 tablespoon = ½ ounce
16 ounces = 1 pint (pt.)
2 pints = 1 quart (qt.)
4 quarts = 1 gallon (gal.)
31½ gallons = 1 barrel (br.)
firkin = 9 gallons
liquid barrel = 32.5 gallons
hogshead = 63 gallons
tun = 252 gallons
1 gallon = a cube measuring 6.135792 on each side.

Wine Measure

18 United States gallons = 1 runlet
25 English gallons, or
42 United States gallons = 1 tierce
2 tierces = 1 puncheon
52¼ English gallons = 1 hogshead
63 United States gallons = hogshead
2 hogsheads = 1 pipe
2 pipes = 1 tun
7½ English gallons = 1 firkin of beer
4 firkins = 1 barrel

Liquid or Wine Measure

16 fluid ounces = 4 gills
4 gills = 1 pint
2 pints = 1 quart
4 quarts = 1 gallon
31½ gallons = 1 barrel
2 barrels or 63 gallons = 1 hogshead

Can Sizes

Buffet or picnic	1 cup
No. 1	1¾ cup
No. 1, tall	2 cups
No. 2	2½ cups
No. 2½	3½ cups
No. 3	4 cups
No. 5	7 cups
No. 10	13 cups

Surveyor's Long Measure

7.92 inches = 1 link
25 links = 1 rod
4 rods = 1 chain
100 links (66 ft.) = 1 chain
80 chains = 1 mile

Area or Square Measure

144 square inches = 1 square foot
9 square feet = 1 square yard
30¼ square yards = 1 square rod
272½ square feet =1 square rod
40 square rods = 1 rood, or quarter acre
160 square rods = 1 acre
4 roods = 1 acre
640 acres = 1 square mile or section
43,569 square feet = 1 acre

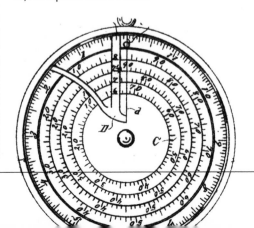

Surveyor's Square Measure

625 square links = 1 square rod

16 square rods = 1 square chain

10 square chains = 1 acre

640 acres = 1 square mile

36 square miles (six miles square) = 1 township

Area or Square Measure: A Comparative Scale

Acre	Roods	Rods	Square Yards	Square Feet	Square Inches
1 =	4 =	160 =	4,840 =	43,560 =	6,272,640
	1 =	40 =	1,210 =	10,890 =	1,568,160
		1 =	30¼ =	27½ =	39,204
			1 =	9 =	1,296
				1 =	144

Square Feet and Feet Square

Never make the mistake of supposing that *square feet* and *feet square* are the same; one foot, yard, rod, or mile, etc., square; or one square foot, yard, rod, mile, etc. are the same, but when beyond the unit measure, the difference increases with the square of the surface, thus:

Fractions of an Acre	Square Feet	Feet Square
¹⁄₁₆	2,722½	52½
⅛	5,445	73¾
¼	10,890	104½
½	21,780	147½
1	43,560	208¼
2	87,120	295¼

Note: 43,560 square feet = 4,840 square yards = 1 acre

A square 208.71 feet on all sides = 1 acre

Land Measure

Farmers often wish to know the contents of a field. To find the number of acres in any square or rectangular field, multiply the length in rods and breadth in rods together, and divide by 160; or, multiply the length in feet by breadth in feet and divide by 43,560, the number of square feet in an acre. Thus:

10 rods by 16 rods = 1 acre

8 rods by 20 rods = 1 acre

5 rods by 32 rods = 1 acre

4 rods by 40 rods = 1 acre

5 yards by 968 rods = 1 acre

10 yards by 484 yards = 1 acre

20 yards by 242 yards = 1 acre

40 yards by 121 yards = 1 acre

80 yards by 60½ yards = 1 acre

70 yards by 69½ yards =1 acre

220 feet by 198 feet = 1 acre

440 feet by 99 feet = 1 acre

110 feet by 369 feet = 1 acre

60 feet by 726 feet = 1 acre

120 feet by 363 feet = 1 acre

240 feet by 181½ feet = 1 acre

200 feet by 108.9 feet = ½ acre

100 feet by 145.2 feet = ⅓ acre

100 feet by 108.9 feet = ¼ acre

43,560 square feet = 1 acre

4,840 square yards = 1 acre

Useful Rules

• To find the number of gallons in a cylindrical tank: Multiply the square of the diameter in inches by .7854, and multiply this product by the height, in inches, then divide the result by 231.

• To find the number of tons of hay in long square stacks: Multiply the length in yards by the width in yards, and that by half the altitude in yards, and divide the product by 15.

• To find the contents of boards, in square feet: Multiply the length (in feet), by the width (in inches), and divide the product by 12.

• The contents of a 16-foot board, 9 inches wide: 9 by 16 = 144 ÷ 12 = 12 square feet.

• The contents of a of an 18-foot board, 13 inches wide: 13 by 18 = 234 ÷ 12 = 1912 square feet.

• To find the contents of scantlings, joists, sills, etc. in square feet: Multiply the length, width, and thickness together, and divide product by 12.

• To find the contents of granaries, wagon beds in bushels: Multiply the number of cubic feet by .8 (for greater accuracy by .8036). A wagon bed 3 feet wide and 10 feet long will hold 2 bushels for every inch in depth.

• Corn Cribs: Good quality ear corn, measured when settled, will hold out at 274 cubic feet per bushel. Inferior quality, 2% to 212 cubic feet per bushel.

• Hay: The quantity of hay in a mow or stack can only be approximately ascertained by measurement. It takes about 350 cubic feet of well-settled timothy hay to make a ton; from 400 to 450 cubic feet of partly settled hay.

• Haystacks: To find contents of a round stack in cubic feet, multiply the square of the average circumference by the average height, and this product by .08; then divide by 350 if the hay is well settled, by 400 or 450 otherwise.

• For an oblong-shaped stack, multiply the average length, width and height together, and divide by the same figures.

• Coal: Hard coal in the solid state averages about 80 pounds per cubic foot, or 25 cubic feet to a ton. Chestnut-size lumps average about 56 pounds per cubic foot.

• Cord Wood: A cord of wood is a pile 4 feet wide, 4 feet high and 8 feet long, and contains 128 cubic feet. Hence, to find the contents of a pile of wood, in cubic feet and cords, multiply length, width, and thickness together, and divide by 128.

• Stone: A perch of stone masonry is 1½ feet long, 1½ feet high and 1 foot thick, and contains 24¾ cubic feet.

• To find the contents of a wall, in perches, find the number of cubic feet, then divide by 2¾ (or multiply by .0404).

INDEX

About the Author

Jerry Mack Johnson grew up on a ranch in West Texas and worked as a cowboy, rodeo clown, professional bull rider, miner, prospector, merchant seaman, oilfield worker, catfish farmer, salesman, and school teacher. He was the author of numerous books of lore, including *Old-Time Country Wisdom & Lore*, *Down Home Ways*, *Country Wisdom*, *Country Scrapbook*, and *The Catfish Farming Handbook*.